PERSIA IN PECKHAM

For Mummy,
and in memory of Daddy.

PERSIA IN PECKHAM

Recipes from Persepolis

Sally Butcher

WITH ILLUSTRATIONS BY
Carlos Calvet

PB

PROSPECT BOOKS

2007

First published in Great Britain in 2007 by Prospect Books,
Allaleigh House, Blackawton, Totnes, Devon TQ9 7DL.

Reprinted, December 2007

BRITISH LIBRARY CATALOGUING IN PUBLICATION DATA:
A catalogue entry of this book is available from the British Library.

Typeset by Tom Jaine. The help and inspiration of Jake Tilson (who
designed the cover) towards a more attractive design of the book is
here gratefully acknowledged.

ISBN 978-1-903018-51-4

Printed and bound in Great Britain by the Cromwell Press, Trowbridge,
Wiltshire.

Contents

INTRODUCTION   9

CHAPTER ONE

STARTERS   31

CHAPTER TWO

BREAKFASTS AND SNACKS   59

CHAPTER THREE

SOUPS   89

CHAPTER FOUR

GRILLED AND ROASTED MEATS   111

CHAPTER FIVE

CASSEROLES   135

CHAPTER SIX

FISH   169

CHAPTER SEVEN

RICE   197

CHAPTER EIGHT

VEGETABLES AND SALADS   221

CHAPTER NINE

DESSERTS   247

CHAPTER TEN

CAKES AND BISCUITS   281

CHAPTER ELEVEN

DRINKS   313

CHAPTER TWELVE

PICKLES AND PRESERVES   329

CHAPTER THIRTEEN

THE PECKHAM INFLUENCE   353

CHAPTER FOURTEEN

THE MEDICINAL PANTRY   381

Glossary   401

Useful addresses   404

Suggestions for further reading   408

Index   411

Acknowledgments

This book is a product of my environment; its contents were absorbed by osmosis and all I have done is to re-hash them.

I thank, in chronological order: my darling Mummy, for instilling a few basic culinary principles in me against (at the time) my better judgment, and Daddy, for making me do things properly; my grandmother/adopted sister Jo-Jo, for being different; Mrs Simpson, for not laughing; the staff and management of the late, lamented Candles Inn, in Westcliff-on-Sea – it may not have done gourmet, but a better crew and a better grounding in catering one could not hope to find; all of my family-in-law, from whom I have been learning since the moment we said 'Salaam'; especially my mother-in-law, Afi, for her humour, tolerance and fabulous cooking; my lovely customers – especially the ones that tried out a few recipes for me.

I must also thank Veronique, my agent. God knows why she took me on, but I am forever indebted. I'd also like to mention my friends, Helen Saberi, for her guidance and support, and Jake Tilson, for his inspiration. A big thank-you too to the Toms of this world: Tom Norrington-Davis for being such an all-round nice guy, and Tom Jaine, my publisher, for sending me back to school.

I thank too Carlos Calvet for his delectable illustrations, and Mr M. Sayeed of Karachi for his Farsi calligraphy.

Most of all I thank Jamshid, my better half, for helping me keep my feet on the ground and allowing my head to remain in the clouds.

Peckham, 2007

7

Introduction

The shop

My husband Jamshid and I opened our shop Persepolis (in Iranian Persepolis is actually known as *Takhte Jamshid* – Jamshid's Throne) as a showroom for our burgeoning Persian import business. But that was just too restrictive; so we did the full-on shop thing instead. And it took on a life of its own, expanding in all sorts of unforeseen directions, displaying goods not just from Iran but many of her neighbours as well. It's not even a proper shop (most shops are pretty boring places, if you think about it). Its layout defies logic, and it's festooned with little bits of yellow paper and blackboards bearing ridiculous witticisms (or, to some, facetiousness). It has been described as more an installation than a shop. As Camberwell Art College is just down the road, we frequently attract students looking for unusual subject material for their projects; we have, furthermore, been photographed and featured in a series of marketing videos (they liked the blackboards); and my (seasonal) gallery of painted water-melons features in various lectures (on the meaning of 'surreal') by a South Bank philosophy professor.

We are proud to be an 'ethnic corner-shop', perched on a windswept cul-de-sac leading to that most glorious of institutions, the Peckham Job Centre. We may not offer the full range of conventional provisions, but a lot of folk depend on us for their daily pint of milk.

Tom Norrington-Davies wrote, 'I am very lucky. Persepolis is my corner shop. But even if it wasn't, I'd happily cross town and country to get there. Otherwise I'd miss the heady scent of their herbs and spices every time I opened my kitchen cupboards. Never mind the slightly worrying addiction to pomegranate juice. Persepolis is an emporium in the true sense of the word. To pigeon-hole it as Iranian would be disingenuous. It feels exotic and local all at once, and this is, in no small part, thanks to Sally Butcher. She is always happy to give advice on everything from chick peas to hookahs with the same warm mix of humour, expertise and enthusiasm. And if the samovar is on you get all the above with a cuppa. Persepolis is the sort of place no neighbourhood should be without.'

What do we actually sell? The criteria are loosely that if we like it we'll consider selling it. Setting aside for a moment our ranges of hand-carved game boards and embossed glassware, musical instruments and *shishe* pipes, there are shelves of somewhat incongruous things – incense, brightly coloured socks, tagines – which aren't strictly Persian.

As we are located on that well-known desert, Peckham High Street, a lot of passers-by assume that we are a mirage – it is not, after all, the most obvious location for an exotic Middle-Eastern bazaar. Peckham residents are puzzled as to why we set up camp on their doorstep when a lot of other shops left years ago, although since we took a stand there have been a lot of initiatives to rid Peckham of its Del Boy/Yardie reputation. Persian customers are equally puzzled as to why we didn't open a 'Super' in Kensington like everyone else (very Iranian, this – if one little Persian person opens a shop somewhere, another five will come and open up next door). But we are fond of our urban village, so critics are wasting their breath.

The book

Persian cuisine is as old as the Caucasus, and there are several worthy, Beeton-esque tomes full of the country's finest regional fare. But nothing *new* has come out of the Persian kitchen for about a thousand years. The book of the shop started as a much-requested, nay, demanded, collection of the recipes which we have featured in our monthly (more often, quarterly) newsletters. It takes Iran as the centre

غذاهای مخصوص ایرانی

of its culinary universe and then roves freely around the Middle East, as well as visiting the shop's own neighbours in Peckham just for fun. These are full of wonderful Caribbean and African spices and vegetables and inevitably these ingredients have crept into our food.

This is meant to be a user-friendly and enjoyable guide to Iranian food. I am anxious to emphasize right at the beginning that while I obviously recommend that the whole world should shop at Persepolis, I have suggested alternatives to some of the more exotic ingredients which the recipes require. There are now Iranian shops in all the major cities of Britain, not to mention plenty of companies happy to send out supplies by mail, and so even the stranger ingredients should be easy to source. There is a little black book of suppliers in the section 'Useful addresses' on p. 404 after the recipe chapters.

Iran – a pot history

Iran is hard to get your head around, both culturally and geographically. It has been in a state of constant flux for millennia, its borders expanding and contracting in line with invasion after invasion. I offer this account merely as a point of reference, in case it comes up in the Sunday crossword. Strictly speaking, you do not need to know anything about King Khosrow II in order to follow the recipes.

Convention has Persian history starting with the Achaemenids under Cyrus the Great. They were the first to unite Persia roughly as we know it today. Before their ascension, a motley assembly of (mostly Zoroastrian) tribes had been loosely ruled by the Assyrians. The Achaemenids built a vast and largely happy-go-lucky empire extending from India to Greece, and perhaps would still rule the world today were it not for Alexander the some-say Great, who put a stop to all that in 330BC.

After Alexander's death, the Persian power vacuum was filled by the Seleucids, a wishy-washy bunch of Macedonians. But they did not have what it took to hang it all together, and after 200 years of dithering they

gave in to the Parthians from the north-east of Iran. This lot were quite impressive. They held off the Romans, and were peaceable enough. But they too were overthrown, this time (in AD226) by the Sassanids from the south of Iran (descendants, in fact, of the Achaemenids). The Sassanian empire ruled the region for nigh-on four centuries (and is perhaps rightly known as the Second Persian Empire), until the Arabs came along in AD637 and changed the face of Iranian history.

Ah, well, the Arabs. Gosh, did they bring a lot of baggage with them – most of it good stuff, it has to be said. They brought their alphabet, and for a while their language, and a whole load of learning, which opened the doors to many scientific and mathematical advances. And they brought Islam, which was soon embraced as the new religion of the land.

Their rule lasted another four centuries, but towards the end of this period there were mutterings of rebellion and tribes seeking devolution. After a lot of scuffles, up popped the Seljuks, a Turkish nation. They ruled Persia from 1051 to 1221. Their reign was successful in as much as they presided over a period of great artistic creativity. The poets Ferdowsi and Khayam were doing their thing during this time. They came, however, to a brutal end with the invasion of the Mongols under Ghengis Khan and the establishment of the Ilkhanid dynasty – any good that they did the country has been severely undermined by a really bad press over the years, but they undoubtedly deserved their ferocious reputation. From 1335 their empire began to crumble, and by 1380 it was ready for the equally legendary Tamerlane and the Timurids to invade from the north-east. He was a skilled and creative statesman, but in his own way just as brutal as the Mongols.

It was in the sixteenth century that peace was again established with the rise of the Safavid dynasty and what is now known as the third great Persian Empire. This was largely due to astounding leadership from the great Shah Abbas I, who laid down much of the modern constitution of Iran and told the Turks to the west to go away. Under his long reign (1587–1629) art and literature flourished, as did the economy. Enduring trade links were formed with Europe. When he died both the Afghans

and the Russians had a go at invading the place, with varying degrees of success, but then Iran pulled two more rather good shahs out of their hat – Nader Shah (a bit bolshy, but he did grab the Peacock Throne and the Koh-i-Noor diamond from India), and Karim Khan Zand (who, unusually for the time, preferred civic duties to warfare).

The next royal house was that of the Qajars, established in 1779 by Agha Mohammad Khan. He was exceedingly unpopular, and they soon got rid of him, but his successors bumbled on for over a hundred years. This was an era of sadly weak rulers, who allowed themselves to be pulled in all directions by the British, the Afghans and the Russians with promises of this trade deal or that incentive. The ante was considerably upped at the beginning of the twentieth century when oil was discovered in Iran. The people had had enough of foreign interference and forced the Constitutional Revolution, and the setting up of the Majlis – democratic government. This didn't last, but the feelings of unrest did, so when those meddlesome British supported a promising young soldier in his quest for proper revolution, the Qajar dynasty was finally brought to an end. Reza Khan (the father of the last Shah) and the Pahlavis had arrived. Reza Shah was exiled by the British in 1941 (he was a little too fond of Nazi Germany), and his son took the throne, and the rest is.... well, actually it's outlined in the next section.

به سبک جدید

Ten things you always wanted to know about Iran but were afraid to ask

What's the difference between Iran and Persia?

Iran is the more correct and archaic term for this ancient land; Persia is a corruption of the name given to it by those meddlesome Greeks. The words are often used by Iranians now to indicate political affiliation – shah-ists invariably use 'Persian'. At Persepolis, we use both interchangeably, although of course 'Persia' is the more exotic sounding and thus more marketable.

How does Iran compare with other Arab states?

Actually, Iran is not an Arab state at all, nor are the Iranians Arabs, although the deep south and south-west of the country is largely Arabic speaking. Iran is a sort of melting pot of cultural influences – the old 'where east meets west' cliché can easily be applied here. In the west there are Iranian Kurds (from the Iranian part of Kurdistan), and the north is home to the Azeris (Turkish Iranians); while the nomadic Baluchis dwell in the south-east of the country near Pakistan, and the Qashqaie and Bakhtiari nomads, although a dying breed, are still to be found all over the interior. The original Aryans came from the broad area we now know as Iran, and in the Caucasus mountains in the far north you can still find people with blonde hair and blue eyes (hence our word Caucasian). My husband Jamshid had white blonde hair when he was a child, although you wouldn't believe it to look at him now, great swarthy thing that he is.

What is Iran famous for?

Well, apart from cute cats and costly carpets, Iran gave the world poetry and wine, the kebab, the first bill of human rights and the words 'daughter', 'khaki' and 'pyjamas'. Among other things. It did not give the world Saddam Hussein or Osama Bin Laden.

How come we never hear much about the ancient Persians?

The ancient Greeks and Romans seem to have much better marketing departments. Life and civilization in the area we now know as Iran actually predates the Greek and the Roman empires. And the Persians have just as much mythology as the next nation. The problem is that they weren't too clever at documenting it, and a lot of what we know about ancient Iran comes from Assyrian and Greek historians. What is extremely annoying is that the great Persian book of legend, Ferdowsi's *Shahname* (The Book of Kings), receives nothing like as much as attention as the *Iliad* or the *Odyssey* or the *Aeneid*.

Why do the Iranian women we see on television always swathe themselves in black from top to toe?

In fact they don't, but this is one of the most powerful media images of Iran. *Hejab* is the Islamic (and thus Arabic) word for the veiling of women. It is believed in Islam that men cannot be trusted and, to preserve female sanctity and honour, women should be dressed modestly enough so as not to arouse male attention. Most (usually extremely fashion-conscious) Iranian women-about-town will wear a *roupush* (a three-quarter-length belted raincoat) and a headscarf. But the traditional *chador* is perhaps more liberating. It is a uniquely Iranian invention, a huge circle of black cloth which is literally thrown around the body and held closed at the neck with one hand. It is certainly cooler and then, who knows what lies under it?

And what's with the men and those beards?

It's quite simple – fundamentalist Muslims don't shave or trim their beards. Many Iranian men of course have beards and moustaches because they like them, or for reasons of fashion, but really long, bushy facial hair is often a sign of extreme fervour. Men in Iran are allowed a little more sartorial freedom than women, but even they have to observe certain codes: no short sleeves or trousers (sorry, let me rephrase that – they are allowed trousers, just not short ones), and no ties (a symbol

of Western decadence). At a recent election a chap actually ran as the 'tie party' candidate, supporting the return of this most innocuous item (and all sorts of other reformist notions, no doubt).

Why do Iranian Muslims seem to differ from Arab Muslims?

Iranian Muslims are Shi'ite, whereas most of the Arab states are Sunni. The scale of difference may be likened to that between Protestants and Catholics. To summarize, although the proscriptions of Shi'ite Islam are a little less strict than Sunni Islam, it is certainly more doleful. When the Prophet died, the Sunnis turned to the leadership of assorted caliphs and amirs, whereas the Shi'ites followed the direct succession of Mohammad's family. This took the form of twelve 'Imams', the most sacred being Imam Ali, Imam Reza and Imam Hussayn who were all assassinated (martyred). The murder of the latter is a time of great mourning in Iran; the month of Moharram is a dark time, when any form of festivity is frowned upon. The Shi'ites are still waiting for the return of the twelfth Imam, Imam Mehdi. When he arrives he will come as a messiah, in the company of Jesus, and he will bring Judgment Day with him.

So what was the revolution all about?

There are many extensive tomes on the causes of the 1979 Iranian revolution. It is hard for most Westerners to understand why a for-ward-thinking, liberal, and naturally well-endowed country would wish effectively to cancel 500 years of progress by exiling its leader and opting for a religious totalitarian state. In truth many Iranians today still can't quite believe how quickly it all escalated. The causes were many, and deeply rooted in history. To cut an extremely long story short, the Shah's modernist thinking and overly fluffy relations with the West, together with his, by any account, shoddy treatment of Mohammad Mossadegh (a great social reformer of the 1950s who nationalized the Iranian oil indus-try and took it out of greedy Western hands) caused a massive backlash. The people did not want to be modernized by force, and such acts as the

Shah's father's banning of Islamic clothing in the 1930s went down very badly. Even liberated Tehranis took a dim view of the Shah's perceived decadent lifestyle, and the corruption and cruelty of his personal police force (the notorious *Savvak*). The revolution, when it came, was perhaps the most dramatic, if not the most bloody, of the twentieth century – going far beyond the expectations even of most of the reformers. Ayatollah Khomeini was swiftly installed as spiritual leader of the world's first-ever Islamic state. Presidents have come and gone since then, some hardline, some reformist, and Khomeini has been replaced by Khameini; suffice it to say that while nothing much has changed, the restrictions on a lot of areas of public life have eased considerably.

What of the Iran/Iraq war?
Actually, the last thing Iran wanted after the revolution was another fight. It was Saddam Hussein who started it (in 1980) and, as with so many Middle Eastern scuffles, it was all about oil. He reckoned that parts of (oil rich) south-eastern Iran were originally part of Iraq, and he wanted them back, together with control of the Shat-al-Arab waterway. Unfortunately, the West supported him. Eight years of appalling war followed, with each side losing hundreds of thousands of young soldiers and neither emerging the victor. The modern cult of the 'martyr' was born of this period – much is still made of their tombs in Iran today. And the toll on both sides is still being paid – there are still Iranian prisoners of war being held in Iraq, and there are still veterans suffering from wounds sustained then. The war changed the country's social profile. So many young men were killed that many women were left without partners; this explains the sudden rise in the birth rate in the last 15 years. Furthermore, it was during this war that so many Iranians fled their homeland. Those that could, sent their children abroad to avoid the military draft: most have never returned.

So it's not a very good place to go on holiday, then?
Not at all true, although if you are looking to recapture that fortnight

به سبک جدید

of sun, sea and *sangria* in Torremolinos, you're looking in the wrong direction. Iran is a fabulous destination, with lots of sights to see, and plenty of activities for the more adventurous; but you have to respect the country's codes and laws. It is a 'dry' nation, and women must cover up. But it is one of the most hospitable and interesting places on earth. The government is trying to encourage tourism and so has waived the need for a visa for a short visit, but you still need to make sure that you are with an accredited tour company or have a letter of invitation in respect of your job or from Iranian friends.

The Persians – a profile

The Iranians are a funny bunch. This isn't meant to offend – my partner is Iranian and I have, to all intents and purposes, been living as part of his family for nigh on fourteen years; and with the Persian shop as well.... I couldn't possibly say anything to denigrate them without 'spitting in the air', to coin an Iranian expression.

When I say 'as part of his family', I am not joking. During the week, we live with his parents, an extraordinarily Iranian thing to do, but by some stroke of good fortune we all get on famously and I am actually quite content. It is clearly a situation which would not suit everybody, but for us it has worked well and has had some unexpectedly beneficial side effects. I have learnt to speak Persian (albeit Perglish rather than Farsi), to cook Persian, and 'taruffing' by osmosis (see over the page for what this means). In this sense I feel very privileged. But I am still undeniably English, and thus an outsider, so in a good position to make a few observations. If I may be so bold.

Firstly, they aren't half full of themselves. It's not their fault. The Avesta (the Zoroastrian holy writ) itself is full of paeans to the glory that was the Aryan race, and they have become embedded in the Persian psyche. In this, they are like the English: superficially self-deprecating, but with a deep-seated belief that, ultimately, they are superior. But they

are not chauvinist, nor do they bunch into easily identifiable ghettos: quite often, one only finds out that one's neighbour of ten years is in fact Iranian through the most casual of conversations.

Secondly, they're all diplomats at heart, at once astute and placatory. Well, at least they are with people they don't know too well. They will quickly assess what someone wishes to hear, and then iterate it accordingly. They progress far and fast. This, I realize, is how I ended up with an Iranian partner.

Thirdly, their culture is full of the most delightful contradictions and contrasts. Which makes stuff awkward for the outsider. This must be a result of their having conquered so many nations (and *being* conquered a bit, too), and the fact that they are at the heart of the Silk Road and the crossroads of so many other trade routes. For a nation the very constitution of which demands propriety and modesty, they can be remarkably raucous and earthy. In private, of course. And they are scarily trendy. For someone as sartorially challenged as myself, this can be quite intimidating. Iranian ladies are some of the best turned-out in the world, which comes as something of a surprise to the uninitiated who are only familiar with the black folds of the *hejab* from media images. And then, I have to say, for one of the politest countries in the world, they can be surprisingly blunt. I can go shopping with English girlfriends, and the answer to questions along the line of, 'Does my bum look big in this?' will be met by a tactful, 'Why not try a different colour?'; if I shop with Iranian pals, the answer would be, 'Yes, enormous!' If one looks chubbier or older since the last encounter with an Iranian friend, they will say so. It's refreshing of course, once you've got over the shock. Again, they're generous to a fault, but they haven't quite escaped that Middle Eastern thing about haggling.

Fourthly, they are notoriously nosy. Questions like, 'Why don't you have any babies yet?' and, 'How much do you earn?' rank alongside, 'How are you?' as standard and acceptable greetings. This is quite funny. When you get used to it.

Next there's the hypochondria. Good health is of course a gift, and

به سبک جدید

perhaps it is because they realize this that such a big issue is made of illness and medicine in Iran. My father-in-law has recently bought a blood-pressure measuring device and, à propos the previous paragraph, his standard greeting is now, 'Hello! How are you? Roll up your sleeve.' The first sign of a sniffle, and they are mostly off to bed, while a trip to the doctor is a major outing involving one's finest clothes and quite a lot of the family. It is also thought a failed trip unless 'the invalid' is able to brandish at least one pot of antibiotics as talismanic trophy. What's more, my adopted family shudders when I go out without a coat, eat ice-cream for my sore throat and hot curry to chase away colds. They cannot understand why I am not moribund.

Finally, there's this whole *taruf* business. What a minefield that is. As all Persian social intercourse revolves around a firm grasp of *taruf*, we foreigners invariably get a crash course in it very early on. Take the business of entertaining guests for example. Iranian lady visitors will always insist on helping to clear up after dinner; this is not just a vague 'Oh, let me...', but a vigorous and physical assault on the sink which requires forward-planning and a battalion of well-briefed relatives to avert. The options (which are easy conventions in English society) of letting them help, or pretending that you always leave the washing-up until the next morning, are not available as this will stoke immediate rumours about how slovenly you are. It's an absolute hoot. And then, when you do get the hang of it, you are often wrong-footed. Iranians do not expect foreigners to *taruf,* and so can often assume that all offers are made with the utmost sincerity. This has occasionally found me frying eggs at 3 a.m., in my pyjamas, on behalf of my peckish beloved ('Let me go and cook you something, darling....'), or doing five hours of ironing ('I'll do it...no, really, I love ironing.').

But at the end of the day, none of the above are *difficulties* – they're just *differences*. And there's nothing so strange as the English anyway.

Meet the In-Laws

The real stars of this book are of course Jamshid and his family, so it only seems fair to introduce them properly.

After a happy (for which read spoilt) childhood, Jamshid was sent to France at the age of fourteen to escape the dangers of the Iran/Iraq war. After a couple of (badly behaved) years at boarding school in Paris, he moved to a (totally unsuitable and strict) college in a little village outside Waterloo in Belgium, where his parents and three brothers eventually joined him. After a couple of years (equally badly behaved, 'but he is a tri-lingual maths prodigy', she added quickly), he moved to England, married, reproduced (twice, the Noodle and Dan, henceforth known as the 'steps'), divorced, went into catering, met me.

His parents were more or less childhood sweethearts. They were both born and raised in Kermanshah in the west of Iran. One of the oldest settlements in the country, this is a town with marked Kurdish influences and a strong sense of regional identity. Father-in-law (Cyrus) has three brothers, all of whom upped camp to America to live the dream. He also has two lovely sisters, one of whom is a physicist and lecturer at Tehran University, and the other, Tatty-Jun, is a teacher in West London. Cyrus himself is a civil engineer, a big-hearted, extraordinarily clever man (albeit a *nagsheh bozorgh*, which is Persian for 'a bit of a character'). Actually, clever doesn't do him justice – he is wise.

My mother-in-law, Afsaneh/Afi (which means 'myth' in Persian), is a former teacher. She has four sisters, one of whom died a few years ago; of the three surviving, only one is married, the effect of which is that Jamshid and his brothers have always had a clutch of doting maiden aunts at their disposal. She also has two brothers, one of whom, Mohsen, works with us in the import business. Afi is very compact (short but not to be under-estimated), feisty, pretty lady. If I have a figure and complexion like hers at 65, I shall be well chuffed. She manages to be both imperious and one of the hardest grafters I have ever come across.

She is quite the boss of the family. Most importantly, for the purposes of this book, she is a terrific cook.

The family is very close. No. 2 brother Omid and wife Tara (both 'something in marketing') live nearby with their romper-stomper, Alex. No. 3 brother Navid (another engineer) and his new bride Anahid live in the family 'compound' in Peckham. Baby brother Amir (he's 23) and girlfriend Liz come and go all the time.

Like many Iranians, Afi and Cyrus gave up a life of ease, professions they enjoyed and a beautiful house so that they could bring their sons to safety and the perceived benefits of a Western education. It has been a long journey, born with fortitude and grace and, like so many Iranians, behind their smiles there is always the intangible, sad flicker of a fire which used to burn in another land and another life.

The evil eye

A confession. I have been sufficiently Iranified to absorb quite a lot of Persian superstition (the more attractive bits at least). Iranian culture still embraces many ancient practices, as opposed to British culture, which still bears traces of archaic beliefs and superstitions, but tends to try and laugh them off, nervously.

There is still a widespread belief that there are forces at work in the universe which need appeasing, and that for every action there is an equal and opposite reaction. This almost certainly derives from the Zoroastrian view that there are two powers at work in the world, good and evil, and that a balance needs to be achieved. To this extent, a run of bad luck is met with certain actions to counteract it and, when good luck prevails, apart from thanks being offered to God, certain rituals are also followed to make sure that the luck continues and isn't spoiled by the beneficiary's complacency or the jealousy of others. The 'bad luck' is known as the 'evil eye', *cheshm,* and an astonishing amount of 'stuff going wrong' is blamed on it. If you are having a successful run at anything, and

غذاهای مخصوص ایرانی

things start breaking or malfunctioning, it is considered a good omen, as it indicates that the 'evil eye' is being diverted from you to harmless inanimate objects. Similarly, a run of really bad luck is usually blamed on insufficient positive 'vibes' or thoughts. It is believed that even the subconscious feelings of a neighbour, whose grass is browner, can cause a negative ripple in the space/time continuum (well, something like that anyway) and cause your grass to wither.

What to do...what to do? Well the simplest way to avoid tempting providence is to litter your conversation with *'en sh'Allah'*, 'if it be the will of Allah', as in 'See you soon, *en sh'Allah*,' or 'When he grows up he will be a great doctor, *en sh'Allah*' (all Iranians want their offspring to be doctors). The reference to Allah is heartfelt, but the habit again reflects a more primitive belief. You can also hang a *cheshm* by the door of your house or car: these (traditionally blue glass) artefacts bear an eye symbol on them, as if to say, 'Hah! Got there first!' to any visiting bad-luck vibes, and thus repel them. The very superstitious wear them as jewellery as well.

The most surefire way of avoiding 'bad eye' is to burn *espand*, wild rue. This pungent, bitter herb is one of the most lingering smells of Iran (and Afghanistan, where there are actually street vendors who will burn rue on your behalf). It is burnt at Nowrooz, at weddings, and at any celebration, and also at funerals and times of national mourning. A little of the herb is sprinkled on some lit charcoal, quite often mixed with frankincense or *golpar*, the weird spice derived from Persian hogwort. The censer is taken around the house or building, so that all may get a whiff of its smoke, and various words are spoken over it. Some offer a religious incantation, others a more traditional imprecation for help. I burn it in the shop frequently. If it is a quiet day, I burn it to make sure that we will not have a whole string of them. If it is a busy day, I burn it to preserve the trend. It has a not-unpleasant smell, and is reputed to cleanse the air. Just by including this passage in the book, I am mentally burning *espand* in the hope that you will enjoy and benefit from my scribblings. In Peckham, they probably think I am a witch doctor; in

seventeenth-century Britain, I would have been burned at the stake. Regardless of what one believes in observing such quaint rituals, the action of so doing reinforces a sense of balance in the individual, and an awareness of one's place in the grand scheme of things. Its overall effect is to make for a more considerate and responsible society. Which can't be a bad thing.

Eating the Persian way

I learnt to speak Persian over dinner. Not the dinner of one evening, you understand, but rather the collective mealtimes of 13 years with the family-in-law. (It rather conceitedly came from a deep-felt belief that in all that foreign rabbiting they were talking about me...which of course they weren't.) The point is that the tradition of communal eating is still very much entrenched in the Persian lifestyle, and society is all the richer for it. That is not to say that there are not Iranian families in the diaspora who eat in the Western manner: in shifts, rushed, the stuff of convenience – but these are the exception.

Iranians don't just eat meals, they feast, every mealtime. None of this eating on the hoof, anything-will-do, pass it through the microwave stuff. Food is planned and prepared lovingly, and served as a spread with all the trimmings. It is not unusual for a housewife to spend all day shopping and gearing up for a dinner (lunch is eaten in Iran, but dinner remains the main meal of the day).

And anyone who happens to be in the area is expected to partake of it. The Persian poet Rumi wrote: 'The mature man who delivers a discourse is like a man who has laid out a feast; his table is spread with every imaginable dish. No guest goes hungry, goes without food: and there is something there to suit every taste'. It would actually be abhorrent to most Iranians to eat if they knew that someone nearby was hungry. Food is a gift which tastes better shared. The food of a family was traditionally shared with not just the servants but also the poor of

the neighbourhood. Local beggars were often to be found outside the houses of the wealthy at feeding time. That is how the dervish survived – he would dangle his *kashkul* (beggar's bowl), knowing that it would be filled wherever he went. Few Iranian families have servants now, of course, and wandering dervishes are slightly fewer on the ground (at least in Peckham) – but still Iranians go by the sharing ethos. If you walk into a Persian shop, and the shopkeeper is having a sup of tea, he will immediately offer you his cup; similarly, Iranian customers buying a snack to eat in a shop always offer it around.

A typical Iranian meal consists of rice or bread with *khoresht* or kebab, although when there are guests the hostess will invariably prepare two or three different dishes. On the *sofreh* (table cloth) too will be pickles, yoghurt, fresh herbs, onion and lemon. Food is most often eaten with a spoon and fork, but the traditional method of eating with scoops of bread is still employed when the food or the company is right. Iranians do own dining tables, and they know how to use them; but it does not take much for them to shed the veneer of Western 'civilization' and eat on the floor. I've always been a floor person, but it can be hard for the uninitiated. It is great fun watching Iranian-American relatives who have 'been away for too long' struggling with the dilemma of rank discomfort set against the embarrassment of having to ask for a tray. The business of sitting *down* is a great leveller, however, and makes for much more sociable mealtimes. Chatter is loud and non-stop (usually all the louder for having the telly on in the background). There is invariably a lot of teasing and gossiping. It is to me reminiscent of the ancient Spartan dinner clubs (not that I actually attended many), where youngsters would be expected to endure night after night of rib-digging, fun-poking jokes at their expense to toughen them up. Characters are built at the Persian dinner spread, plans are made and empires rise and fall. It is nothing short of a major tragedy that family dining in Britain is on the decline. This is hardly an original lament, but I believe that the social costs of its demise will be astronomical. I have witnessed the moral grounding, together with etiquette and basic language training

that these occasions provide for young Iranians; not to mention the sense of family and belonging that it instills. It is priceless.

Whilst there are plenty of 'new Iranian men' out there who do things like wash-up and cook, these activities are usually reserved for private indulgence within the dynamics of a couple's relationship. Publicly and within the family at large, men don't do domestic stuff. At a proper Persian gathering, the women actually withdraw after dinner (to the kitchen), and the men can then smoke/drink/play backgammon or what they will. The women clear away, wash-up, and (sorry, but there's no other way to put this) bitch. Iranian kitchen conversation is not for the faint-hearted. This is not so removed from English habits, although we are sadly spending less time in our kitchens now. My own grandmother never actually sat down to eat with us (family legend has her too busy drinking gin and smoking, slander in truth as she actually just liked to be in her kitchen); my mother complains that when she first married she assumed that she should behave the same way until my father actually asked why on earth she wasn't eating with him.

The gentle art of corner shopping

This is not a tirade about supermarkets: their price fixing, the spies they send out into nearby small shops, the often miserable and unhelpful staff and the general absence of anything remotely philanthropic in their mission statements. We won't mention any of these. This is, rather, a paean to all things small and corner-shaped.

It goes without saying that a small shop where the owner is very hands-on is likely to be more carefully and caringly run. The product range may not be as large, but goods are lovingly sourced and merchandized, and the shopkeeper will usually happily engage in discussions as to the merits of this, or how to prepare that. If you are a regular, and ask nicely enough, the shopkeeper will also go to great lengths to find and stock particular products for you.

Small shopkeepers (whether they like it or not) invariably get to know their customers, and exist in symbiosis with their neighbourhood. Thus if something goes wrong with the balance, if Mrs. Smith varies her routine or Mr Brown doesn't turn up one day, or little Lucy is covered in bruises, the shopkeeper is often the first to know. In a successful neighbourhood, this imbalance leads to appropriate remedial action. This does not and cannot happen with supermarkets. And (like hairdressers) shopkeepers get trusted with some amazing, or hysterical, or horrifying confidences. The counter can occasionally confer on the shopkeeper a lot more responsibility than he'd like. The corner shop has a pivotal social role.

Which brings us to your responsibilities. The little shop needs you. It needs you to support it in every way you can. Otherwise, it will not survive. It is not that we are at war with the supermarkets, it is literally a case of 'they're big, we're small', and unless we take a stand we will be assimilated. I love the way my good customers use our shop. Everything they can possibly buy from us, they do. Only once they have trawled the little shops nearby, will they visit the supermarket to acquire what is left on their list. Corner-shop goodies may not last as suspiciously long as those from the supermarket, but this need not be a bad thing. Buying and cooking fresh food more often has in fact to be a good thing. There is something faintly chilling about the once-a-week-shop, and something faintly scary about people who are organized enough to live this way.

Is the customer always right? Not invariably. Some are very rude; others are away with the genies. To help you get more out of your corner shop, here are our top ten no-nos in terms of customer behaviour.

❀   Leave your bad temper/arguments/grumps at the door.

❀   Just because a shop looks foreign, it does not mean that you can haggle (unless you are a real joker and routinely try it at McDonald's and BP as well). Iranians do haggle, but it is habitual rather than serious, and if they are assured of your best attention

به سبک جدید

they will usually leave happy. If you do wish to haggle, let the shopkeeper know in advance so that he can put his prices up and then lower them under pressure just to humour you.

❀ Any shopkeeper worth his salt knows that one of the keys to attracting regulars is to indulge their children. So we give them lollies and play games with them; but that does not mean they can run amok. We offer a special child-laminating service for the worst offenders, but if they're that bad we usually recommend you leave them tethered outside.

❀ The mobile phone. We get customers who come in while talking on their mobiles, ignore your, 'Hello there, can I help?', proceed to give whoever is the other end a running commentary of the shop or to discuss their mutual shopping requirements, and leave again, without having acknowledged us or uttered a single civil word. It is slightly surreal.

❀ We don't take kindly to being shouted at by either British people who assume we are foreign and thus of poor English, and that shouting and waving their hands will help us understand a bit better (we always play along with this charade – it's such fun) or by foreigners who assume that shouting will have the same effect as the Babel fish and instantly render us capable of understanding Lithuanian or Cantonese.

❀ We can't stand stupid thieves. Every shopkeeper knows he is going to get the odd shoplifter. You can usually spot them a mile off, even the professionals. They try to look oh-so-casual, as they walk in with their big, empty sports bags; or they wait until they think that you are busy and then charge in and out very quickly. There is almost a perverse pleasure to be had in observing their art (even as you are calling the police). But stupid thieves pose a problem – it's like a double-whammy of an insult.

❀ The ignorance that breeds racism is difficult to live with. I am as English as they come, but even I get all manner of abuse because I speak a funny language and work in a shop with foreign writing

on it. The shopkeeper is not a fair target for such despicable behaviour; it has got to stop.

 There are certain activities which are not part of browsing in a shop. We would ask you to desist. We list such things as in-line skating, extreme ironing, spitting and porcupines in our schedule of prohibitions, but you would think that people realized that smoking, swilling booze and bringing along your rottweiler are all pretty daft ideas in a food shop. There's some rum 'uns out there, I tell you.

 It doesn't matter if you're open 23 hours a day, there will still be a queue of folk who want to visit during that one hour you are closed; or who will turn up 5 minutes before you open and bang on the shutter (while you're still eating your muesli); or 5 minutes before you shut (a very Iranian trait, this: they are quite proprietorial towards their pet Iranian store, i.e. they rather sweetly behave as if they own it). Try to get to know your corner-shop's opening hours.

 Smile more, please. Not only those who enter, but you, madame, on the passing bus, and you, sir, adjusting your collar in the reflection in the window. This may be a mirror of your vanity; it may, too, offer a glimpse of the wares within; but it is also my window on the world. And you are not smiling enough.

به سبک جدید

EARLY EVERY MORNING
SHE WOULD COME OUT FROM
THE HOUSE WHERE SHE
LIVED AND WALK DOWN
THE STREET
TO WORK

CHAPTER ONE

CHAPTER ONE

STARTERS

'Starters' is a bit of a formal expression for the average Iranian menu. It is true that the Tehran smart-set has developed some depressingly Western habits over the years, and they do delight in serving up a proper three-course repast when the occasion suits. Before a traditional Persian meal, however, it is more likely that a range of light and wholesome morsels will be offered, something akin to *meze* or *tapas*. The word *meze* is in fact Persian in origin, deriving from the noun *mazeh* or taste – a fact of which I was blissfully ignorant until the lovely Helen Saberi, herself the author of a wonderful book of Afghan food, enlightened me. As Iranians believe in nutritional balance, so their starters are designed to complement the meal which they are about to consume: fresh herbs to excite the appetite, live yoghurt to fortify the digestive tract, bread and cheese to line the stomach.

The Persian bread basket – *naan*

We mistook the full moon as a loaf of bread and raised our hands to the sky.

Rumi

Bread is big in Iran. In every sense. It is far more important than rice, which is often regarded as the staple food of richer folks. *Everybody* in Iran eats bread, and many will not contemplate a meal without it. It is eaten with cheese at breakfast, wrapped around kebab for lunch and used for mopping up stews with the evening meal; in many areas it takes the place of cutlery.

Persian bread, of course, bears no resemblance whatsoever to dear old Hovis; it comes in large (often up to half a square metre), flat sheets or long, oval slabs. And it is ripped, not sliced.

At this stage we should point out that what we have done in this section is in effect quite anomalous. A hundred or so years ago, many households in Iran *would* bake their own bread to order. The wood- or peat-fuelled oven was constantly alight and central to the running of the household. Joseph Knanishu describes the process very well in his wonderfully bigoted travelogue *About Persia and its People*. He describes how dough was left near the fire to rise, and then divided into balls, rolled flatter than a pancake, 'spread over something made for that purpose' and whacked onto the inside of the oven wall, 'as far as a lady's elbow and sometimes as far down as the length of her arm'. The dough would stick; after a couple of minutes it would be cooked through and easily collected and brought up to cool.

Now, of course, most houses no longer rely on a large, smoky bread oven for warmth, and the business of cooking flat breads in a normal domestic oven is an approximation, at best. Hardly any modern Iranian housewives will bother to make bread as there is a baker on more or less every corner in every town and village in Iran, and they all bake fresh bread throughout the day. Away from the homeland, it is not always possible to get off-the-peg Persian *naan*, even in London, so a recipe may not come amiss. You may however see the workings of a traditional bread oven in many Iranian restaurants around the country – it is indeed the cornerstone of a good kebab house.

There are three basic types of bread baked across Iran, *lavash* or *taftoon*, *barberi* and *sangak*, though with dozens of regional variations. I have to admit that baking is my Achilles heel, and so I went to the expert for help with this book – our own bread supplier at the shop. He was a little evasive at first – this turned out to be less from a reluctance to help and more to do with the fact that he could not see any mystique

or art in his creations. For the *naan-e-taftoon* recipe, Abu Reza, thank you. By way of useless information, the Arabic term *abu* means 'father of' (and *om* 'mother of'). It is a matter of honour in certain sections of the Arab community for parents to assume the name of their eldest child. Thus Prince Charles becomes 'Abu William', and the Queen would be 'Om-e-Charles'.

Abu Reza's *Naan-e-Lavash/Taftoon*

This is everyday bread – it is this above all others which is the staple of the Iranian diet. The first time I had it I actually thought it was cardboard, but it grows on you. And it is incredibly versatile. *Lavash* and *taftoon* are basically the same bread, *taftoon* being just a little thicker. They are both traditionally cooked stuck to the inside of a clay *tanoor* oven (but we will use your domestic oven on this occasion). They may both be eaten hot or cold, although *taftoon* is better warm, and *lavash* better cold. Home-baked bread usually comes out nearer to *taftoon* than *lavash* – but it is really up to you as to how thin you roll it. This bread keeps well – either wrap it in a plastic bag, or cut it and freeze it.

> *1 teaspoon dried yeast*
> *about 300ml lukewarm water*
> *500g plain flour*
> *1 teaspoon salt*
> *2 teaspoons oil*

Sprinkle the yeast on to the warm water, and let it sit for 15 minutes. Next, put the flour in a bowl with the salt and the oil, and then slowly

add first the yeasty water, beating with a wooden spoon, and then the rest of the water, splosh by splosh, until it comes together. When it starts to cohere, ditch the spoon and go with your hands. Knead the dough for about 5 minutes until it becomes decidedly gloopy, and then cover the bowl with a lightly damped cloth. Leave it to rise for a couple of hours.

At the end of the 2 hours, knead for a further 5 minutes, before breaking off a lump of the dough the size of a small apple or large plum. Roll it into a ball. Repeat until you have divided all the dough, and then re-cover the balls and set to rise for a further half an hour.

Heat the oven to gas mark 9 (240°C). Sprinkle both your board and your rolling pin with a little flour, and then roll out each ball of dough just as flat and thin as you can. If you are a true paragon of the domestic arts, you can cook these breads directly on the floor of your oven; if you suspect that your oven may in fact have a teensy bit of last night's pizza or last Sunday's beef dripping still lurking, best use a baking tray. Bake the sheets one at a time (or more if you have multiple baking sheets) for 1–2 minutes – when they are golden and crisp, remove them from the oven.

غذاهای مخصوص ایرانی

Naan-e-Barberi

نان بربری

This is a slightly fatter bread, and where *lavash* can seem rather strange to the uninitiated, this bread is a dream. Usually eaten warm, it is like a Persian ciabatta. It is good as an accompaniment to food, but also can be used as a pizza base. It is usually made in ovals 50–60cm long, but also comes in a tear-drop shape, or in small rectangles.

10g fresh (or 5g dried) yeast
300ml lukewarm water
500g plain flour
¼ teaspoon sugar
1 teaspoon salt
2 tablespoons oil
melted butter to glaze
seeds of choice (sesame, nigella or caraway are all good)

Either cream the fresh yeast with the water, or get the dried going as instructed on the tin. Leave to work for 15 minutes. Mix the flour, sugar, salt and oil in a bowl, and add the water bit by bit, beating with a spoon. Then knead it with your hands – a good 10 minutes' cardio-vascular workout. Press into a ball, cover and leave to work its magic for a couple of hours.

After this period, knead for another 5 minutes and then form the dough into four flattened ovals. Make a few ridges across the bread, brush with the butter and sprinkle with seeds. Leave for another half an hour, and then bake in a pre-heated oven (gas mark 9, 240°C) for 15–20 minutes, or until risen and golden brown. Eat fresh, or keep covered and sprinkle with water before re-heating to serve. This bread does not keep as well as the indestructible *lavash*.

Naan-e-Sangak: Stone-Baked Wholemeal Bread

This is really the showpiece of the Iranian bread world; it has a strong nutty flavour, and a chewy texture which intrigue the taste-buds and the whole process of baking this at home really gives one the impression of being a true domestic goddess, homely and in tune with one's rustic roots. It is not too difficult to recreate the stone-baked thing at home – you just need to find a selection of fairly evenly sized, smooth pebbles – 5cm in diameter or more is good. These will obviously need washing thoroughly, and then oiling thoroughly before use. You will also need the mother of all baking trays (strong enough to bear half a beach, at least).

> *1 teaspoon dried yeast*
> *100ml lukewarm water*
> *350g wholemeal flour sifted together with 110g strong white flour*
> *1 level teaspoon salt*
> *cold water*

Sprinkle the yeast on to the warm water and allow it to sit for about quarter of an hour. After this, pour it into a big basin, add in the sifted flours and salt, mixing all the while, and then blend in enough cold water to make it all hang together. Obviously you will have to knead with vigour – the mixture should start to come away from your mixing bowl and feel quite rubbery. Cover the bowl with a clean damp cloth and leave it to stand for three hours; then knead it again and let it sit for a further hour.

Preheat the oven and your 'mini-beach' at gas mark 9 (240°C). Divide the dough mixture into two and stretch and pummel it into submission as two flattish, squareish sheets. Either oiling or flouring your hands

before working with the dough should give you an easier time of it. Cook the sheets one at a time. Place it over the pebbles; after three and a half minutes, turn it over and bake for a further three and a half minutes. When the bread is cooked it should be a rich brown colour and lift easily from the pebbles. This bread is best consumed whilst still warm, but it may be reheated by sprinkling with water and popping in a really hot oven for 30 seconds.

A few words about herbs or *sabzi*

The first things that will be brought to any meal table are bread, cheese and fresh herbs.

Herbs get everywhere in Iran; not only do they feature prominently in all sorts of dishes, they are eaten just as they are, in great handfuls. Not for the Persian housewife the mouse-like sprinkling of dried greenery that passes for herb use over here. Many Iranian dishes are so laden with fresh or dried herbs that they assume a rich green hue. The main stars of the show are parsley (*jaffaree*), coriander (*geshneez*), chives (*tareh*), spinach (*esfanaj*), fenugreek (*shambahlileh*), dill (*chiveed*), mint (*na'nah*), tarragon (*tarkhoun*) and basil (*reyhan*). Then there are all sorts of carefully measured mixtures of herbs, used variously for herb omelettes (*sabzi kookoo*), casseroles (*sabzi ghormeh*), soup (*sabzi ash*) and rice (*sabzi pulao*); you may prepare your own mixtures, but they are widely available pre-mixed in Persian stores, both in dried and frozen form.

The *sabzi* basket

Every traditional Persian household keeps a mixture of fresh clean herbs in the fridge ready to be served with main meals or wrapped in sandwiches. This *sabzi khordani* comprises parsley, coriander, mint, tarragon and basil most commonly, together with spring onions and

radishes, but there are hundreds of other ones which creep into the basket from time to time, many of them members of the cress family. Herbs are bought by the bunch, trimmed carefully away from their stalks, swooshed around in a bowl of cold water and then left to soak for at least half an hour, during which time any dirt sinks to the bottom. They are then scooped out into a colander, and allowed to drain. They are best stored in the colander (which allows them to breathe) – just rest an inverted side-plate on top and pop the whole thing in the fridge. They should keep for around a week. It takes a while to get used to eating raw herbs, especially some of the more aromatic or pungent ones – but they are so beneficial in so many ways – coriander acts as an appetizer, and tarragon, basil and mint act as an aid to digestion; parsley is an invaluable source of vitamin K and, of course, masks any unpleasant odours on the breath.

Baby *Chelo* Kebabs Wrapped in *Lavash* Bread with Relish

These minced meat kebabs are really one of the mainstays of the Persian kitchen; Iranians are essentially carnivores, and have a deep rooted affinity with fire, and so meat cooked on fire is always bound to meet with favour. They are normally eaten as a main course with bread or buttered basmati rice and a grilled tomato. They look very easy to make, but they are not – mastering the technique of getting them to stick on the skewers, I have always thought, is an activity worthy of some torturous culinary TV game show. In Iran they are quite broad but flat, and are moulded on to thick, flat skewers – they have two distinct

sides, so that it is easy to turn them on the fire. These little ones are easier to make, and you do not even have to cook them on skewers or real fire. These quantities will serve 6 people as a first course.

500g minced lamb
1 medium onion, grated
½ teaspoon bicarb of soda
salt and pepper
½ teaspoon smoked paprika (not authentic but adds nice barbecue
*   flavour)*
little wooden skewers
For the relish:
1 green chilli
2 medium onions
dash olive oil
2 dessertspoons carrot jam (quince or plum also acceptable)
1 dessertspoonful malt vinegar

12 small lavash *bread (if necessary cut larger sheets to shape – you*
*   need strips of around 8cm x 15cm)*
sabzi *(see above)*

Mix the mince with the onion and other ingredients – you should knead well so that the fat from the meat starts to soften and it all becomes quite sticky. Using wet hands, roll the mixture into sausage shapes of around 2cm thickness and 10cm in length, inserting a skewer along the length of each. Pop them into the fridge to chill whilst you make the relish. Wash and chop the chilli, and chop the onions; fry in a little olive oil until softened, and then add the jam, followed by the vinegar. Season to taste, and set to simmer on a low heat.

Cook the kebabs – preferably over charcoal, but under a domestic grill will do (and if you haven't bothered with the skewers, you can just put them in the oven on a tray).

Smother a little of the relish on to each sheet of *lavash*, and then wrap a kebab in each. Pop them all on to a tray and rest them in a warm oven for 10 minutes, so that a little of the dripping from the lamb starts to seep into the bread. Serve on plates strewn with herbs, preferably with pickled Persian cucumbers and a pot of thick yoghurt.

Kashk-e-Bademjun: Aubergines with Whey

This is a versatile little recipe: it will see you from canapés at lunchtime, through an impressive dinner-party starter to late-night supper – that is to say, it will enhance your culinary portfolio.

Kashk is almost impossible to get in England, unless you happen to live next door to a dairy farmer who can help you out. You can always use lightly salted yoghurt in its place – it's not the same, but it does. *Kashk* is whey (the murky water left after you've made your butter, cheese, or yoghurt) which has been dried and then (usually) rolled into balls: in Iran it is used reconstituted in soups and other dishes to thicken and flavour – it has a very strong, cheesy taste. (If you can imagine mixing Parmesan with yoghurt, you'll be approaching the *kashk* experience.) In Afghanistan it is often eaten just as it is and is regarded as a great delicacy. There is a story as to how it was first created, although this may be the stuff of pre-urban legend. It is said that Attila and his chirpy little Huns invented it; superlative horsemen, they would often spend days in the saddle, carrying provisions on or under their saddles – milk thus carried (in skins) first soured and then separated and solidified, so that after a long campaign they would be left with prime *kashk*.

2 large aubergines
salt and pepper
2 medium onions
a little butter and olive oil
½ cup kashk *or yoghurt*
1 tablespoon dried mint
2 sheets taftoon *bread or similar*

I suggest *taftoon* bread (see p. 35 above) because you want bread not so thin that it flops nor so thick that it dominates. These quantities are enough to make 10 small servings.

Wash your aubergines, cut off and discard the little hats (calyxes), and chop them into 1cm cubes (a purist would skin them, but I always think that skin adds greater texture, colour and certainly more nutrients to a dish). Sprinkle them with a little salt, and leave for half an hour or so to draw out the moisture.

Chop the onions and fry three-quarters of them gently in butter and oil in a pan; as they start to soften, add the aubergine, and cook until soft and lightly browned. Add a couple of tablespoonsful of water to the pan, cover, and leave to simmer a little longer, before either mashing it roughly with a fork or blitzing it briefly in the blender. You are not aiming for a purée and it should retain a little chunkiness. Pop back in the pan to sizzle through and swirl with the *kashk* or yoghurt. Cut 10 discs (use a cake cutter, or cut round an inverted glass) from the *taftoon* breads (small for canapés, larger for supper) and warm them in the oven for a couple of minutes before smearing each one with some of the aubergine mixture. Crisply fry the remaining onion together with the mint and sprinkle on top of each disc as a garnish.

به سبک جدید

Potted Shrimps with Saffron and *Sabzi*

Contrary to the current media bias, the Persians aren't a particularly fishy bunch, and so this recipe really is a fusion of ideas. Potted shrimps are, of course, Olde Englishe, devised to keep these morsels fresher for longer. The blend of fish with butter, saffron and luscious herbs make this a dish fit for shahs as well as fisherfolk. Cheating is permissible – using dried herbs instead of fresh is okay, and substituting prawns for shrimps will probably be more or less essential as the real thing is hard to find. This is a useful dinner-party starter as you can make it up to four days beforehand. This will be enough for 5 or 6 people (including some for the cat).

> *a very big handful each of coriander, parsley and chives (fresh or dried)*
> *a small handful of fenugreek (fresh or dried)*
> *350g good quality butter*
> *600g prawns*
> *¼ teaspoonful ground saffron steeped in boiling water*
> *2–3 wholemeal pitta breads*
> *a little olive oil for frying*
> *black pepper and lemon to garnish*

Prepare your herbs: discard the stems, and soak the leaves in water for at least half an hour so that any sediment can settle out. Drain and chop them fairly finely. If using dried herbs, you still need to soak them for half an hour. Fry the herbs in hot oil, rotating vigorously so that they all get coated and do not blacken (this will take 7–8 minutes), then set them aside.

Clarify the butter by melting it then simmering it gently for around 5 minutes; just as it threatens to brown, whip it off the heat and trickle it through a kitchen towel. Keep a bit back, but pour the rest into a frying-pan: when it is hot again, toss in the prawns, drizzle on the saffron and cook for a few minutes. Stir in the herbs, sizzle a bit more, and then divide the mixture between six ramekin dishes, sealing each one off with a little of the reserved butter. Chill for at least a couple of hours. Prepare *nachos* by toasting the bread so that it puffs slightly, and then cutting each piece into eight. Heat some olive oil in a frying-pan and fry the bread until crisp. Drain on a kitchen towel and cool. Present the ramekins with a plate of lemon wedges, a basket of the *nachos*, and the pepper mill.

Saffron – a few facts

The King of the Spice World, saffron is as costly as gold, and is even weighed by the carat in certain bazaars. It consists of the stamens of the crocus flower and, as it takes about 15,000 flowers to produce 100g, it is hugely labour-intensive. It is now widely believed that it originated in Crete, but before long had made its way to Persia and from there spread its fragrant, vibrant trail around the world. It even made it to our dank and dismal isle – Saffron Walden is indeed named after the spice that was formerly harvested there, and there is a growing saffron industry to this day in Wales. But the best saffron in the world comes from Iran – even the Spanish concede that theirs lacks the strength of colour and aroma of the Persian crocus.

Its uses are many – it is used as a dye for clothes, as ink, medicinally and in food. It is undoubtedly important in other countries – a bedrock of Spanish cuisine, and colouring the defining image of the Buddhist monk – but it has stained Iranian culture and cuisine through to the core. It wanders across nearly every page of this book, nearly as frequently as salt and pepper. My mother-in-law reckons that I am a

saffron slut – I use it to almost vulgar proportions. But it has in its heady smell all the warmth and magic of hot climates and carefree times, and it is the colour of happiness – it is hard to resist. Furthermore, since I started incorporating it in my diet, my hayfever, allergies and eczema have rarely made an appearance.

> Laughter, reunion and coming together smell of saffron, while tears and distance have the stench of onions.
>
> Rumi

It is best used ground – but resist the temptation to buy ready-ground, as this is often adulterated with Ahura Mazda-knows-what. It is easy enough to grind it yourself in a pestle and mortar, or whizz it in a coffee grinder. Once ground, keep it in a dry, airtight jar. When a recipe calls for some, pour a little boiling water on to a saucer, and add ¼ – ½ teaspoon saffron – the spice thus steeped in the liquid will go further and mix well with other ingredients. And saffron used like this really does go far – if you accidentally make too much, just pour the liquid into a little pot and keep it in the fridge until next time you need it. One final tip: always wear yellow clothing when cooking with saffron, or at least a pinny.

Yoghurt

ماست

Like many Middle Eastern countries, Iran eats a lot of yoghurt. The chances are the product evolved simultaneously in several countries across the region as a fortuitous accident: no fridge...hot climate.... It was swiftly established as a favourite and, furthermore, even thousands of years ago it was widely understood to be an aid to the digestion. The fact that it contains live, friendly bacteria was a great aid in times when the provenance of meat was not always of the best. Yoghurt is a good accompaniment for heavy, meaty dishes because it is 'cold' in nature (see Chapter Fourteen), and helps to balance things out. For the same reason it is never eaten with fish.

In Iran most housewives make their own yoghurt. It is really not my intention to portray Iran as a nation populated by mini-Martha Stewarts, with every domestic skill mastered, no cake stall or crochet pattern too much, but generally (and for reasons I hardly need spell out) they are more capable and industrious than Western housewives. I would not presume to hold them up as paragons of domesticity – it is simply a fact that they learn more homely skills at mother's knee than we do, and there are one or two skills (yoghurt-making being one such) which we could well do with adopting, or at least rediscovering.

You will need: a large bowl and a large saucepan; a largish piece of muslin/fine cotton material (I use a bit of an old summer skirt); and 1 old blanket-type thing.

2 litres full fat milk
1 little tub cheap plain yoghurt (preferably live, although not
actually essential)

به سبک جدید

Firstly bring your milk to the boil in the pan – don't let it boil over, but keep it just 'bubbling under' for around 5 minutes. Take the pan off the heat, and allow to cool until you can just about stick your finger in it without squealing. Mix a little of the milk together with the yoghurt in the big bowl, and then, whisking all the time, pour in the rest. Cover the bowl with cling film or a plate, and wrap the whole thing in an old blanket. Nestle it somewhere warm for at least 8 hours (overnight) – an airing cupboard is ideal, or a warm bathroom. At the end of this time you can eat the yoghurt just as it is, but it is even nicer strained – just spoon the yoghurt into the middle of the muslin/cloth, tie all four corners firmly together, and dangle over the sink for a couple of hours – the watery element will drain away leaving lovely creamy yoghurt. If you are a real yoghurt aficionado, then before you finish one batch, use a little of it as a starter culture for the next batch.

The Iranians have developed quite a range of dishes which blend yoghurt with other things – I have outlined but a few below. It is quite fun to make a trio of these 'dips' and serve them alongside each other, either as a starter or a fitting accompaniment to a rich meaty feast.

غذا های مخصوص ایرانی

Borani-ye Esfanaj – Yoghurt with Spinach

Borani is named after one Pourandokht, a very popular queen of olden Iran. Apparently she was inordinately fond of yoghurt with things up it, and this dish was her favourite of them all.

> *1 large onion*
> *oil or butter for frying*
> *a smidgin of ground turmeric (optional)*
> *1 x 500g tub thick(ish) yoghurt*
> *salt and pepper*
> *1.5–2kg fresh spinach, washed and chopped (or 2 packs frozen)*

It couldn't be simpler – just chop and fry the onion gently in the oil, add the turmeric and the spinach and sauté for around 5 minutes. Allow to cool thoroughly, season to taste, then mix well with the yoghurt. Serve chilled with *lavash* bread or crudités, or as an accompaniment to kebabs.

Must-o-Khiar – Yoghurt with Cucumber

This dish does of course crop up in the cuisine of every country east of
Athens and west of Tokyo (think of the Greek *tsatsiski*, or the Indian
raitha), but that does not make it any the less authentic with Persian
food. In Iran they benefit from having the weensiest cucumbers with
the most wonderful fresh flavour – gorgeous to eat on their own with a
sprinkling of salt: these are available in England in Middle Eastern shops,
but a run-of-the-mill cucumber will do. A proper Iranian housewife will
peel the cucumber and, if using the larger variety, will de-seed it as well.
I rarely can be doing with any of that I must admit.

> ½ regular cucumber (or 4–5 baby ones)
> 500g strained yoghurt
> salt and pepper
> olive oil
> sprinkling mint
> finely diced onion (optional)
> 12 diced walnuts (optional)
> handful sultanas (optional)

Authenticity would demand that you grate your cucumber – I chop
mine because it does not get as bruised and will therefore last a bit
longer. So, chop the cucumber, mix it into the yoghurt and add the
other ingredients to taste. I rarely use sultanas and walnuts – this is
another convention in Iran designed to alleviate the ill-effects of having
too much 'cold' food (see Chapter Fourteen) as they are both 'warm'.
Incidentally, in Iran this dish (without the fancy bits) is the traditional
accompaniment to a glass of vodka – vodka is 'hot', and the yoghurt
offsets this.

Must-e-Moussir – Yoghurt with Spring Garlic

Fresh spring garlic is available in Britain, but this recipe is more usually made with dried spring garlic (often mis-translated as shallots), and this is available in good Middle Eastern shops. If you cannot find spring garlic, then regular garlic with a little onion mixed in will give a reasonable approximation of how this should taste. This is perhaps the most popular of all the yoghurty dishes – it is fair to say that Iranians are generally very fond of their garlic.

> *200g dried spring garlic (or ½ bulb of the regular variety with 1*
> *small onion)*
> *500g thick yoghurt*
> *dash of olive oil, plus salt and pepper*

Soak the *moussir* (garlic) overnight; to be honest I usually soak it for 48 hours, changing the water several times. Chop it very finely, and then mix with the other ingredients. The olive oil is merely to give the dish a thick and glossy appearance – it is not essential. Eat with herbs and warm bread.

Smoked Salmon with Persian Pesto

This is based on one of my cousin Stephen's recipes. Poor chap's a banker, but he really should have been a chef.

I always keep a jar of some sort of pesto in the pantry – it is amazingly versatile. This one with tarragon is useful for all sorts of fish and chicken dishes. The use of dried whey instead of Parmesan is optional – I originally devised it because my mother-in-law loathes cheese with a ferocity which beggars belief. This is a great starter to have on the hoof, at drinks parties or as part of a rolling buffet, because although it is messy it still qualifies as finger-food. But it also makes a grand supper for Sunday evenings (which I am sure you will agree have a self-indulgent, mellow quality about them which eludes other evenings). These quantities will serve 4 to 6 people as a starter.

1 bunch fresh tarragon (2 large handfuls)
handful fresh parsley
3–4 cloves garlic
75g pumpkin seed kernels (pretty colour, and better for you than pine nuts)
good olive oil
30–40g dried, crumbled kashk *(or dried* labneh/Parmesan*)*
salt and pepper
1 sheet taftoon *or other knobbly flat bread*
2 tablespoons mascarpone
smoked salmon

Pick through and wash the herbs, and then shake them dry (good idea to put a couple of sprigs aside for garnish). Best to use a blender for the next bit, but you can do energetic things with a pestle and mortar

if you wish. Buzz the herbs together with the garlic and pumpkin seed kernels. Now, by hand, whisk in enough olive oil to make the resulting green gunk look like a sauce (about 200ml should do), and finally mix in the *kashk* (whey) or Parmesan. Season to taste.

Preheat the oven to gas mark 6 (200°C). Spread the *taftoon naan* with some pesto, and pop it in the oven for about 3 minutes. Whip it out again, smear with mascarpone, and then drape the salmon languidly across the top. Garnish with reserved sprigs of herb, and swirls of lemon or lime. Serve immediately – but make sure you get your share afore it leaves the kitchen, because there won't be any left later on.

Variations on pesto: dill is good in pesto. I mix a handful of dill with a handful of parsley and the garlic as above. Instead of pumpkin seeds, I use 50g dried broad beans which have been soaked overnight and then drained. And I add half a teaspoon of ground saffron steeped in boiled water (cool before adding) along with the olive oil and *kashk*.

Tom's Broad Beans

باقلا به سبک تام

As corner-shop-to-the-stars, we get regular visits from real chefs who *actually know what they are doing*. And as we are rather fond of food, it is always a pleasure, nay, an honour, to pass the time of day chin-wagging on all matters cooking-related. One of our most frequent visitors is Tom Norrington-Davies, food columnist for the Saturday *Telegraph*, and it is actually one of his recipes I have shamelessly purloined. He assembled this when he was guest chef at the Flavas of Peckham festival one year, and as it is (almost) entirely made of ingredients from our shop, it seems only appropriate to reproduce it here. This serves 4 as a starter.

به سبک جدید

400g shelled (shucked) broad beans, preferably baby ones
2 teaspoons dried or fresh dill weed
dash of good olive oil
salt and black pepper
200g–250g really good mozzarella cheese, cut into 1cm cubes
2 beef tomatoes and 1 small onion (optional garnish)
1 large sheet lavash *bread (or other really flat bread)*

This is a last minute job, but it couldn't be simpler. Sauté the broad beans in olive oil, add the dill and a twist of black pepper, and then finally add the mozzarella, stirring constantly. Add a bit of salt if required – I am a bit of a Grinch when it comes to salt, so you may well find yourself adding more than I have recommended to many of my recipes.

Halve the tomatoes through the length of the core, and then slice them very thinly into half moons. Range the slices like flower petals round the edge of four plates: slice the onion, and drape it prettily on top of the tomatoes.

Cut the *lavash* into four squares, and heat through in the oven for a couple of minutes before putting one square in the middle of each plate. Divide the beany mixture between them.

Variation: this is a great little dish just as it is, but if you want a bit more 'meat' to your starter, add some pancetta or lardons of bacon or chopped halal salami at the bean-sautéing stage.

A Bit More About the Original Persepolis

It wasn't originally a corner shop. Persepolis Mark 1 was built around 2,500 years ago as a sort of stately pleasure dome, a palace fit for the Achaemenid kings of the age. In Persian it is known as Takht-e-Jamshid, Jamshid's throne, named after the great priest/king who is credited with founding the Iranian nation. In truth he probably had nothing to do with Persepolis, although as he lived 700 years, he might well have passed through on a day-trip.

The city was built to be the capital of the Persian Empire, but it was so hidden away in the mountains that in practice most business was

به سبک جدید

run from other towns. But symbolically it was the heart of all things Persian. It was also possibly the most opulent settlement the world has ever seen. It was to Persepolis that all subject nations came each *Nowrooz* (New Year – see p. 174) bearing tributes for the king. The first king actually to sit on the throne was Darius I; his string of successors terminated in 330BC with the assassination of Darius III and the arrival of that arch hooligan, Alexander 'the Great', who managed to burn the palace down during a drunken orgy one evening. But all was not lost...the spirit of the place was nurtured by a secret brotherhood down through the centuries until it could be suppressed no more and finally re-emerged as a proud and glorious corner shop in Peckham.

The remains of the original Persepolis are perhaps Iran's greatest tourist site, and they are startlingly beautiful, albeit utterly ruined. The tall, tall columns rising in ghostly fashion from the plain, together with the sheer size of the site, convey the majesty of what was – it does not take much imagination to hear the vast 'halls' once again echoing with the sounds of celebration and victory. Persepolis embodies the dignity and pride of what it is to be Iranian, in spite of the efforts of the last Shah who, in a misguided attempt to shore up his monarchy, staged a gloriously over-the-top pageant of Iranian history in front of dozens of world leaders.

Tahcheen – Chicken and Rice Cake

تَچِین

This is a highly unusual and satisfying dish to make. Cooked in larger quantities it is a good and economical way of making a little bit of chicken go far. Actually we normally make big trays of it at home and eat it as a main course with lots of salad and relishes. But because it is so unusual, it is great to serve cooked in individual portions either as a starter or an accompaniment to another dish. If you don't have ramekins, make it in a larger dish and cut it into wedges or cubes. This will feed 6 people as a starter.

2 small skinless breasts of chicken on the bone
1 onion, roughly chopped
salt and pepper
2 cups basmati rice
some ghee or butter
⅓ teaspoonful ground saffron
2 eggs
250ml natural yoghurt

Wash the chicken and place in a pan with the onion and some salt and pepper, cover with water, bring to the boil and set to simmer for around half an hour or until the chicken is just coming off the bone. Remove the chicken from the stock, set the stock to one side, and then strip the meat from the bone. Prepare your rice as usual (preferably with ghee, even though it is very naughty), but without overcooking it or allowing *tahdik* (a crispy crust – see Chapter Seven) to form. Mix the flaked chicken thoroughly into the rice, and turn the mixture into greased ramekins or a buttered oven dish. Strain 250ml of the reserved stock into a mixing jug, sprinkle in the saffron, and then whisk in the yoghurt,

به سبک جدید

followed by the egg. Pour the resulting 'slurry' over the rice and chicken, and then cover the dish/es with a piece of greased foil. Bake in the oven at 200°C/gas mark 5 for one hour, then turn the heat down to 180°C/gas mark 4 and bake for a further hour. Bring the remaining stock to the boil and serve alongside the dish, with plenty of herbs, pickles, raw onion and garlic.

To make this dish as a main course for 6 people, use one whole chicken, 750ml of yoghurt, 3 eggs and 6 cups of basmati rice – and a bit more saffron. Otherwise the method is the same.

To make a vegetarian version of this dish, blanch 1 finely chopped floret of broccoli and 1 bunch of roughly chopped spinach in approximately 500ml of vegetable stock, and then proceed as above, substituting the vegetables for the chicken.

غذاهای مخصوص ایرانی

CHAPTER TWO

CHAPTER TWO

BREAKFASTS AND SNACKS

An experienced Iranian housewife will usually have a fridge full of easily assembled or heated snack foods. My mother-in-law will often spend all day Sunday cooking, preparing proper food for her family to replace all those skipped breakfasts and fast-food lunches of the week ahead.

The Iranians are inveterate snackers and their cuisine amply supports this habit. Not only do they eat proper breakfasts, lunches and dinners, they are lucky enough to live in a country where the stuff of healthy snacks is abundant – seeds, nuts, fresh and dried fruits, every household has jars and bowls of these. It has to be said that the seed thing is at first quite incomprehensible; I have still not acquired the oral dexterity required to open and shell the wretched things, and usually end up having to spit the whole soggy mess out. Furthermore, after entertaining any group of Iranians, I have to spend many an extra hour sweeping up – the floor is always a sea of discarded shells. But these seeds (melon, sunflower, pumpkin, courgette) are just so popular; when you share your life with an Iranian you learn to check every pocket before filling the washing machine.

Nuts in Iran are often eaten raw, fresh, straight from the tree and still in their skins. Again to the uninitiated palate, these can taste odd – bitter and cloying. But it makes you realize just how old most of the nuts that we eat in the west probably are.

Iranian fresh fruit is tastier than its European cousins – most Iranian produce is in fact organic. It is freshly picked, and strictly of the season – none of these suspect winter strawberries, or summer pomegranates that are to be found in our supermarkets. It benefits from being sun-ripened.

Fruit is eaten at every opportunity – with cheese at breakfast, during the day, before dinner, and quite often in dinner – there are very many savoury dishes in Iran which incorporate fruit. Any Iranian housewife worth her salt will always keep a full fruit basket, because when guests come a-visiting, that is the first thing that they are offered. (Followed by tea. And then sweets, and nuts. And you will have to make an effort to consume it all, otherwise offence will be taken.)

Even 'fast food' tends to be healthier in Iran (although there are now a good few burger joints opening in the bigger cities); traditional street food (with the exception of kebabs) tends to consist of things like freshly cooked beetroot, chestnuts, salted boiled turnips (see Chapter Nine).

Lorry Food One – *Tuna Chelow*

چلو ماہی

Lorry Food, I should explain, is my nickname for the cuisine of some of Iran's greatest chefs – its lorry drivers. The first time I became aware of this unlikely fact was one winter night as we unloaded our first ever truck of dates from Iran. Unloading a lorry when you are self-employed and have no staff is no joke: you have to bully and cajole all your friends, neighbours and family into helping, and still it just seems to go on hour after hour, case after case. At about one in the morning the driver, who had until then been helping us, retired to his cab and reappeared in the traditional house-clothes of an Iranian chap – baggy Kurdish trousers, slippers – it seemed that he was retiring for the evening. We immediately protested that he should wait for dinner (which was on schedule for around three in the morning). Smiling, he opened the side compartment under the main body of the lorry and withdrew first

a stretch of well-worn carpet, then a deckchair, and finally a Primus stove. A few battered pots and pans followed, and then, blow me if he didn't produce a professional chef's roll of utensils. Before too long the kettle was on for tea, while he dug out the ingredients for dinner: basmati rice, canned Persian baked beans, fresh herbs, chillies, onions and a can of Caspian's finest (cousin of) sturgeon. Through force of circumstance, rice cooked in this way always tastes better – Iranian classic cuisine demands that you wash rice thoroughly, when in fact it is more nutritious and tasty when left alone. Soon this enterprising nomad had concocted dinner for all seven of us, and did it taste good. We were cold, dirty and tired, easily impressed if you like, but still that meal remains seminal to my view and interpretation of Iranian food. This chap knew what he wanted to eat, and nothing was going to stop him from enjoying that meal at the time and in the manner he desired. The style, the ritual, the essential hospitality of the Iranian – it was all there on a rug in the middle of a Peckham street, surrounded by boxes, thousands of miles from its country of origin.

> *1 cup rice per person (but really this is great with leftover rice too)*
> *1–2 cans (preferably Persian) tuna*
> *home-baked beans (see recipe on p. 155) – but any canned, baked large*
>   *beans in sauce will do*
> *quartered raw onion and fresh herbs*
> *chillies and raw garlic (optional)*

Cook the rice; flake the tuna and mix it in. Warm the beans and stir these through as well. Sprinkle with black pepper, garnish with fresh herbs, and eat with the onion (using the wedges as a spoon is quite fun). Grated cheese on top is another optional extra.

Like most rough and ready recipes, you can make this quite elegant – reduce the quantity of rice for example, and serve it instead with *barberi* bread; use fresh tuna; grate mozzarella and fresh basil on top... but this is and always will be Lorry Food One.

Lorry Food Two

After the above experience, I have of course made it my business to discuss the menus from each lorry driver's itinerary (much to their amusement). For this recipe the driver uses a sort of dried salami, which obviously travels well, but he said that it is just as good with canned luncheon meat...so I suggest you try this with Spam, which is readily available since its relaunch, and similar in flavour to Iranian canned meat products. Some of the other ingredients he had clearly 'borrowed' from our lorryload of pickles – which makes it all the more fun. In his case, he broke his stale *lavash* in pieces and dropped it into the frying-pan with the tomatoes and meat – but I prefer croûtons.

> *2 cloves garlic, roughly chopped*
> *dash of oil*
> *2–3 slices stale bread, cubed*
> *1 onion*
> *5–6 Persian (or other) gherkins*
> *1 small can Spam or other luncheon meat, cut in 1cm cubes*
> *4–5 large tomatoes, roughly chopped*
> *1 teaspoon tomato paste*
> *chilli sauce (optional)*

Firstly you should fry the garlic in some oil; set the garlic to one side, and then fry the cubed bread in the same oil. Once it has browned, set this aside as well. Again in the same oil, fry the onion, add the pre-fried garlic and the gherkins, and then the Spam. Once the onion has started to brown a little, add the tomatoes, and stir in the tomato purée and chilli sauce. Cook for another five minutes so that the juices of the tomatoes start to run; season to taste. Strew the croûtons over the

top, and then eat from the pan, with extra (preferably fresh) bread for mopping. Our driver had this last part down to a fine art – he mopped so well there was no subsequent need to wash the pan.

Importing stuff

The import trade came as a revelation. It is extremely hard. As much as my heart soars at the prospect of bringing fresh and unusual produce to the British table, it sinks at the thought of yet another consignment arriving at the airport at two in the morning, or another container of jumbled goods which we know will be six hours in the unloading. Although I refer to our own experiences here, the same is true for any small company importing food from outside the EU; it is not for those of a naturally irate disposition.

Our goods are sourced in Iran by my father-in-law, using a chain of connections he has forged over many years. Usually, initial deals will be struck during a 3–4 day marathon in the bazaar in Tehran. This is followed by farm and workshop visits up and down the country, where quality and packaging can be discussed. Just for the record, it actually doesn't matter how much we discuss and proof-read labelling for our goods – our suppliers still write whatever they want to write on the foods. Some of their efforts at translation are priceless, and we would not change it for the world; thus these almost metaphysical lines from Jahan Tea:

> We expect the customers to buy Jahan Tea in packages which bear special sign. Customer is our best friend. He is not dependent on us, We are not dependent on him. He is not alienated from us, He is part of us.

Our containers of goods are sent directly from the relevant factory, but the lorry-loads are mixed and are thus assembled by us – we contract a driver, and dispatch the consignment from Tehran. Bureaucracy in Iran

به سبک جدید

is 'colourful' – it can take days to find the right official to sign the right documents – but Middle Eastern muddle-headedness has nothing on the panjandrums of the EU, and things always get done. Far from breathing a sigh of relief, it is actually once the goods have set off that one starts to sweat. The first-ever lorry we sent vanished for six weeks in Eastern Europe (the usual transit time from Tehran to Peckham is one week) – it turned out that the driver had broken his leg, conveniently near the house of a long-lost relative, and had stopped there to recuperate. Not unnaturally, those six lost weeks caused Customs to raise their officious eyebrows, so then we had to wait for them to fly in an expert from Volvo to disassemble the lorry nut by bolt (for the privilege of which, make no mistake, we were charged in full). Another of these drivers got to Europe, realized he didn't have the right visas, so dispatched a friend of his to bring our lorry over. The problem was that said friend, whilst having the right visas, had absolutely nothing resembling any form of driving qualification. Allah must have been smiling on him, because he arrived with our goods safe and sound.

Our first-ever container docked at more or less every port in the Far East before making its eventual way to Felixstowe (it took two months as opposed to the scheduled one). We have had to learn to rant and rave, and to assume the worse from the moment of dispatch; international 'spedition' companies, as they like to be called, can often be an unhelpful combination of avaricious and stupid.

But the headaches really begin when the lorry or container arrives in this country. Perhaps the authorities view anything from Iran as direct from the Axis of Evil; it invariably attracts unwonted attention. You should see the paperwork. Gallows humour might suggest we declare the guns, drugs and immigrants *toute de suite...*

Like all importers, we use freight clearance agents to handle the customs entries for us – it is specialized work, and, like the proverbial sailor, we tend to have a different one in every port. The ideal scenario for imported food is that it gets immediate paperwork clearance and, after the statutory X-Ray, is waved on its way. It is of course right and

reassuring that Port Health wants occasionally to inspect or sample something, but less so when a week's delay is built in, or the dock company breaks 20–30 cases during a careless 'out-turn' (for the labour for which we are also invoiced), or that we get charged demurrage (space rental) for their tardiness and inefficiency.

As for airfreight, this is the stuff of nightmares. We cannot avoid it. The fresh fruits and pastries we import are fragile and would not withstand the trip by road or sea. But freight-handling is often unsatisfactory (more trenchant critics might say lazy and corrupt). Consignments arrive late, short and damaged; there is always a queue to collect one's goods – our record is 12 hours – even though our produce is highly perishable. On airport nights our drivers often don't sleep, such is the rush to get the goods to our customers in prime condition.

For all the difficulties, this is our reward: an exotic fruit on a tree in Iran on Monday morning can in theory be in your fruit bowl by Tuesday evening. We can bring the spice which was in the bazaar a month ago straight to your pantry. Cardamom-scented sweets from a baker in Tehran will still be warm for a party on the morrow.

A luggage bearer

به سبک جدید

The *Kookoo Burger*

Kookoo sabzi is one of the Great Four herb-based Iranian dishes, along-side *ghormeh sabzi*, *ash reshteh* and *sabzi pulao*. It is quintessentially an omelette *aux* not-very-*fines-herbes* – it is so thick with herbs that it is a rich green in colour. It is usually eaten as a sandwich ingredient, in soft bread with tomatoes, herbs and pickled cucumbers, but it is great on its own or as an accompaniment. This version of it sees it transformed into funky burger format, and is very popular with juniors.

> *1 bunch coriander plus 1 of flat-leaf parsley*
> *few sprigs fenugreek*
>> *(or use a bag of* sabzi kookoo *dried herb mix, available from*
>> *Iranian supermarkets, instead of the previous three items)*
> *1 small bunch spring onions*
> *6 eggs*
> *1 dessertspoonful flour and ½ teaspoonful baking powder*
> *salt and pepper*
> *olive oil for frying*
> optional extras:
>> *100g lightly broken walnuts, or*
>> *100g soaked barberries, or*
>> *100g soaked raisins, or*
>> *100g toasted pine nuts*
> *slices burger cheese*
> *mayonnaise*
> *soft burger buns*

Trim and soak your herbs and leave to dry a while. Wash and chop the spring onions, and then chop the herbs (if using dried herbs, soak them

and then squeeze out as much of the moisture as possible). Beat the eggs well, and then blend in the flour, baking powder, seasoning and any of your chosen optional extras. Fry the herbs and spring onions in hot oil for around five minutes, turning constantly, and then pour the egg mixture on top. Cook on a lowish heat for around 15 mins, and then either toss the omelette (show-off!), or pop the pan under a hot grill for 3 minutes or so. Slide on to a plate, and then cut into burger-sized pieces. Halve and toast your buns lightly, and then assemble them – a swirl of mayonnaise, a *kookoo*, a slice of cheese and a pile of fresh herbs. Serve with chips and relishes.

Variations on the Theme

Kookoo sabzi is the most famous of a whole range of *kookoos*. The permutations are endless, but other popular ingredients are cauliflower, potato, lamb's brain, French beans, and sugar – the recipe can be made as a sweet breakfast or pudding option (see separate recipe below). But my favourite *kookoo* is aubergine – *kookoo-ye-bademjan*.

> *2 large aubergines*
> *salt and pepper*
> *8 eggs*
> *1 tablespoon flour plus 1 level teaspoon baking powder*
> *100g walnuts, lightly broken*
> *1 chopped onion*
> *2 tablespoons olive oil*
> *½ teaspoon ground saffron, steeped in boiling water*

Top and tail the aubergines, and remove most, if not all, of the peel. Cut into cubes and then blanch in boiling water for around 15 minutes: drain and then mash with a little salt and pepper. Whisk the eggs with the flour and the baking powder, and stir in the walnuts. Fry the onion

in the oil, and then add in the aubergine, breaking it up and mixing it with a wooden spatula. Pour the saffron into the eggs, and mix the whole egg concoction into the aubergine. Cook on the ring for about 8 minutes before moving the frying-pan to under a hot grill to cook the top of the *kookoo*. Again, cut into wedges and eat hot or cold.

Sweet *Kookoo*

Sweet omelettes and sugared scrambled eggs are common in other parts of Europe (notably France and Belgium) and, once you get over the unexpected mix of flavours, they are extraordinarily tasty. You can serve this as a pudding, with a sharp fruit compote and dollop of crème fraîche perhaps. But it is just great with coffee over the Sunday newspapers. You need, per person:

> *2 large or 3 small eggs*
> *2 teaspoons sugar*
> *1 teaspoon flour*
> *½ teaspoon cinnamon (optional)*
> *butter or ghee*

Beat the eggs, and add the dry ingredients. Melt a knob of butter or ghee in a frying-pan, and pour the eggy mixture in. Cook for a minute or two on the stove, before transferring to the grill and cooking the top – or you can turn the omelette over and continue to cook on the ring if you are dextrous enough. Serve on its own with some warm breakfast bread, or as an accompaniment to ham ('jambon' made with halal chicken and beef is popular in Iran), in which case you may want to streak a little maple or date syrup over it.

Takht-e-Jamshid Eggs

نیمرو به سبک تخت جمشید

The Iranian style of eating is generally more conducive to comfort and social exchange than our somewhat stuffy Western habits. Nothing better exemplifies this fact than our favourite fried eggs.

As we learnt in the last chapter, the real name for Persepolis is Takht-e-Jamshid – the 'throne of Jamshid'. Jamshid was a powerful priest-king way back at the dawn of Persian legend; he is also the current proprietor of the Peckham branch. The modern Jamshid has laid claim to this recipe as his own, but I suspect that something like this has been cooked by hungry priests, kings, warriors and other Jamshids through the centuries. It's the stuff of Sunday brunch, and it's awfully easy to make.

> *olive oil (the very best quality that you can find)*
> *1–2 smoked sausages per person (as Iranian-style 'calvas' are*
> *   practically impossible to get in the UK, we recommend*
> *   frankfurters or their halal equivalent); if you are vegetarian,*
> *   halloumi cheese does a very nice stand-in for the sausages*
> *2–3 cherry tomatoes per person (or 1 large one)*
> *freshly ground black pepper*
> *2 eggs per person*
> *ground turmeric*
> *fresh or dried dill (but if you don't like dill, oregano is quite fun too)*
> lavash *or* barberi *bread for scooping and mopping*

Heat the oil in a large, preferably heavy-bottomed, frying-pan. You will need enough to cover the bottom of the pan to a depth of 1mm. Slice the sausages diagonally into 2.5cm chunks (or, if you are using halloumi, 1cm cubes will do), and sauté them gently. Add the tomatoes

به سبک جدید

and pepper, and continue to fry for a minute or two more. Make a few holes in the mixture with the back of a wooden spoon and crack the eggs in. Splash the yolks with hot oil and then sprinkle the top of each with turmeric (about one-eighth of a teaspoonful per egg) and a pinch of dill. Once the eggs have cooked underneath, flash the whole pan under the grill for a minute, and then rush it to the table with warm bread and a basket of *sabzi*. Yes, that's right – eat out of the pan – it tastes just so much better.

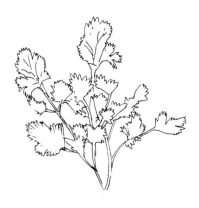

غذا های مخصوص ایرانی

Breakfast Rice

پلومخصوص صبحانه

Breakfast risotto made with dates and saffron. Strangeness aside, it's great for those occasions when you really don't know what you want to eat – when otherwise it's cornflakes. It's based on a recipe from up north (Iranian, that is, not Yorkshire), a region which is often the source of much merriment on account of its rice-eating habits. This will feed 4 as a sizeable snack.

100g raisins
200ml cold Earl Grey tea
3–4 cardamom pods, cracked slightly
½ teaspoon ground saffron steeped in boiling water
150ml milk
butter
200g fresh Iranian dates, stoned
100g arborio rice
1 tablespoon sugar

Soak the raisins and the cardamom pods in the tea for a minimum of 6 hours. When you are ready to cook, firstly add the saffron water to the milk so that it can infuse. Drain the raisins, reserving the tea. Melt a knob of butter in a pan, and add the raisins, cardamom and dates; fry gently, and then add the rice, turning it so that it all gets coated. Stir in the sugar, and then slowly add the milk, stirring constantly; when it is all absorbed, do the same with the tea. In all, the rice should take about 25 minutes to cook through.

Serve with hot tea.

به سبک جدید

Salad *Oliveiyeh*

سالاد الویه

This is a twist on a dish popular in many countries. A sort of posh potato salad, it undoubtedly originated in Russia – the Spanish even call their version *ensaladilla à la Russe*. And I remember something really exotic called Russian Salad appearing at Abigail-style parties during the heady days of my 1970s childhood. Anyway the Persian version is popular right across the land, and is eaten as a snack, at parties, and as a sandwich filling. As with all dishes, some of the ingredients are debatable, one housewife using peas and carrots and the next throwing up her hands in horror at the very thought of them. We obviously think our version the best, and it's pretty simple. This makes a very big bowlful.

1.5kg peeled potatoes
butter
English mustard
2 breasts cooked chicken (bit of a waste to use breasts really, and so
  the meat from a couple of legs and thighs would be adequate. This
  is obviously a good way of using left-over roast chicken.)
400g mayonnaise
either 1 large tin garden peas or 1 small bag frozen peas, blanched and
  drained
1 jar (750g size) Persian pickled cucumbers
1–2 bunches spring onions
one large bunch coriander or parsley (according to taste)
one bunch fresh tarragon (optional) or two desertspoonsful dried
  tarragon
6–8 hard-boiled eggs
salt and pepper and lemon juice

غذاهای مخصوص ایرانی

Boil the potatoes and then mash them roughly with just a little butter and a couple of teaspoonsful of mustard. Flake the chicken meat into the mixture, and add the mayonnaise and the peas. Reserve four cucumbers, and drain and dice the rest. Chop the spring onions and wash and chop the fresh herbs (put a bit of each to one side for garnish). Leave one of the eggs to one side and roughly chop the rest. Stir the cucumbers, herbs, eggs and onions into the potato mixture with a dash of lemon juice, and season to taste. Pack into a deep dish or, if you are serving it immediately, on to a suitably grand platter, smooth the top and make pretty with sliced gherkins (remember, those four you kept back), and sliced egg (likewise). A sprinkling of green stuff is good as well. This is a good filler for buffet spreads, but we usually wrap it in *lavash* bread for extemporized sandwiches on the hoof.

Iranian Sandwiches

Whilst *lavash* bread can be wrapped around anything to create a sandwich of sorts, if you offer an Iranian a sandwich, he will expect a small (20cm or so) baton of French-style bread with one of a number of popular fillings. *Oliveiyeh* is just one of these – also popular are *kookoo* (see p. 68), *cottelettes* (see p. 88), mortadella, tongue and frankfurters (see the *Bandari* recipe p. 85). They are assembled with finely sliced, seasoned cucumber and tomato, a good handful of fresh herbs (usually just coriander and parsley) and, most importantly, thinly sliced Persian gherkins. These sandwiches are sold at public events throughout Iran, and are hugely popular with ex-pat Iranians at ex-pat Iranian events in Britain and America.

Iranian picnics

Picnicking is extraordinarily popular in Iran. It is probably all Omar
Khayam's fault – just take those classic lines:

> A Book of Verses underneath the Bough,
> A Jug of Wine, a Loaf of Bread – and Thou
> Beside me singing in the Wilderness –
> O Wilderness were Paradise enow!

Poem after poem of the classic era (twelfth to thirteenth centuries AD)
extols the virtues of *al fresco* eating (usually, of course, with copious
quantities of wine), and much classic art is dedicated to the same theme
– young lovers or groups of friends sharing food under a tree or in a
courtyard. They do of course (for most of the year) have the climate for
it, and the people possess a sort of childlike spontaneity which sees little
outbreaks of picnicking by the road, in car parks – anywhere there's
room for them to sit down, and anytime they're a tad peckish. It is not
unusual for my mother-in-law to cook a full meal (rice and all), decide
it is a nice day, wrap the whole lot up and cart it off to the park.

It is the more delightful because the habit persists even though
the prohibitions of the revolution in 1979 effectively shut down huge
sectors of public life. The covering of women to a large extent sent them
scurrying indoors – those that could afford it installed every known
comfort at home and pulled up the drawbridge. Social life, previously
based in the bazaars, streets and cafés, mutated to something based
on the home and the family, and just a few trusted friends. But as soon
as the weather changes after the long, dark days of winter, and until
the evenings start to draw in again at the time of the autumn equinox,
they're out there – whole tribes of relatives, dotted all over the grass of
every park across Iran, picnicking. And it is picnicking in style – even
Crichton would be impressed. There are *kookoo* and *dolmeh* and *lavash*
and *sabzi* and cheese. There's a Thermos full of tea, and another full of

fragrant fresh fruit frappé, a bag of *torkhmeh* (seeds) and the ubiquitous bowl of fruit with baby cucumbers. And usually either the barbecue comes too, or they will use a municipal barbecue area. Many towns have designated picnic areas under the trees, with raised platforms upon which to spread a rug, each a discreet distance from the next to allow a degree of freedom and privacy.

Dolmeh

دلمه

The thing about stuffed stuff is that all the fillings are interchangeable. Everybody does it differently anyway. There is vast scope for experimentation, and it is rewarding. My mother-in-law rarely just stuffs one thing – she will make a range of different stuffed vegetables and leaves, sometimes all with the same filling, sometimes with different fillings but the same sauce. Although I have ranged these dishes in the snack aisle, (largely the fault of mother-in-law's ungrateful progeny, who grumble that it is not real food and will not themselves contemplate an evening meal composed of such things) they could just as easily feature in the main course or starter sections.

Opinions vary as to which bit of the Middle East may lay claim to the very first stuffing – every country east of Athens seems to have its own version and tales of derivation therefrom. I'm inclined on this occasion to give the Iranians the benefit of the doubt. Anyway, Iranian stuffed stuff (or *dolmeh*, to give its proper name) is actually some of the best, and the act of stuffing is common practice in most Persian kitchens (whereas I always get the feeling that in certain other countries, it is something they just do for tourists).

به سبک جدید

Stuffed Peppers

Most *dolmeh/dolmades/yemistakia/*stuffed vegetables are traditionally filled with a mixture of rice and meat. We've filled this one with a mixture of barley and vegetables just to be different. In fact I regard the meat in *dolmeh* as being largely superfluous, although it is quite a good carrot if you are trying to persuade someone of a nervous culinary disposition to try them for the first time.

I adore peppers, as they are so very useful and obedient. You can stir-fry any mixture of vegetables, add a few seeds and some goat cheese, and tip the whole thing into a halved pepper. Thirty to forty minutes in the oven and you have the most scrumptious, nutritious and thrifty supper. And the oils in vegetables like avocado and green peppers are incredibly good for the skin and joints.

Pot barley is one of the forgotten secrets of English cookery and another of my favourite ingredients – it's versatile, and wholesome, and easy to play with. In truth, in Iran they really only use pearl barley, and then only for soup, but at least they use it. This will be enough for 8 as a starter.

9 capsicum peppers, assorted colours, one of which is chopped
200g pot barley (washed and picked over)
1 large onion, diced
2 green chillies, or ½ really hot red chilli, finely minced
½ teaspoon green cumin seeds
3 cloves garlic, minced
little knob of ginger, finely chopped
2 sticks celery, diced
olive oil
600ml of good vegetable stock

غذا های مخصوص ایرانی

½ bunch each coriander and parsley, washed and chopped
4 large tomatoes, washed and chopped (I practically never bother
*   skinning tomatoes. Here, a real 'chef' probably would.)*
salt
1 tea-cup good tomato juice or passata and 3 tablespoons Persepolis
*   patent tomato sauce (p. 331)*

The chances are that you won't find peppers that will be considerate enough to 'sit up and beg' (unless you blanch them first, thus losing important nutrients), and so I usually halve the peppers from top to bottom, taking care to leave part of the stalk attached to each, and then de-seed them. However, if you want to do it properly, chop a little bit off the bottom of each pepper (so that it has a flat base) and remove its stalk/hat as well. Blanch the peppers and their hats in boiling water for about 3 minutes, remove and set aside.

Sauté the onion, garlic, chilli, cumin, ginger, celery and the chopped pepper together in a little olive oil, and when they start to soften, add the barley. Stir the mixture constantly so that all the grains get coated and sealed, and then add the vegetable stock. Turn the heat very low, and cover the pan. When you see that the stock has all been absorbed, slowly add a further 600ml of cold water. Cover and cook as before. You may need to add a bit more besides. The barley is ready when it is edible without being soggy (after about 40 minutes). It needs still to have a bit of crunch to it as we're going to cook it some more. As you take it off the heat, mix in the majority of the herbs and the chopped tomatoes. Check the seasoning – if you are using stock cubes, these are usually pretty salty anyway. Place your peppers in a shallow oven dish, and then fill each with the barley mixture. Mix together the tomato juice and Persepolitan sauce, and pour around the bottom of the peppers in the dish. Cover with foil and bake on gas mark 5 (180°C) for 40 minutes.

Serve sprinkled with herbs, accompanied with warm bread, yoghurt and salad. This dish is also rather good topped with some melted cheese, or with mascarpone.

به سبک جدید

Stuffed Vineleaves

I don't know why vine leaves have such cachet, an aura of foreignness about them. I mean, they're everywhere, thanks to Greek tourism – most British market towns have a taverna of sorts, and every taverna offers stuffed vineleaves. I tasted my first 'dolmade' at the age of perhaps eight, yet still to this day it feels like exciting food. Anyway, in spite of Greek claims, I have a feeling that this really is a Persian invention – they have always displayed creativity with vine products.

Fresh vine leaves are good to use, but you will need first to blanch them in boiling water for around 15 minutes. Vine leaves in jars can be used, but tend to be tough – you should wash them and then steep them in boiling water for 10 minutes to soften them. This leaves my favourite, the vacuum pack, which are miraculously ready for action, although, as the leaves are usually preserved in salt, a good rinse is called for.

Let's be radical and leave the meat out again. This dish is actually vegan, and almost fat free, but carnivores will never notice. And once you've mastered the rolling part, it's easy.

This will be enough for about 40 vineleaves,

250g rice (long grain is the norm, but short grain is acceptable)
1 large onion, very finely chopped
4 tomatoes, finely chopped
2 tablespoons dried mint
1 tablespoon dried oregano
1 teaspoon ground cinnamon
big handful fresh parsley, finely chopped
1 teaspoon ground black pepper
1 level teaspoon salt

3 tablespoons olive oil
250g vine leaves (1 vacuum packet), well rinsed
juice of one lemon
3 tablespoons grape syrup (optional, but much nicer with)

Mix the uncooked rice with the onion, tomatoes, herbs, spices, seasoning and one tablespoon of the olive oil. Spread a few of the vine leaves out on a flat surface – if any of them have holes in, 'patch' them with smaller leaves. The dull side with the veins showing should be face up, and the stalks should be pointing towards your tummy. Place a heaped teaspoon of rice mixture in the middle of each leaf, near where the stalk and the leaf connect. Roll the two nearest points of each leaf once (away from you) around the mixture, and then 'tuck in' the side bits of the leaf, before continuing to roll away from you. Each parcel thus made should be compact, but not too tight as the rice will expand during cooking. Repeat the exercise until all the whole leaves have been used. Invert a plate in the bottom of a large saucepan (probably best not use the antique Dresden), and line it with any defective or part-leaves. Arrange the stuffed vine leaves close together over the inverted plate, and layer up until they are all snuggled in. Put another inverted plate on top of the *dolmeh* to weigh them down, and then pour in about 750ml of cold water together with the rest of the olive oil, the lemon juice and the grape syrup. Bring to the boil and then set to simmer – they need to cook for around 1 hour and 20 minutes. Remember to check there is enough cooking stock in the pan at all times: top up with water as required. If there is any left-over rice mixture, you can just cook it as normal rice, or use it in other *dolmeh*.

Serve hot or cold – rather good with yoghurt.

You can always use cabbage leaves – just make sure you boil them for around 10 minutes first to make them malleable.

به سبک جدید

Stuffed Aubergines, Mother-in-Law's Recipe

As a concession to inveterate meat-eaters, we'll be totally authentic and use some meat in this recipe. The pairing of minced lamb and aubergine is particularly good – aubergine is the blotting paper of the vegetable world, and so readily absorbs the subtle juices of the lightly spiced lamb. This will feed 4 as a generous supper.

for the aubergines:

4 large aubergines

salt and pepper

100g split peas

150g pudding rice (or other rice of your choice)

1 large onion, chopped

2–3 cloves garlic

500g minced lamb

1 teaspoon ground turmeric

1 teaspoon ground cinnamon

2 teaspoons dried marjoram or oregano

1 teaspoon dried savory or mint

2 tablespoons tomato purée

1 can tomatoes/concasse

for the sauce:

the chopped middle bits of the aubergine

1 medium onion

2 cloves garlic

1 tablespoon tomato purée

1 tablespoon Persepolis patent tomato sauce (or just use two of purée)

350ml (or thereabouts) chicken or vegetable stock

olive oil, salt and pepper

Wash, top and tail the aubergines. If they are truly massive, slice them in half across the aubergine equivalent of their waists – you are aiming to have 4–8 rounds, each 5–6cm high. With a small, pointy knife, scoop or cut out the inside of the aubergines, although you should leave at least 1 ½ cm of flesh all the way round – the vegetables will otherwise collapse during cooking. Salt the inside of the aubergine rings, and set aside. Finely chop the flesh which you have removed, salt this as well, and rest it on some kitchen towel.

Now for the filling. Cook the split peas and the rice in boiling water until both are soft (I usually cook them together in the same pan); drain well. Fry the onion and garlic in some oil, and when they have softened add the minced lamb. Continue to cook, stirring well, for around 5 minutes, before spooning in the spices and herbs, followed a few minutes later by the tomato paste and the tomatoes. Add in the split pea and rice mixture, turn the heat right down, cover and cook for 15–20 minutes, stirring occasionally.

In the meantime, you can make the sauce. Dry the chopped, salted aubergine flesh. Fry it together with the onion and garlic until it is well cooked (verging on mushy). Add the purée and/or tomato sauce, and then buzz through the blender. Put back in the pan, and then add the chicken stock, stirring well so that it combines into a thick, luscious sauce. Taste and season as required.

Wipe the insides of the aubergine rings, and sit them in an ovenproof dish. Pack each one full of the meat mixture, and then pour the sauce around aubergines into the base of the dish. Cover with foil, and bake on gas mark 4 (180°C) for about an hour and a quarter, checking halfway through cooking time that there is enough stock left in the pan.

Yoghurt is the natural accompaniment to this dish, alongside some *lavash* for mopping up.

Aubergine Sandwiches

This is a very naughty recipe. I generally hold that fried chicken (and the fast-food outlets that purvey it) is one of the greatest evils facing modern society today, but I have to admit that this dish would be another contender, were aubergines ever to become as popular as chicken.

Some foods taste better when they are stolen. Not shoplifted, but innocently sampled when the chef's back is turned...and that is how this dish evolved. From stolen fried aubergine. But it is so nice that now I sometimes cook aubergine just for this purpose.

To make about 6 wraps you will need:

2 medium aubergines
salt and pepper
oil for frying
3 sheets lavash *bread (or other flat bread)*
mayonnaise
cucumber and spring onion in julienned strips

Wash and top the aubergines, then slice thinly lengthways. Sprinkle with salt and pop on to a piece of kitchen towel. Cover with another piece of kitchen towel and leave for around half an hour to drain. Wipe the aubergine, then fry in hot oil until each slice is soft and golden brown. Drain on yet more kitchen paper. Warm your chosen bread, and spread it with mayonnaise. Place the aubergines in a thin layer on top, and then the vegetable striplets and a grind or two of black pepper. Roll up and scoff; and if the oil doesn't run down your chin, you probably haven't done it properly.

Nice variation: add a rasher of grilled bacon (halal is available) to each wrap.

Bandari Sausages

سوسیس بندری

'Bandari' anything in Iran tends to be colourful (though slightly risqué or down-market). Literally it means 'of the docks'; this invariably implies that it is from the south of the country, where the warmer climate and the constant flow of sea traffic to ports such as Bandar Abbas have led to a vibrant cultural mix. Bandari music in particular is very popular (just as British sea shanties were a century or so ago) – it has evolved from being the preserve of nautical bods to one of the most popular musical genres. Its fast and infectious beat means that it is invariably the choice at weddings and birthday parties.

And this recipe is equally popular, with its spicy flavours and easy-to-find ingredients. It will serve 2–3 people as a snack.

500g potatoes (new are good, so are waxy ones like Maris Peer)
250g frankfurters, chilled or canned (if using the latter, you want
*   250g drained weight)*
olive oil
4 cloves garlic, chopped
3 green chillies (or ½ habanero chilli)
1 teaspoon ground turmeric
½ teaspoon smoked paprika
1 teaspoon coriander seeds, lightly crushed
salt
250g good (organic, even) tomatoes
2 tablespoons Persepolis patent tomato sauce (see p. 331, or use 1
*   tablespoon purée and 1 tablespoon tomato ketchup)*

Scrub the potatoes and cube them (1½–2cm). Bring to the boil in a pan of water, cook for 5 minutes and then drain. Cut the frankfurters

به سبک جدید

into 2cm lengths. Heat a dash of olive oil in a frying-pan, and fry the frankfurters along with half the garlic; as the garlic starts to colour, scoop it out together with the frankfurters and set them both aside. Then fry the drained potatoes in the same oil, turning them constantly. Once they start to stick and brown, season with salt, stir the sausage and garlic back in, and turn off the heat.

Next, make the sauce. Fry the chilli and the remainder of the garlic in another dash of oil, add the spices and the chopped tomatoes, followed by the tomato sauce or purée/ketchup. Bubble for a few minutes, until the sauce starts to look quite glossy and thick. Smear it over the frankfurters, and dive in.

The dish is usually eaten just with *lavash* bread (to use as a scoop and mop up the sauce), but you can beat 1–2 eggs per person with a dash of milk, pour it over the sausages and make it into a tasty (albeit fiery), thick omelette.

A Bit More about the Persian Music Scene

A lot of my shop customers ask me tricky questions along the lines of, 'What's Persian music like?' It's a perfectly reasonable question, but one that I normally answer somewhat facetiously with another question, 'What's British music like?' Iranian music comprises a bit of everything (except, unsurprisingly, country and western). Classical Persian music is famous for its purity of sound and often extemporized abandon. Whilst there is plenty of orchestral music, instruments are most enjoyed in trios, duets or solo pieces. Their names – *neh*, *tar*, *santour*, *kamancheh*, *dapth*, *sittar*, *oud* – and shapes are exotic, their sound haunting. Perhaps most exciting is the *tonbak* – the Iranian drum. Traditional vocal work is also exciting, with singers such as Shajarian piercing the soul with their mournful 'daad eh bidaad' – laments.

Of folk music there is plenty in Iran, from the ballads of the Khorassan, to the foot-tapping, fast and furious Kurdish beat and the

happy, frenetic Bandari. Iranians love to make music, and to dance, and although there may be extensive restrictions on dancing in public at the moment, any sort of happy private gathering usually involves music for dancing. A great number of Iranians can actually play a musical instrument or two – when I want backing musicians for one of our storytelling evenings, I have but to ask a few customers before I find what I want.

Iranian contemporary music is as diverse as the next nation's. A lot of the music made in that well-known Iranian state, California, is deliciously cheesy pop, and if boy bands are few, there are any number of medallioned solo male artists and scantily clad, pouting females trying to make it. To be fair, California is home to a number of deeply and importantly talented Persian mega-stars – Googoosh and Leila Forouhar are *the* Iranian divas, childstars of the fifties who are still superstars in their sixties, and then there's Siavash Ghomayshi, the singer-songwriter, Dariush, Ebi and Moein, the soulful ballad spinners, to name but a few. But the music now coming out of Iran itself is much more interesting. Since we opened the shop we have had heavy rock, rap, jazz poetry, dj compilations and techno reaching our shelves. Admittedly a lot of it is banned in Iran, but still it gets heard and gets exported. The Iranian underground music scene is big, and if a few of its cult figures have had token spells in prison, their sheer popularity usually ensures a happy ending. The biggest musical sensation of recent years has been Group Arian, a bunch of brave and talented youngsters who sing like angels. After something of a battle, they were allowed to retain their female backing vocalists, and their audacity has spawned a whole load of young mixed singing groups.

Cottelettes

When I am stressed, I always make soup: my mother-in-law, I have noticed, makes these delicious potato and meat croquettes – they are fiddly but extraordinarily more-ish. They are a great breakfast favourite for Iranians – both in the conventional sense and during Ramadan, when those fasting will often break fast with them. They are rolled in *lavash* bread with handfuls of herbs.

Once you have mastered the basic idea, you can do all sorts of things with this recipe, adding tomatoes, cheese, herbs, mushrooms, a pinch of *je ne sais quoi* and a spoon of what you will. This will do a breakfast for 6–8 people.

4 large floury potatoes, peeled
1kg minced lamb
1 medium onion, grated
1 teaspoon turmeric
3 dessertspoons roasted chick pea flour
2 eggs
salt and pepper

Cut the potatoes into chunks, boil until soft and then mash them with just the tiniest bit of butter. Season to taste. When cool, mix in the other ingredients really well, and then with wet hands form the patties into long, flat oval shapes. Fry in hot oil until brown on both sides.

CHAPTER THREE

ش

CHAPTER THREE

SOUPS

T he Persian word for chef is *ash-pas*, which literally means 'soup-maker'. Soup is important in Iran, a nutritious and economical way of feeding lots of people and an essential tool in the battle against the vicious cold of the winter months. It's odd that Iran exists in the imagination as a land of mystery and warmth – 'it's exotic, so it must be hot', the line of thought runs – but in fact most of Iran experiences the sort of white Christmas that we can only dream about.

Halim – Chicken Porridge

This at first seems quite the weirdest dish; in fact it remains so at second and third...that is, if you have been raised on Ready Brek. But it is utterly delicious, and combines a double-whammy of comforting carbohydrate with the culinary hug that chicken soup gives you.

In Iran it is eaten as a hearty breakfast; it is in fact so satisfying that it also great for lunch or supper, and in very tiny doses would make a great dinner-party starter. Three points to note: first, most Iranians actually make this dish with wheat instead of barley, but in truth they are largely interchangeable; second, they would always use hulled grain, but as most of the goodness is in the husk, we prefer to leave it on; third, the dish is also nice with lamb or turkey.

These quantities will make absolutely loads.

500g pot barley
1 medium chicken, skinned
sugar and salt
butter
ground cinnamon

Soak the barley overnight; if you forget, or haven't read this recipe properly before attempting to make the dish, you'll simply need to cook it for much longer. Place the chicken in a large pan, cover with plenty of water, add salt and boil for around an hour. Strain off the stock, and strip all the flesh from the chicken. Put the barley in the pan together with the water in which it has been soaking, add the chicken stock and the flaked chicken, bring to the boil and then set to simmer for at least two hours. (In Iran they really would get up before dawn to get this dish underway, but if you are having it as breakfast we recommend making it the day before.) Check it at regular intervals – you may need to add a drop of boiling water if the liquid content is insufficient. The barley is cooked when it is all soft and gloopy; when you are happy this is the case, take the dish off the heat. Now comes the fun part – traditionally you would pound this in a pestle and mortar but, to be perfectly honest, we put it through the blender. Return the gloop to the pan (it should have a slightly reluctant pouring consistency) and warm through. To serve, melt the butter (around 40g per bowlful) in a saucepan and let it simmer until it starts to darken and hiss. Ladle the porridge into bowls and drizzle a little butter on top of each; sprinkle each with cinnamon and a dessertspoonful of sugar. If you are not eating at one sitting, it will keep in the fridge for around four days – just make sure that you sizzle your butter freshly every time.

This is truly the breakfast to see off all other breakfasts.

غذا های محصوص ایرانی

Ash Reshteh – Herb, Noodle and Bean Soup

This is probably the best soup in the world; it really is the tops...if not to die for, then at least worth an acrimonious squabble over the last bowlful. It is a luscious conglomeration of herbs, beans and noodles, and has the advantage of being vegan (without the whey, that is). It is warming in winter, but because it is so wholesome and pure, it is great in summer too. It is also a great favourite during Ramadan (of which, more below).

Like most of our recipes, there are many ways to prepare it, so this is our own family recipe. You can play with it and improvise as you wish – for example, you may prefer to use dried herbs (which you will need to soak for half an hour before use), or canned kidney beans/chick peas (which obviously need a lot less cooking); and you may like to use stock instead of water, although I think that the herbs have such a lovely flavour of their own that this is superfluous. If you cannot find the soup noodles, substitute a pasta which will hold its shape, such as the Greek *kritheraki*.

This will be enough for around 12 bowlsful.

2 large onions
2 bunches chives (or 2 leeks) thoroughly washed
splash olive oil
2 teaspoons ground turmeric
200g kidney beans, soaked for at least 6 hours
200g chick peas, soaked for at least 6 hours
½ bunch coriander
½ bunch parsley
1 bunch spinach
200g dried mung beans

به سبک جدید

200g brown lentils
200g reshteh ash – *Iranian soup noodles*
1 dessertspoonful dried mint
salt and pepper to taste
liquid whey or plain yoghurt (optional)

Chop and fry one of the onions together with the leek or chives in a little oil, and then add the turmeric. Add around 2 litres water and bring to the boil. In a separate pan, bring the kidney beans to the boil, cook for 10 minutes and then drain. Add both the kidney beans and the chick peas to the soup pot, and set to simmer.

In the meantime prepare those herbs – this is very fiddly work, and I always find delegation an attractive option. Discard the woodier parts of the stalk of the herbs and spinach, and soak them for at least 20 minutes. Scoop out of the water, drain and spin-dry (if you have a salad spinner), then chop them: not too finely, as the soup requires texture and definition.

Once the kidney beans and chick peas have been cooking for around an hour (and are to all intents and purposes cooked), add the mung beans and the lentils. After a further 20 minutes, add the chopped herbs, and another 20 minutes after that, the noodles. Cook through for a further 20 minutes – if it seems impossibly thick, thin with a little boiling water. Season to taste.

Chop and fry the other onion, and then add in the dried mint, and cook together until crisp.

Serve the *ash* with a swirl of whey or yoghurt, and garnish with the minted onion.

Ramadan, month of feasting

Yes, OK, I know it's actually all about *fasting*...but explain why we sell more food during Ramadan than any other month.

Ramadan is the ninth month of the Islamic calendar, supposedly the month when the Koran was received, and henceforth celebrated as a month of contemplation and personal revelation. Muslims are meant to fast between the hours of sunrise and sunset every day for one moon (i.e. lunar month) – they abstain from eating, drinking, smoking, and, er, intimate relations. They often rise to eat before dawn (a meal known as *sahari*), and then eat *iftar* or breakfast (traditionally dates, halva and tea) at dusk. During the evening they may prepare lavish meals, or graze on and off as the mood takes them. There is great emphasis during this month on sharing food, both by way of eating with your friends and of giving to the less fortunate. It is very common in Iran for the faithful to congregate in mosques or *masjid*s (prayer houses) to eat communally. It is regarded as a good act not only to fast but to help those who are fasting, and to provide *iftar* for those in need.

To us over-consumers in the West, the whole thing sounds like torture, notwithstanding the fact that the Christian faith also has its time of denial in Lent – how many people you know actually give anything up for Lent? In fact most Muslims look forward to Ramadan. A true believer steps back from the rat-race, makes use of the time to meditate on his place in the world, and to ponder where he might make improvements. It is a time for extra prayer and charity; it is in fact like one big, faith-wide group hug. The abstinence itself can be very hard, especially as Ramadan is a movable fast – it moves forward through the calendar 10 days each year – and so during the summer months when the days are longer, the fast can be for up to 18 hours a day. But it does reward those who last the month with a real sense of achievement. The end of Ramadan is marked with an almost euphoric festival, *eid al fitr,* and those who have fasted can celebrate, exchange gifts, feast and visit friends.

Of course fasting isn't a bad thing for the health either. Young children, those who are infirm, pregnant, breast-feeding or travelling are not permitted to fast, and even older children are only allowed to fast until midday. For those in full health, the month can act as a de-tox period, when the price of 11 months of over-indulgence can be reclaimed.

In Iran, as you might imagine, the public observance of Ramadan is compulsory. The country runs on standby for a month, with businesses operating during limited hours. Restaurants are closed during the day, and open consumption of anything is banned, even for tourists: in fact, any form of flouting the Islamic law meets with particularly severe punishment during this period. That is not to say everyone fasts – what is done in the privacy of the home is entirely up to the individual – but fasting and abstinence has been part of Persian medicine and culture since Zoroastrian times, and comes quite naturally even to the non-devout. Most Iranians at least pay lip-service to the ritual by fasting for a day here or there. *Eid al fitr* is big in Iran, but whereas in Arabic countries it is perhaps the most important day of the year, for Iranians nothing can supplant *Nowrooz* (New Year – see p. 174).

For Iranians living abroad, there is a certain sentimentality about Ramadan (that is for those to whom Islam is not a compete anathema); even those ladies about town with their killer heels and that jack-the-lad DJ Massoud are to be found discreetly breaking fast at the Iranian *masjid*. One evening's listening to the chin-wagging in the hopelessly crowded women's section of any London mosque during Ramadan will teach you everything you need to know about contemporary Persian society – all life is there. It pulls the community together – and knowing how aloof Iranians can be from each other, this is rather a nice feature.

> Oh you who believe! Fasting is prescribed for you, as it was prescribed for those before you, so that you may guard against evil.
>
> *The Koran*

Pomegranate Soup

This goes to the heart of what Iranian cuisine does best – the juxta-position of the most amazingly unexpected ingredients, and their transformation into surprisingly wholesome food. This soup is droolingly good.

3 medium onions
a little oil or ghee
1 teaspoonful ground turmeric
½ teaspoonful ground cinnamon
1 cup split peas
2½ litres good stock (good water would do)
500g minced lamb
salt and pepper
1 cup kritheraki *or pudding rice*
½ bunch each parsley/coriander, washed and chopped
handful of fresh mint, washed and chopped
1 bunch spring onions, washed and chopped
1 dessertspoonful sugar
1 cup pomegranate syrup

Peel and chop two of the onions, and fry them in a little oil. Add the turmeric and cinnamon, followed by the split peas, and then add the stock. Bring to the boil, and simmer for about 10 minutes.

Meanwhile, grate the third onion into the minced lamb, add a little salt and pepper, and knead together.

Next, add the chopped herbs and the *kritheraki* or rice to the soup, and then, once it comes to the boil again, the pomegranate syrup and the sugar. Shape the meat mix into the babiest of meatballs and plop

به سبک جدید

them in as well. Now let the whole thing bubble very gently for half an hour. This *ash* is nice garnished with crisp fried onion and mint (see p. 94) or, if they are in season, you could strew a few plump pomegranate seeds across the top.

Ash-e-Miveh – Fruit Soup

This is lots of fun, and has a guaranteed 'ooh-aah' factor. It encapsulates both the enterprising and the thrifty nature of Persian cuisine, as it enables the mid-winter chef to produce a sensational and nutritious store-cupboard soup bursting with the flavours of all the seasons. It looks complex at first reading, but is really quite a doddle. It is one of those joyous recipes that you can adapt to what's lurking in your pantry at any given time. You can use dried herbs, thus sticking to the true store-cupboard ethos, but if fresh are available, why not?

It's what I would consider to be touchy-feely food – sensitive to your needs, and hugging your tastebuds. I like it with little meatballs, but it is just as good *au naturel*.

> *100g each of dried chick peas, red kidney beans and mung beans (or you can use canned instead)*
> *200g* aloo bokhara *(dried yellow plums) or prunes*
> *150g dried apricots (try to get the chopped, dried variety rather than the gooey, often sulphur-coated Turkish-style ones)*
> *150g yellow sultanas or raisins*
> *100g barberries (or cranberries)*
> *1 large onion*
> *1 teaspoon ground turmeric*
> *a little oil for frying*

1 small bunch each of coriander, parsley, spinach and chives (or
    spring onions)
salt and pepper
for the garnish:
1 small onion, chopped
1 small apple, finely chopped
1½ tablespoons dried mint
yoghurt (optional)
for the meatballs (optional):
1lb minced lamb
1 small onion, grated
salt and pepper
1 teaspoon each oregano and mint
½ teaspoon ground turmeric

If you are using dried kidney beans and chick peas, soak them overnight. Kidney beans should be blanched prior to use. The plums and apricots need to be soaked for around an hour, and the sultanas or raisins and the barberries or cranberries for about half an hour.

Chop and sauté the onion in a little oil, add the turmeric and around 2 litres of water or stock. Drain the soaked beans and add them to the pan. Cover and simmer for about an hour. Meanwhile, trim the stalks from your herbs, soak, drain and chop them. When the hour's up, you should drain and add in the apricots and plums/prunes, the herbs, and salt and pepper to taste. Bubble away for another 30 minutes, then drain before adding the sultanas and barberries. If you are adding meatballs, mix all the ingredients together, and with wet hands roll them into tiny balls (of no more than 2cm diameter) and plop them in. Cook for a further 30 minutes. Check seasoning again, and add a little lemon juice if it is not sharp enough. Prepare your garnish by frying the onion, apple and dried mint together until it is nicely browned. Serve the soup swirled with yoghurt if you wish, sprinkled with the mint garnish, and with a basket of warm bread alongside.

A little lesson in Farsi

Farsi is a fairly easy tongue for the Westerner to learn. It is Indo-European (i.e. part of the family of languages stretching from India to Europe) and as such, although syntax and inflection can be complicated, its grammatical forms and vocabulary are at least familiar. It is perhaps only the superimposition of the Arabic alphabet which deters the casual language scholar, and indeed that is the hardest part to master for anyone wishing to learn Farsi. There are pitfalls for the student of any language – the most common in Iranian is perhaps the difference between 'Chetoree?' and 'Sheturee!', the first being 'How are you?', and the second, 'You are a camel!' It is a language rich with potential ribaldry, and Iranians, while deeply appreciating anyone learning their language, are swift to hoot with laughter when 'things go wrong'. And there is 'performing parrot syndrome', where your accent and phraseology are appalling, but because they are comical or endearing, nobody bothers to correct you.

Learning the language is one thing; learning how to use it and getting your head around the myriad Persian maxims and metaphors is another matter entirely. Take the *ash* above for example. *Ash* is so much at the heart of the Persian kitchen, and the kitchen is of course the heart of any home, that it is hardly surprising that Farsi is littered with saying involving soup: thus the 'chick pea in every *ash*' is a nosy person, 'it's your aunt's *ash*, so you'll have to eat it' for something you cannot get out of, and 'making such an *ash*.....' is when you embroil yourself in something from which you are unlikely to be able to extricate yourself. Easy enough. But what about, 'I ate the ground and my father came out' (banging your head so hard you see stars)?

The below is by way of utterly frivolous distraction, but it is a famous Persian urban myth based, I believe, on a letter actually sent by an employee of NIOC (the National Iranian Oil Company) to his English boss many years ago. It neatly illustrates the complexity of the Persian vernacular.

Dear Mr. Smith,

I, the undersigned, have worked at NIOC in London for three years. But since Mr. Ahmadi has transferred here, everything has changed. I don't know 'what a wet wood I have sold him' that from the very first day he has been 'pulling the belt to my lift'. 'With all kinds of cat dancing,' he has tried to become the 'eyes and the light' of Mr. Green. He made so much 'mouse-running' that finally Mr. Green 'became donkey' and appointed Mr. Ahmadi as his right hand man; but 'my eyes did not drink water', and I knew that all these were 'hat-play', and that he was trying to 'put a hat on my head'. I put the 'seal of silence to my lips' and did not say a thing.

Since then he has just been 'putting watermelons under my arms'. Knowing that this transfer 'was only good for his aunt', I started begging him to forget that I ever came to see him. I said, 'You saw camel, you did not see camel', but he 'was not getting off the devil's donkey'. 'What headache shall I give you?' I am now forced to work in the mail room with all kinds of 'blind, bald, full and half-height people' – 'imagine how my bottom burns'.

Now Mr. Smith, 'I turn around your head', you are my only hope, my 'back and shelter'; 'I swear to you by the fourteen innocents' 'please do some work for me': 'in the resurrection day I'll grasp your skirt.' 'I have six head bread eaters.' 'I kiss your hand and legs'.

Your servant,
Mr. Davoodi

Mr. Smith replied: 'My liver is barbecued'.

به سبک جدید

Soup-e-Jo – Barley Soup

This is an ultra-comforting soup, and it tastes ever so naughty, although with the exception of the dash of cream it is pretty wholesome stuff. It seems to crop up as a starter in Iranian households, although it is so filling that I think it is better as a supper or lunch dish. It is most definitely winter fodder. Jamshid's aunt Tatty-jun ('jun' after any name in Iran translates as 'dear' so-and-so) first introduced me to this dish, and as hers is still the best I have tasted, my recipe is based on hers.

I suspect that this is not, in fact, indigenous Iranian fare. Legendary food-writer Margaret Shaida has suggested that it might have come out of Russia with the White Russians. There are a number of extremely popular but vaguely familiar 'Persian' dishes in the recipe folder of the average Iranian housewife – another such is Stronagoff (sic – as it is invariably called), a dish of spiced minced lamb with *gheimeh* potatoes (chips) and cream...sound a bit familiar? Then there is *piroshki*, those strange little Russian pasties, and Salad *Oliveiyeh* (see Chapter Two). Anyway, as a national of a country which rates chicken curry amongst its favourite 'traditional' dishes, I am hardly in a position to criticize – I am merely making an observation.

> *300g pearl barley, rinsed and soaked (half an hour will do)*
> *3 leeks, washed and chopped*
> *3 onions, chopped*
> *butter for frying*
> *3 large carrots, scrubbed and grated*
> *2½ litres (preferably home-made) chicken or lamb stock*
> *1 tablespoon brown sugar*
> *1 tablespoon vinegar*
> *juice of 3 fresh lemons*

*150ml (or so) of soured cream, or single cream at a pinch (but you
   will need a little more lemon juice if you use this)*
salt and pepper

Drain the barley well. Fry 2 of the onions and all of the leeks in a drop
of butter in a big, heavy pan. Once they are cooked and just turning
colour, add one of the three grated carrots and the barley. Cook for a
couple of minutes more, stirring constantly, and then pour in the stock.
Bring to the boil, cover and then set to simmer for a couple of hours.
Check the liquid content from time to time – if it looks too gloopy,
add a little boiling water.

In the meantime prepare the garnish: melt the butter in a pan,
and fry the remaining onion and carrot until it soft and starting to
brown. Add the sugar and the vinegar, and continue to cook until quite
caramelized.

Just before you want to serve the soup, check the seasoning, and stir
in the lemon juice and the cream. Serve with the caramelized carrot
ranged in pretty patterns on top.

Chilled Cucumber and Herb Soup

Variations of this are common in Middle Eastern countries. It is one of those dishes which just make sense – the combination of cooling ingredients, yoghurt, cucumber and summer herbs, goes together like fish and chips, or kebab and *lavash* if you like. But I think that it is generally acknowledged that it is Iranian in origin, and certainly their version of it is the most interesting.

Whatever the provenance, it makes a dreamy summer starter, and comforting fridge-food at any time. This will feed 4 people to begin a meal.

> *1 handful fresh mint*
> *1 handful fresh dill*
> *1 large cucumber*
> *800ml thick plain natural yoghurt*
> *150ml sour cream*
> *100ml water*
> *50g raisins (optional)*
> *50g shelled walnuts (optional)*

Pick through, wash and drain your herbs before chopping them roughly. Top and tail the cucumber before grating it – retain the ensuing juice to add to the soup. Beat the yoghurt, cream and water together, and then stir in the herbs and cucumber, together with the raisins if you opt for them. Season to taste and chill well. If using walnuts, chop them coarsely and stir in just before serving. Serve with herby ice cubes if you want to look flash – finely chop some mint and freeze with water in an ice cube tray. Garnish with a few sprigs of mint or dill as you wish.

Eshkeneh – Persian Egg and Onion Soup

This is very similar to French onion soup – but whereas the French version has a respectable culinary pedigree, this is a staple of peasants in Iran. Many Persians, being inveterate snobs, deny ever having sampled it. This is a shame, as it is quite delectable and very easy to prepare. With the right garnish, it polishes up a treat. This should be enough to serve 6 hungry peasants.

6 medium onions
1–2 dessertspoons ghee (or butter)
1 teaspoon ground turmeric
2 dessertspoons flour
1 litre water
juice of 1 lemon
salt and pepper
1 egg per person
optional extras (but not all at the same time):
75 g broken walnuts, or
200g fresh spinach, washed and roughly chopped, or
500g pitted sour cherries (or soaked prunes/apricots)
   (personally, I usually go with the spinach)
for the garnish:
1 onion, finely chopped
2 dessertspoonsful dried mint
2–3 slices stale bread
2–3 eggs

Slice the onions very finely and then fry them in hot melted ghee or butter. Once they are quite soft and starting to colour, add the turmeric,

به سبک جدید

and the walnuts (the first on the list of optional extras). Cook for a few moments more, then stir in the flour. Add the water, stirring constantly, and continue to heat so that the soup starts to thicken. If you have opted for the fruit or the spinach rather than the walnuts, now is the moment to add one of them. Season to taste, and simmer for another 20 minutes.

Prepare the garnish. Fry the onion in a little oil until it starts to brown. Add the mint, and cook until the mixture darkens; set aside. Beat the eggs for the garnish with a sprinkle of salt and pepper. Cut each slice of the bread into six, dunk the resulting squares into the egg, and then fry in hot oil until browned. Keep them hot.

Just before you want to serve, gently crack the eggs (from the list of main ingredients) one by one into the *eshkeneh*, bubble for a few minutes until they start to set, then carefully ladle the soup into warm bowls (obviously ensuring each person gets an egg). Float 2–3 eggy-bread croûtons in each bowl, and then top with a criss-cross of the minted onion mixture. Serve with fresh warm bread and raw onion.

Chicken Soup with Quince, Celery and Saffron

It may the basis for much of their humour, but Jewish culture does not have a monopoly on the chicken soup thing. At the first sign of a sniffle, Iranian mothers are out with the soup-pot, shovelling vats of (actually rather tasty) chicken broth down the throats of anyone who crosses their path. An Iranian housewife on a mission is most certainly not to be messed with. Although I have learned a lot of deeply useful herbal lore from my mother-in-law, I still try to conceal any incipient illnesses as I am never quite sure what will be administered should I admit to any symptoms.

Home-style, remedial chicken soup sees a skinless leg of chicken cooked up with every vegetable that the fridge or garden can yield; 'birds nest' noodles are added (like vermicelli), and the dish is served with wedges of lemon. The cook will stand over you with a menacing wooden spoon until you have finished every last drop.

Our version rests on the same principles, but with (hopefully) a little more finesse. Although it is good for snuffles (quinces are good for the chest), it is also a good supper dish. If quinces aren't available, apples may be substituted.

This should be adequate to feed 6 invalids.

6 small skinless joints of chicken
3–4 dried limes
100g yellow split peas
1 teaspoon turmeric
½ teaspoon saffron steeped in boiling water
salt and pepper
butter or ghee
1 head celery, washed and cut into 3cm lengths

3 large quinces
1 large onion, roughly chopped
large handful parsley, chopped

Firstly wash the chicken and place it in a saucepan with the onion: cover with about 2 litres of water, and add the turmeric, dried limes, split peas and saffron and a token sprinkle of salt and pepper. Bring to the boil, and simmer for around half an hour. Heat a splodge of butter in a frying-pan, and gently fry the celery. When it has softened, remove it with a slotted spoon and drain on kitchen paper. Peel and core the quinces, and then cut each into eight vertical slices, which you should then halve again, this time horizontally. Fry these in the frying-pan for around 6–7 minutes, turning occasionally. Add both the celery and the quince to the soup, along with the parsley. Now is a good time to check the seasoning. Cook through for another half an hour, or until the chicken is falling off the bone and the quince is very tender.

Serve with the pepper mill, wedges of lemon or lime, and some warm bread for dunking.

Ash-e-Mash – Spiced Mung Bean and Meatball Soup

I don't really think we do enough with the little mung bean – he's pretty, and incredibly versatile. It doesn't help that someone gave him the wrong name – he's actually a pea trying to compete in a big bean world. He's very nutritious, and has the advantage of being a pulse that cooks relatively quickly. Mung beans are part of Persian cuisine, but more in the east of the country – they are extremely important in neighbouring Afghanistan and Pakistan. Many of my customers have never made this soup, nor do they feature *mash-pulao*, rice and mung beans, in their culinary repertoire. There is sufficient here for a big potful.

2 onions
4–5 cloves garlic
2 green chillis, or ½ habanero chilli
1 leek, cleaned and chopped
1 teaspoon ground turmeric
300g mung beans, washed and picked through
1 bunch spinach, washed and chopped roughly
½ bunch each coriander and parsley, washed and chopped roughly
salt and pepper
for the meatballs:
2 medium onions, 1 chopped, 1 grated
2 cloves garlic, chopped
500g minced lamb
salt and pepper
1 teaspoon each cinnamon and cumin
½ teaspoon ground chilli
3–4 chopped tomatoes, and 1 tablespoon tomato paste
1 tablespoon kashk *or yoghurt*

Fry the onion in a little oil, and then add the garlic, chilli, and leek. When the leek has softened, add the turmeric and the mung beans, and top up with 2 litres water. Bring to the boil, cover, and turn down to simmer. After around half an hour, add the herbs and the spinach, season, then cook for another half an hour.

Next the meatballs. Fry the chopped onion with the garlic. Mix the other onion with the lamb, a little seasoning and the spices, and with wet hands form into tiny meatballs and drop them into the pan with the fried onion. Add the tomato paste, stirring constantly, followed by the tomatoes. Turn down the heat, cover and simmer for 10 minutes, and then take off the heat and drizzle the *kashk* or yoghurt across the top.

Pour the *ash* into bowls, and place the meatballs in the centre of the table so that people can help themselves. The meatball and tomato mixture should be spooned gently on to the soup. The dish needs plenty of warm bread for dipping.

While I rather like the DIY assembly of foods at the table, I have noticed that some Persians prepare meat garnishes slightly differently. So try this. Instead of making the meatballs, fry one onion with the garlic and spices as above, then 250g minced lamb. Once the lamb is sealed well, add the tomato paste (but omit the fresh tomatoes) and ½ teaspoon saffron steeped in boiling water. Cook through for about 10 minutes, stirring well. Season to taste. Serve the meat strewn in a cross over the surface of the soup, followed by *kashk* or yoghurt.

غذاهای مخصوص ایرانی

CHAPTER FOUR

ثتى

CHAPTER FOUR

GRILLED AND ROASTED MEATS

Mullah Nasruddin bought himself a delicious piece of steak in the market, and on his way home he had the good fortune to come upon one of his friends, a chef, who gave him a fitting recipe for the meat. Sadly as the mullah neared his house, a huge crow swooped down and stole the steak. 'Ha!' cried the mullah, waving at the skies, 'You won't enjoy it, bird, for I still have the recipe.'

The Persians have a thousand-year love affair with fire, dating back to the time of the ancient Zoroastrians (see p. 126) who were reputedly fire worshippers – although this is not really true. Still, today, food cooked over fire (kebab) is the food of choice for nine out of ten Iranians. My father-in-law lights a fire every single night, and given half a chance will cook over it. It is picturesque, but can be quite tiresome when you've just dusted. He is not unique, and for this reason one of our best-selling commodities is charcoal. It is not that they are secret pyromaniacs, but rather it is a deeply felt tradition.

Meat

Iranians come in lots of different shapes, sizes and colours. There are certain giveaway features, but it is still often hard to spot them in a crowd. It is an irony not lost on them that the home of the original Aryan race has become so racially mixed. It is hardly surprising – it is a vast country, and a crossroads at that. You can still find true Caucasians in the north, with blonde hair and blue eyes, but elsewhere, especially in the south, the Arabic influence is very clear. There are devout Muslims, luke-warm Muslims, lapsed Muslims, Zoroastrians, Christians, Buddhists and Jews, all living very happily together. Sectarian tension within Iran is almost non-existent. There is a certain Persian-ness about them which transcends details of which god they worship. All of which of course has nothing to do with your burgers.

My point is that a surprising number of Iranians living abroad, regardless of their religious beliefs, prefer to eat halal meat. Not that all halal meat is actually good – it is just what they are used to. All meat in Iran is of course halal, but most importantly the flavour and quality of meat in Iran is generally much better as well, and it is most assuredly this which the ex-pat Iranian is seeking.

For the uninitiated (which was me until I became attached to an Iranian), halal is just a method of slaughter much the same as kosher practices. Animals are given a drink of water (it is important that they do not die thirsty), and then their throats are cut – it is believed that this is the most humane way to kill them. The national cuisine does not feature any recipes for pork, as pork is regarded as a dirty meat (pigs 'wallow in their own excrement'), and is thus *haram* – forbidden to the good Muslim. Meat in Iran is generally either lamb or chicken, with turkey or duck thrown in for a bit of variety. Beef is eaten, but it is not widespread.

The meat you buy to follow any of these recipes will largely depend on where you live. In Peckham, most of the butchers are halal, and some of them purvey truly excellent meat. Furthermore they are more than happy to discuss your requirements and trim your cuts accordingly. Having said that, when my mother-in-law wants minced lamb, she usually buys a boned leg and minces it herself, just to be certain she is getting the best quality. Organic mince is also usually a good bet if it is fresh.

Big *Barberi* Burgers

همبرگر پهلوان در نان بربری

2 onions
1 kg good quality minced lamb
salt and pepper
1 teaspoon ground cumin
2 teaspoons ground cinnamon
2 teaspoons ground turmeric
6 medium tomatoes
6 baby cucumbers (or ½ regular one)
6 Persian-style pickled cucumbers (non-sweet)
1 bunch spring onions
juice of one lemon
handful fresh chopped parsley
3 tablespoons plain yoghurt
2 tablespoons mayonnaise
few drops Tabasco (optional)
1 tablespoon tomato ketchup
2 sheets barberi *bread (or any semi-flat-just-slightly-risen bread)*
150–200g grated cheese of choice

This recipe will feed six 'healthy' eaters. Firstly grate the two onions and mix and pummel them into the lamb together with some salt, pepper and the three spices. Cling-film the mixture and pop it in the fridge to chill and firm up.

For the Shirazi salad, dice the tomatoes, cucumber and gherkins, together with the bulbs of the spring onions (reserve the tops to go into the sauces). Squeeze the lemon juice over it, season and stir in the parsley.

To make the sauces – chop the tops of the spring onions and whisk

به سبک جدید

them into the yoghurt together with some salt and pepper and a dash of olive oil. In a separate bowl, mix the mayo and ketchup along with the Tabasco (if using).

Remove the burger mix from the fridge and, with a rolling pin if necessary, roll it out flat on a piece of greased foil so that it is roughly the size and shape of the bread. Lift the meat on the foil and turn it out on to your grillpan, griddle or barbecue – a couple of minutes either side should suffice. Once it is cooked a little, you should find it is easily turned with a couple of spatulas, but if not just halve it. In the meantime, heat the *barberi* bread in a hot oven for around two minutes. Smear one sheet with the yoghurt mixture, and then spread a layer of salad on top. Lift the burgers on to the top of the salad, sprinkle the cheese on top of that, and then spread the other sheet of bread with the pink sauce before lowering it on top. Congratulations – you now have the world's silliest burger, not to mention one of its biggest. Cut it into squares or wedges to serve. You can of course cook smaller burgers and cut the bread to fit – but this is a lot fiddlier and less fun. We hardly need to suggest serving this with French fries, or you could try the spiced chips on p. 191.

Iranians and Islam

Like most religions, Islam is meant to be a code for life. Unlike most Islamic countries, the Iranian government enforces this code, or 'sharia' law – it is still the world's only Islamic state, ruled by a theocracy. But that is not to say that all Iranians observe this code – like all other nationalities, they come in lots of different varieties. Few are actually atheists, although there are plenty who *profess* to despise Islam. I think it fair to say that most Iranians regard Islam in the same way that they regard their parents – it is in their blood, they know that it is right, they feel at home in a mosque…but they have to have their little rebellion. I know Iranians who drink and eat pork, and then fast for Ramadan. I know Iranians who never drink, or eat pork, but neither pray nor fast.

غذا های مخصوص ایرانی

Most Iranians in the West live Western lifestyles, and just occasionally touch base with the mosque to remind themselves of what it is all about. Which is about the same relationship as the average Jew or Christian has with their spiritual home. Iranians will however defend their faith – woe betide anyone who criticizes Islam. For implicit in that criticism would be a criticism of Iran. Islam is now so wrapped into the culture of this multi-faceted country that it partly defines the people, regardless of whether they embrace it or not.

After so many invasions and cultural sea-changes, Iran has developed a unique ability to soften, translate and transform the input of other nations and religions. She has developed her own inner eye, as if able to peel away all the layers of history and perceive at once all the very best that has gone into this land. Iranians are not always comfortable in their own land, but they are very much at home with the idea of being an Iranian in the universe at large. This has a lot to do with the concept of *ghayb*, which Jason Elliott in his exemplary travel writings calls the 'mirror of the unseen' – the belief that 'everything existing in the visible world is the imperfect mirror of a hidden reality into which the human being may occasionally glimpse.' It is a comforting thought. And it explains perhaps why Iran has such a strong character.

Mullah Nasruddin

به سبک جدید

Lamb Fillet Kebab (*Kebab-e-Barg*) with Pomegranate Salsa

کباب برگ با سالاد تند انار

This is one for your barbecue portfolio, but it is nice at any time of the year, which is good because barbecues are usually in the summer, and pomegranates usually come out to play in the winter.

This marinade is good for any tender cut – cubed leg of lamb responds just as well – but *kebab-e-barg* is uniquely made with lamb fillet and is a dish famous as much for its texture as its flavour. It is an expensive dish, and so in Iran is usually eaten alongside other kebabs as part of a mixed grill. The original Iranian 'salsa' is called Shirazi salad, and comprises finely diced fresh herbs, onion, cucumber and tomato with salt and pepper and lemon. Please note – this dish is best marinated overnight.

fillet of lamb (neck or loin) – each fillet can be split into 2 or 3
  portions: served without any other meats you will need to allow
  1½ – 2 of these portions of meat per person
2 onions
2 lemons
butter, salt and pepper
for the salsa:
1 luscious, large pomegranate (in summer, you could use redcurrants)
1 medium cucumber, finely diced
2–3 tomatoes, finely diced
1 green pepper, finely diced
1 hot chilli, chopped
½ bunch each of mint and coriander, washed and chopped
1 bunch spring onions, finely diced
salt and pepper, olive oil and lemon juice

غذا های مخصوص ایرانی

Trim your meat of any excess fat. You may then either split the fillet along its length i.e. into two or three long rashers or, perhaps more efficiently, cut the fillet across into three or four equal chunks, and then almost sever through each chunk two or three times from alternate directions to form a concertina which may then be opened out. Any which way, the resulting strips of lamb should then be bashed lightly (best to use the palm of your hand – a tenderizer can be too harsh for such a delicate cut) and placed in a shallow dish. Finely grate the onions – this is one occasion when you can actually whack them in the blender, as the more watery they are the better. Pour the onion slurry all over the meat, cover the dish and pop in the fridge for the night.

A couple of hours before you want to eat, add the juice of one of the lemons to the meat and onion mixture, and stir. This is also a good time to make your salsa. Firstly, make sure that you are wearing pomegranate-coloured clothes (or perhaps put an apron on). Cut the pomegranate in half with a sharp knife, and with your fingers gently prise free the seeds, pulling off any pith as you go. Mix them together with all the other ingredients, stir well, cover and chill.

To cook the kebabs, thread each strip, again like a concertina, on to a skewer, season and grill/barbecue. Or you could just pop the meat under the grill. Melt a little butter, mix with some of the lemon juice and baste the kebabs with this during cooking.

Serve either with saffron rice or *lavash* bread, with plenty of fresh herbs, wedges of lemon and the salsa.

به سبک جدید

Jujeh Kebab – Spring Chicken Marinated with Lemon and Saffron

This is an essential addition to your barbecue portfolio, with flavour to drool for. And it is really, really easy to make. This is enough for four people.

2 poussins, skinned and chopped into 4cm pieces
2 onions, very finely chopped
½ teaspoon ground saffron
1 bottle Iranian lemon or lime juice, or the juice of around six fresh lemons (or ten limes)
salt and pepper, plus a dash of olive oil

Place the chicken in a sealable container, and add all the other ingredients. The saffron should be sprinkled on to a saucer of boiling water and allowed to cool before it is mixed in. You only need to add as much lemon juice as it takes to cover the meat – but this probably will be most of the bottle. Mix the ingredients well, cover, and leave in the fridge to marinade overnight. Cook over fire if possible, although you can cook it in an oven (200°C/gas mark 5) on a baking tray – it will take around half an hour this way – or you can grill it (around 20 minutes, turning it from time to time).

Serve with basmati rice, fresh herbs, Shirazi salad (see the previous recipe), pickles and raw onion.

Steak with Fenugreek and Chive Butter

There is not a lot to say about this. This is a book about a taking a Persian twist on life – well, at least on the food of life – not a 'how to cook' manual, of which there are many excellent varieties in a bookshop near you. So I'll leave the steak bit up to you. But if you want a really flavoursome melt to stick on top of it, see what follows. For each person, you will need to supply:

> *1 steak*
> *1 tablespoon softened butter*
> *black pepper and a pinch of salt*
> *1½ teaspoons chopped fresh or dried fenugreek leaf*
> *1½ teaspoons chopped fresh chives*
> *juice and grated zest of ¼ lime*

Mix the butter with pepper, the herbs and the lime. Shape it with wet hands – if you are making it for a few people, it is best to form a cylinder, as you can subsequently slice it into little discs – and roll it into twists of greaseproof paper. Pop into the fridge overnight (or the freezer for half an hour) to firm up.

Salt your chosen steak lightly, and grill to your preference. Dot a disc of the herb butter on to the steak and serve immediately.

به سبک جدید

Sausages and Lentils

No, there's nothing wrong with bangers and mash; but sometimes it's good to be different. Lentils are great with sausages anyway – many of our European cousins feature the pairing in recipes.

There are two types of sausage to be found in Iran – the frankfurter (pronounced 'fraunkfouurterrr'), which is often chopped into fry-ups (see the Bandari Sausages recipe in Chapter Two), or enjoyed in hotdog format, and the *saucisse*, which is nowadays a highly processed, rather worrying meat form, round and fat and often stuffed with cheese. This recipe owes little to either of those but is rather a culinary collage of sausage lore, using Persian ingredients. Its nearest relation is perhaps the spicy *merguez* of North Africa.

I absolutely adore sausages, but I find most supermarket varieties woefully greasy and salty, so make no apology for the inclusion of this recipe. You can of course make it in sausage skins, but few homes have sausage machines, and it is just as tasty without. I sometimes use caul fat to wrap around the sausage-meat (in the context of this book use lamb caul, but pork is more available and versatile). This should feed 4 for a family TV supper.

for the sausages:
350g minced lamb
100g beef or lamb fat (cut into little pieces)
1 teaspoon salt
1 teaspoon harissa paste (or 1 teaspoon fresh minced chilli)
½ teaspoon smoked paprika
2 cloves garlic
1 level teaspoon ground cumin
½ teaspoon ground cinnamon

½ teaspoon turmeric
½ teaspoon ground cardamom
1 block of caul fat (optional)
2 dessertspoonsful cold water
for the lentils:
250g Puy lentils, washed and sorted
1 large onion, peeled and chopped
2 cloves garlic, peeled and chopped
dash of olive oil
10–12 tomatoes (mushy, unloved ones are fine here, or use tinned)
2 dessertspoons tomato paste
2 dessertspoons Persepolis patent tomato sauce (optional, see p. 331)
1 teaspoon turmeric
1 teaspoon cinnamon
½ bunch each coriander and parsley, washed and roughly chopped
salt and pepper

Firstly the sausages. They need to chill a little before leaping on to the fire, so to speak. Put the lamb and fat into the blender with all the other ingredients (except the caul fat, if using) and give it a quick whizz. It should come out looking like, well, sausage-meat. Cover it and put it in the fridge.

Next the lentils. Pop them into a pan, cover with about three times their volume of water and bring to the boil. Simmer until cooked – usually around 20 minutes – and then drain. Fry the onion in the olive oil, add the garlic and when both are golden throw in the tomatoes, paste, sauce and spices. Mix in the lentils and the chopped herbs, season to taste, and pour it all into an oven-proof serving dish, which can in turn go into the oven (set on low) to keep warm.

Back to the sausages. Take a tiny globule of the mixture and grill or fry it – this is the only sure way of checking that you are happy with the seasoning. Adjust accordingly. If you are using caul, pull a lump off, stretch it out into a sheet, and pull it up around a 'sausage' shape of

sausage-meat. Repeat until the mixture is finished. If caul is not for you, just roll the meat into sausage shapes, or press into patties, and grill or griddle them. They should need around 8–10 minutes cooking altogether – turning them at the halfway point.

Serve the sausages on top of the lentils. Accompany with a good crisp salad and some warm *lavash* bread.

If I were a cool chef instead of a hopelessly over-eager cook, this would be one of my signature dishes.

غذاهای مخصوص ایرانی

Liver, Heart and Kidney on Sticks

I don't think that any of us really eat enough liver (except my cat). Just a little bit, once a week, and you'll soon have hairs on your chest. It contains chromium, selenium, copper, iron, molybdenum (one of the newer fellas, I think: one they didn't have when I was doing biology at school), vitamins A, B, D and folic acid – I knew you'd be impressed.

In fact all offal is good for us in moderation and Iranians are mighty partial to it. In the winter in Iran you can even buy skewers of it wrapped in bread from street vendors. It is usually lamb's heart and kidneys which are used, but you can use calf's or lamb's liver.

It is of course best cooked over charcoal, but it is also a tasty snack just grilled or griddled at home.

There is no mystique about cooking offal. It usually has a membrane, which needs to be stripped off; you should also wash it well and remove any gristle or fat. Cut heart and kidney into 2cm cubes, and liver into ribbons 3cm wide. Thread on to skewers. Sprinkle with salt and grill for a few minutes each side. Eat with plenty of lemon or lime juice – or try the simple onion 'salad' below. You will need the following per person.

½ an onion, finely sliced
handful of your favourite fresh herbs (I'm a coriander buff – but
    parsley, mint and dill are all good)
juice of ½ lemon
salt and pepper

Chop the herbs finely, mix with the other ingredients, cover and leave to 'marinate' for at least 30 minutes. Use as a bed for chunks of freshly grilled meat.

Zoroastrians (Zarathustrians/Zartoshti) – the non-fire-worshippers

Zoroastrianism is perhaps one of the most mysterious and least understood faiths in the world today. And yet it was the first-ever monotheistic religion, and its influence was huge. It has had an enormous impact on Western culture, and it underwrites and underpins the (at times very thin) strands which hold Iranian society together.

There are few books on the subject (of which the best is the fabulous *In Search of Zarathustra* by Paul Kriwaczek), and the holy scripture of the Zoroastrians, the Avesta, is effectively impossible to obtain. To be fair, the original exists only in the form of fragments and oral tradition, but the best translation (by James Darmesteter, 1882) has mysteriously gone out of print in recent years. Sections are available on the Internet (see Bibliography), but the situation still gives the impression that the Zoroastrians are extraordinarily secretive. It is true that parts of the texts could be open to misinterpretation but, when properly understood, they are a key to one of the most peaceable and attractive religions on earth. And one which offers the original 'green' code of practice.

Zoroaster was the prophet of Ahura Mazda (God), and although there are wildly differing opinions as to where he came from and when, it is widely believed that he was born somewhere near Balkh (in modern Afghanistan) in the fifteenth century BC. He was the first man to suggest that there was one divine creator, and to propound that good and evil walk the earth side by side and that man has to make a conscious choice for the good. The immutable truths that he saw around him – the changing of the seasons, the rising of the sun, the flowing of the waters – suggested to him that Nature should be held as sacrosanct (he thus incorporated many of the ancient beliefs in water goddesses such as Anahita and wood sprites). One of the main tenets of Zoroastrianism is that its followers should in no way interfere with the environment. For this reason they never bathe in running streams (for fear of polluting the water); nor do they cremate or bury their dead (for fear of polluting the

air/earth respectively) – traditionally, the dead are left at allocated sites for the vultures to eat. The rhythms of nature led him to suggest that there is a powerful force for the good in all things, *asha*, and mankind needs to strive towards good thoughts, good words and good deeds, using *vohu manah* – good mind – to combat the works of Angra Mainyu, the Devil, and his agents, the *divs* (evil spirits), and the *drugs* (lies and liars). Fire is sacred to Zoroastrians – it is seen as representative of Atar, the ancient god of fire, who is later portrayed as the son of Ahura Mazda; ultimately it represents the path of the righteous, the Light. For this reason the Zoroastrians do worship in fire temples, where an eternal flame is tended by priests – but it is no more the fire itself that they are worshipping than Christians do the Cross in churches. The sacred symbol for the faith is the *farvahar* – the figure of Zoroaster set against outstretched wings with three rows of feathers representing the thoughts/words/deeds thing.

There are perhaps 100,000 Zartoshti left in Iran today, mainly living in and around Yazd, home of the biggest and most sacred temple. They are tolerated as part of society, and allowed to practise their faith in peace. When asked about them, even President Khatami smiled indulgently and replied that of course he respected them – his grandfather had been one. There are many more world-wide, most notably in India – the Parsees were Zoroastrians who were persecuted and left Iran around 1000 years ago to set up their own colony. But the legacy of Zoroastrianism is much more widespread – it was, after all, practised as a national religion in Iran for nearly 2000 years, and travellers took elements of it all over the globe. The unimaginative Romans plucked

به سبک جدید

the cult of Mithras (a sort of general to Ahura Mazda) and made it their
state religion; and its effect on the early Church must also have been significant (strange that the symbols for both are such a similar shape).

An awareness at least of this most ancient of creeds is essential for
anyone wanting to understand the Iranian nation of today – the respect
for fire and the belief in *asha* are indelibly stamped on its collective
psyche.

Persepolitan Roast Stuffed Chicken

مرغ گازی شکم پُر با روش تخت جمشید

I cook nice roast chicken. As one does. With all the trimmings. The
children love it, and the other-half dutifully proclaims it is just the
best. As they do. And I am sure that this scenario is repeated in most
households up and down the land. I mean, it's actually quite hard to
fail to cook nice roast chicken, and there's nothing much about it not
to like. But then there's Persian-style roast chicken, stuffed with an
aromatic, textured, melt-in-the-mouth blend of fruit and nuts (none of
that sage and breadcrumb stuff that tastes like herbal kapok). This is a
dish apart, an exceptional roasted offering for an exceptional Sunday,
with flavour enough to elevate it to dinner-party status if required. And
it's really not that hard to make. This serves 4–5 people.

> *100g barberries, soaked (or cranberries)*
> *50g prunes, soaked and pitted*
> *50g dried apricots or peaches, soaked*
> *50g walnuts*
> *50g nibbed nuts (almonds and pistachios)*
> *50g sour (or morello) cherries*
> *150g butter*
> *1 teaspoon ground cinnamon*

غذاهای مخصوص ایرانی

½ teaspoon ground cardamom
1 tablespoon tomato purée
salt and pepper
1 plump chicken
1 teaspoon ground saffron, dissolved in boiling water
4–5 potatoes, peeled and cut into 1cm chip-shapes

Drain the soaked fruit and pat it dry. Roughly chop the walnuts, prunes and apricots or peaches. Melt 50g of the butter, and fry the fruit and nuts together, stirring well, for 6–7 minutes. Add the cinnamon, cardamon and tomato purée, cook it a little more and then take off the heat.

Season the inside of the chicken, pop it into a roasting tray and then cram the stuffing inside. You should at this stage produce a bodkin from the folds of your pinnie and carefully truss said chicken – but I always resent such instructions in recipes, as I chose the cookery option, not the needlework...so I don't often truss: I just fold over and hope for the best. Melt the rest of the butter, add the saffron mix and drizzle this over the skin of the bird. Cover with foil, and roast in a pre-heated oven (gas mark 4, 180°C) for about 40 minutes. In the meantime, sauté the 'chips' in a little butter and oil until they are golden. When the 40 minutes are up, remove the foil from the chicken, baste it well, dot the potatoes around the side, and put back in the oven for another 25 minutes on gas mark 5 (190°C) until the potatoes are cooked through and the chicken skin crisp.

Serve with vegetables and roast potatoes if you like, or you can do it the Persian way and serve it with plain or fancy rice.

It goes without saying that this is quite a versatile stuffing – I have used a variation of it for the quail in the section on rice, but it is also great with duck, turkey, or even a boned shoulder or leg of lamb. And you can play around with the components of the stuffing as well – substitute other dried fruits or nuts as available – the important thing is to retain a degree of sharpness in the ingredients you use.

به سبک جدید

Very Big Meatballs – *Kufteh Tabrizi*

If you have hordes of very big, very hungry mouths to feed, these are the recipes for you. This is great party food as well. It is impressive, filling and you can do most of the making in advance.

The idea of *kufteh* is to mould minced meat mixed with soft rice or pulses around a hidden treasure, be that eggs, nuts and fruit, or vegetables. The most famous *kufteh* are from the northern town of Tabriz; they are absolutely huge. The first time I was served any sort of *kufteh Tabrizi*, I am afraid I just burst out laughing. They are on average perhaps 12–15 cm in diameter – a far cry from the dainty little numbers we scatter over pasta or get out of 57 varieties of tin.

The first recipe I offer below is pure ostentation in the kitchen. But every curious cook should make it at least once, just as you should also have a crack at that sparrow within a jackdaw within a dodo (whatever) combination.

Kufteh Number One

To feed 4–5 people.

> *a small chicken or poussin, boned (ask your butcher to do this for*
> *you, but keep the bones for stock) stuffed, glazed and cooked in the*
> *Persepolitan manner (see previous recipe – but skip the potatoes)*
> for the 'sauce':
> *2 chopped onions*
> *½ very hot red chilli (or 2 green chillis), chopped (optional)*
> *1 red pepper, finely chopped*
> *1 teaspoon ground turmeric*

1 tablespoons tomato purée

1 tin tomato concasse

1 tablespoon Persepolis patent piquant tomato sauce (or just add an
*   extra spoon of purée)*

450ml bottle sour grape juice (or just add ½ litre extra stock and the
*   juice of 2 lemons)*

salt and pepper

3 litres good chicken stock (use the bones from your poussin)

for the meat mixture:

2kg minced lamb (or beef)

200g (raw weight) pudding rice, cooked and cooled

200g (raw weight) yellow split peas, well cooked, drained and cooled

2 teaspoons ground cinnamon

2 teaspoons ground turmeric

2 teaspoons dried oregano

2 teaspoons dried tarragon

2 eggs

2 onions, finely chopped, fried and cooled

1 teaspoon salt

1 teaspoon pepper

Firstly, you need to make sure that your Persepolitan chicken is not only cooked, but cooled. You are going to wrap the meatball around it, you see. It is probably prudent to roast it a day in advance.

Now, make the sauce by frying the onions, chillis and pepper in a little butter, adding the turmeric, and then a few minutes later stirring in the purée, Persepolis sauce, tomatoes, sour grape juice and stock. Season to taste and set it to simmer.

Next make the meatball mixture. Simply blend all the ingredients. The secret of a good *kufteh* is in this blending – you really need to pound the living daylights out of it, work up a bit of a lather if you will. The idea is for the warmth of your hands to melt the fat of the meat a little and get it inextricably bound with the starch of the rice and peas

until the mixture is really, really sticky. You can put the whole lot in the blender, but you should still give it at least 5 minutes of manual massage to get those juices running.

Make a well in the meat mixture, and place the cooled, roasted poussin in it. With wet hands, mould the *kufteh* meat around the chicken, until it is completely covered. Lower it ever so gently into the simmering sauce, cover and cook for an hour or so, turning once during cooking. Towards the end of cooking, remove your prize meatball and whack the heat up under the sauce to reduce it.

This can be served with rice or bread, hot with the sauce or cold the next day: the one essential is to serve it with a great deal of pride.

You can of course just omit the chicken, and make smaller meatballs filled with the stuffing that was used in the previous chicken recipe. Even in Tabriz, the 'chicken within a meatball' is only served on high-days and holidays.

Kufteh Number Two – Broad Bean Balls

These are seriously tasty, much smaller and much easier to make. Forget the once-in-a-lifetime show-cookery of the previous recipe; you will want to make these every week. This is also enough to feed 4–5 people.

for the balls:
250g pudding rice (soaked for around 30 minutes)
1½ kg fresh broad beans, depodded and skinned or shucked (or 1 x
    400g bag frozen – defrost and shuck)
500g minced lamb
1 egg

1 onion, grated
2 tablespoons dried dill
2 teaspoons dried tarragon
½ teaspoon salt and 1 level teaspoon pepper
for the cooking liquid:
1 onion, chopped
1 teaspoon turmeric
1 litre good chicken stock
for the sauces:
100g thick yoghurt
50ml sour cream (or single)
3–4 cloves garlic
2 teaspoons dill
1 dessertspoon lemon juice
salt and pepper

tahini dip (see p. 227)

Blanch the rice and broad beans for about 15 minutes. Drain and cool. Mix with the other *kufteh* ingredients – a whizz in the blender is good, or 15 minutes of hard manual labour – until everything is really sticking together.

Fry the onion for the cooking liquid in a little butter, add the turmeric, and pour on the stock. Bring to the boil.

With wet hands, roll the beany mixture into approximately 3cm spheres, and plop them into the simmering stock. Cook for about 45 minutes – the *kufteh* obligingly rise to the surface when they are done. Scoop them out, and bubble the stock to reduce it a bit.

To make the yoghurt dip, just mix it with the dill, lemon, garlic and cream, and season to taste.

I serve this on bulghur wheat (see below), with the stock served separately and the yoghurt and tahini dips on the side. But these broad bean balls are also quite fun served with tahini sauce in a pitta pocket.

به سبک جدید

Warm Bulghur Wheat

Bulghur wheat seems only to be found in the bits of Iran which abut Arabshire – it is more authentically an Arabic/Kurdish ingredient. It is versatile, though, as it's so quick to prepare, and you can have it hot or as a salad. To enjoy hot, fry 1 bunch of (cleaned and chopped) spring onions in a little olive oil, add a chopped green pepper, and when they are soft, add 250g medium- or coarse-grain bulghur wheat. Stirring constantly, add ½ – ¾ litre of vegetable stock and bubble until all the water is absorbed and the wheat cooked (about 20 minutes). Season to taste. Chop 2–3 handfuls of your favourite herbs (parsley and coriander are good) and stir them through the wheat.

CHAPTER FIVE

شڪ

CHAPTER FIVE

CASSEROLES

When the Iranians aren't cooking over fire, they tend to eat *khoresht,* or stew. Now our word stew, or even its rather grander cousin, casserole, is resonant of school dinners, Bisto-flavoured bowls of overcooked ingredients, food as a punishment. In Iran it is an art-form, and there are hundreds of varieties. Some, like the rich, sharp *ghormeh sabzi,* are national classics, and others, like cardoon casserole, are regional favourites, unheard of in other parts of the country. Some are eaten with rice, and others with bread. They are mostly gloriously simple to make – one-pot affairs. Jamshid's family eat a lot of *khoresht,* and so we have developed very much our own style of preparing them.

Sorting through sour grapes preparatory to making verjuice.

Khoresht-e-bademjun – Chicken and Aubergine Boats

Unless you happen to dislike aubergines (and, let's face it, they are subject to rampant loathing and ardent passion), you will find this to be one of the most popular Iranian dishes to present; it is one of the great Persian comfort foods. There are two ways of making it – in the north of the country it is made with a rich herby sauce but, most commonly, it is made with a tomato base. Usually it is made with a whole chicken cooked on the bone, with the aubergines sliced, fried and added at the end of the process. For sheer oohs and aahs, we have added our own Persepolitan twist, which puts slivers of chicken breast inside hollowed-out aubergine boats, which we then float in their own tomato-dark sea. This will serve 4 people.

4 largish aubergines
salt and pepper
olive oil
4 chicken breasts, skinned and off the bone, cut into slivers
2 medium onions, sliced
1½ teaspoons turmeric
¼ teaspoon smoked paprika
1 teaspoon ground cinnamon
1 teaspoon tomato purée
½ – ¾ bottle sour grape juice
2–3 tablespoonsful sour grape pickle (or use fresh)
1 can tomato concasse

Prepare the aubergines by scoring round each one, 1cm from the top

and 1cm from the bottom. Peel away the skin between the two scored lines. Then, using a sharp knife, cut a line straight down the length of the vegetable between the two lines, so that the point penetrates just to the middle. Carefully reach in and bring out the sacs of seeds which are inside. Set them to one side. Sprinkle salt both on to the outside and the inside of each aubergine, and then settle them between two layers of kitchen paper so that any water which is drawn out is absorbed.

In the meantime, cook the chicken. Fry the onion in a little olive oil, and then stir in the chicken. Cook until sealed. Add the middle bits of the aubergines which you withdrew earlier, the spices, a little salt and pepper and then, after a few minutes more, the tomato purée. Add the fresh or pickled sour grapes (if using), tomato concasse, and about half a bottle of sour grape juice. Cook for around 10 minutes more, and then take off the heat.

Pat the aubergines dry, and then either deep fry for a few minutes (a luxury – you will need to use clean oil, and the aubergines will render it useless for anything else), or shallow fry, turning them constantly until they soften just slightly and brown just a little. Then set them in an ovenproof dish, and spoon a quarter of the chicken mixture into the middle of each. Pour the surplus sauce into the base of the dish, and cover with foil. Bake in a moderate oven (gas mark 4, 180°C) for around 40 minutes, checking halfway to make sure that there is still plenty of fluid in the base of the dish.

As by now I am sure that you are completely converted to the Persian way of doing food, you will no doubt have a large supply of fresh *sabzi* in your fridge (see p. 39) so serve this dish garnished with herbs (*in extremis,* a sprig of parsley will do), crusted rice cakes (see p. 201) or deep-fried croûtons of *barberi* bread.

Sour grape juice

This is one of the heroes of *la gastronomie Persane*. *Originalement*, at least in Europe, it was known as *verjus*, which in English became the rather more prosaic verjuice. It is somewhere between wine and vinegar in flavour. It is widely believed that in Iran it was cultivated largely to replace wine in food. Ironically, the Persians are generally credited with the invention of wine – 3000-year-old amphorae containing wine sediment have been found in the depths of the Caucasus Mountains. Tales of the drunken revels of old are legion – that great hero Rostam was often so drunk that he had to be helped on to his horse, whilst Hafez mentions wine on more or less every page, and the *Ruba'iyat* of Omar Khayam is more or less a paean to the fruit of the vine.

> One draught of Old Wine is preferable to a New Empire,
> It is best to get out of any way not the way of wine;
> The last of the wine is a hundred times better that Feridun's throne,
> The clay lid of a wine vat better than Kai Khosrow's kingdom.
> *(Penguin version, translated by John Heath-Stubbs and Peter Avery)*

This was a serious relationship. Until the revolution, Iran had a flourishing wine industry (it is no coincidence that there is a grape named Shiraz); in fact it still has flourishing wine 'activity' behind closed doors.

Anyway, in the absence of grape juice of the fermented variety, they turned to the indigenous sour grape to spice up their soups and casseroles – and it has to be said that it is largely more complementary to food than its alcoholic cousin. It is available in bottled form and as a powder in Iranian and many Middle Eastern shops. The fresh variety is available in this country in the late spring/early summer. Fresh sour grapes freeze beautifully, and are so easy to use (just throw them in, stalk and all). If you are unable to get hold of any sour grape products, then a mixture of dry white wine and lemon juice would suffice. But don't forget the Persepolis mail order service.

Arabian Lamb Hotpot, Persepolis-style

This dish is a fusion of Arabic and Persian culinary concepts. That sounds very grand until we confess that it is actually a product of having failed to buy the right ingredients and having lots of people coming for dinner one night. It has to be said that it is very useful having a shop as a store-cupboard, but this dish really does comprise things that most people have in their larders. This will serve 8 people.

1 small bunch each mint and coriander, washed and chopped (or use dried)
a little oil
3 medium onions, chopped
5–6 cloves garlic, finely chopped
1 boned shoulder lamb, cut into 2cm cubes (retain the bone and get your butcher to cut it into 4cm pieces)
2 teaspoons ground turmeric
salt and pepper
2 dessertspoons apple (or cider) vinegar
½ bottle sour grape juice (or 2 tablespoons lemon juice)
2 dessertspoons sour grapes (optional)
1–2 cans chick peas (depending on how much you like them)
1 large can or 1 pack frozen spinach

Sort and wash your herbs or, if using dried, cover with cold water and leave to soak. Heat some oil in a large saucepan and fry the garlic and two of the three onions. After a couple of minutes add the meat and stir until it is sealed all over. Add the turmeric and pepper (we won't add the salt yet – see footnote), fry a little more and then add the vinegar and the sour grape juice. Top up with water until just covered, bring to

به سبک جدید

the boil and set to simmer. In the meantime, retaining a handful of the mint, drain and fry the herbs in a little oil, turning vigorously to prevent clumping (this should take 7–8 minutes). Once they are cooked, add them to the casserole along with the pickled sour grapes, if you opt for them. If necessary, add a little more water to the dish so that everything remains covered. Bring to the boil again, and then set to simmer for at least an hour. After this add the chick peas and the spinach, and cook for another half-hour. Finally, fry the remaining onion and the mint in oil until the mint has darkened and the onion is crisp. Spoon the hotpot into a deep serving dish and strew the crisp onion mixture over the top. Serve with crusted basmati rice (see p. 201), plain thick yoghurt and pickles as desired.

A word about salt

Iranians are inordinately fond of the stuff and, apart from generally using too much of it, they appreciate its culinary pitfalls. Salt notoriously toughens casseroled red meat if you add it to a dish too early, as do ingredients with hidden salt such as tomato or curry paste. So if you want that melt-in-the-mouth, 'no less than three helpings will do' effect, let your lamb or beef cook a while before you season it.

غذاهای مخصوص ایرانی

Khoresht-e-Fessenjun – Duck with Walnut and Pomegranate Sauce

Of all the dishes to come out of the Persian kitchen, this is probably the one with the biggest 'ooh-aah' factor. Iranians will always be impressed by it as it contains such traditionally expensive ingredients. It bears the mark of opulence; by serving it to a dinner guest you are either showing great respect or you are just showing off. Foreigners (non-Iranians) are always bowled over by *fessenjun* – the sheer strength and originality of the flavours leave their mark.

This recipe works with any rich meat or game. I've made it with quail and pheasant, but I also find it great with chunky fish (e.g. salmon) and big prawns. In truth, most Iranians nowadays would probably prepare it with chicken.

You can accessorize this dish with a garnish of baby meatballs, and enhance the sharpness and texture by adding plums. But these are entirely matters of choice. Personally, I usually go with the plums and ditch the meatballs.

This should be a feast sufficient for 4–5 people.

1 duck, jointed
300g shelled walnuts
1 large onion, diced (peeled is good too)
2 teaspoons ground turmeric
½ bottle pomegranate paste
salt and pepper, sugar, and lemon juice (optional)
100g dried bokhara plums (pre-soaked for 1 hour) or substitute
  prunes (optional)
250g minced lamb mixed with ½ grated onion (optional)

Fry the duck in a some hot oil, and allow to cook for five minutes; then remove it from the pan with a slotted spoon and set to one side for a moment. Next grind the walnuts – best to blitz them in a blender, but wrapping them in a teatowel and bashing the hell out of them is another option. Fry the walnuts in the same oil as you cooked the duck, turning constantly until they start to darken; set these to one side. Next fry the onion in the same pan. Now, without burning your fingers, strip the skin from the duck and place the joints back in the pan with the onion. Add the turmeric, salt and pepper and about a pint of water, and set to simmer for about 15 minutes. Then add the walnuts and pomegranate paste, plus the plums if you are using these. If you are doing meatballs, roll the minced lamb and grated onion into 2 cm balls and pop those in as well. Allow to simmer for a further half an hour. Serve on white basmati rice (it's worth getting really nice fragrant rice for this dish), ranging those optional meatballs round the edge, medieval banquet-style. Then sit back and wait for those 'oohs' and 'aahs', not to mention the odd 'darling, you must give me your recipe'.

Ghormeh Sabzi – Herb and Bean Casserole with Lamb

This is Iran's favourite dish. There is a sort of unwritten agreement amongst Iranian housewives that it should be served in every household at least once a week. As far as I know, it isn't actually written into the statute books, but sometimes I wonder.

When it's blowing a gale around Persepolis we like nothing better than to tuck ourselves up around a roaring log fire and recount epic tales of Persian heroes of old (although a video may be nearer the mark): and

that's the sort of evening when we just have to have *ghormeh sabzi*, one of the world's ultimate comfort foods.

The dish is quite stunning. If you have made it correctly, it should in fact be a rich green in colour, and the aroma wafting from it should be enough to get them queuing down the street. These quantities feed 6 hearty or 8 modest eaters.

> *1 shoulder of lamb, trimmed of as much fat as possible (the sheep is a*
> *badly designed animal and it is impossible to remove all the fat), cut*
> *on the bone into 3cm chunks (a nice butcher will do this for you)*
> *2 large onions, chopped*
> *8–9 dried limes, washed and pricked in several places*
> *1 teaspoon ground turmeric*
> *400g kidney beans soaked and cooked (or 2 cans of the same)*
> *1 bunch each of fresh coriander, parsley, chives, spinach and*
> *fenugreek, washed, drained and chopped*
> *salt and pepper*

Place the lamb, onion and dried limes in a pan of water, sprinkle the turmeric on top, bring to the boil and set to simmer. After an hour, stir your casserole a bit, and fry off the herbs in a little oil, stirring constantly so that they cook through thoroughly (5–7 minutes should do the trick). If they are not properly fried they will clump together when you add them to the main dish. Add the herbs, stir the *khoresht* well, and add some seasoning. Set to simmer again, keeping an eye on the liquid level. Twenty minutes before you wish to dish up, stir in the kidney beans.

Altogether we like our stew to bubble away for a couple of hours, but it will be edible after about one and a half. The finished dish should have a thick, rich green sauce and the meat should be falling off the bone.

Serve with plain white basmati rice (sacrilege to contemplate anything else, I am told), and wedges of onion, raw garlic and a pot of thick plain yoghurt.

به سبک جدید

Cheat's Guide: washing and sorting all those herbs is a time-consuming business and even the most dutiful Iranian housewife is not above the occasional shortcut. So you can use dried herbs if you wish – just soak them first and then fry them or, if you are lucky enough to have an Iranian store near you, look out for frozen pre-chopped herbs, frozen chopped and fried herbs or even the whole sauce thing in cans. Not that we endorse such scheming in the kitchen, you understand....

Khoresht Aloo Bokhara – Plum Hotpot with Chicken

This is a really lush casserole – thick and gloopy, sweet and sour, with both crunch and squidge. It should really be called chicken casserole with plums, but as I invariably scoff the plums and peas and sauce, I rarely have room left for the chicken. As a general rule, the meat part of a *khoresht* is largely a detail and so, with a small twist, most of the recipes featured in this book can be made just as successfully in vegetarian or even vegan mode. Here are the quantities for 4–6 people.

*400g aloo bokhara, whole dried plums (widely available at Middle
    Eastern shops now, but you can use dried prunes)*
a little olive oil (or ghee, to be more authentic)
1 large onion, peeled and chopped
1 skinned chicken, cut into 8 pieces
1 teaspoon ground cinnamon plus 1 teaspoon ground turmeric
1 tablespoon tomato purée
sour grapes and sour grape juice
150g yellow split peas (preferably Iranian or Indian)

Put the dried plums (or prunes) into cold water to soak – best to do this half an hour to an hour before you start cooking. Heat a little olive oil or ghee in a saucepan and toss in the onion. Fry for a few minutes, and then add the chicken pieces. Turn the chicken gently until it is lightly browned, and then stir in the spices and the tomato purée. Add a tablespoon of sour grapes, half a bottle of sour grape juice, and 500ml cold water. If you are using *chana dall*, i.e. Indian or Iranian split peas, add them now; common or garden split peas (which are not so good as they cook to a mush, losing their integrity) should be added after about 20 minutes. Bring the chicken to the boil, and then set to simmer for around half an hour, stirring occasionally. Drain the plums and mix them into the casserole, together with some salt and pepper. Cook for a further 20 minutes. Taste the sauce. If it is too sour, add some sugar; if it is not sharp enough, you may add more sour grape juice or a dash of lemon juice.

Devour with white basmati rice, fresh herbs and minted onion salad.

I rather like this as a hot (as in chilli) dish, and so I usually add 1–2 red chillies to the recipe at the frying-onion-stage. The combination of thick, sweet and eye-watering is unexpected but delicious. It is not, however, authentic. Iranians are not known for their love of really hot food, and several have thought that I was actually trying to poison them when I tried to spice things up.

Korma Shalgam – Afghan Lamb and Turnip Casserole Persian-style

Afghan cuisine is similar to Iranian cuisine – they are next-door neighbours and are clearly bound to borrow the odd cup of sugar or recipe from each other. But the Afghans like things a lot spicier – probably something to do with all those lovely mountains, not to mention their neighbours on the other side in Pakistan. Anyway, unlike many Iranians, we really like hot food, and so I make no apologies for including this recipe. It is a favourite with our helper, Mr Mirwais, who says that on a good day, with the wind blowing in the right direction, it is almost a tenth as tasty as his mother's. Rare praise indeed. I especially like this dish because it enhances the flavour of the turnips, rather than drowning them in a sea of root vegetables. This is a truly hearty feast for a cold day. Enough for 6–8 people.

1 small boned shoulder of lamb, trimmed of fat
2 onions, chopped
4 cloves garlic, chopped
1½ really hot red chillies or 3–4 hot green chillies, chopped
a little oil of choice (ghee to be more authentic)
2 teaspoons cumin powder
2 teaspoons ground turmeric
½ teaspoon smoked paprika
2 teaspoons cinnamon powder
1 can tomato concasse
250g yellow split peas
½ bottle sour grape juice (or three tablespoons lemon juice) and some
*   pickled sour grapes if available*

4 medium turnips, peeled and quartered
4 medium carrots, peeled and quartered
2 teaspoons tomato purée
salt and pepper
fresh coriander, chopped

When you buy the shoulder of lamb you may well ask the butcher to bone it for you. Make absolutely sure you keep the bones, and ask the butcher nicely to cut the bone into enough manageable chunks to go round, otherwise there will be an undignified scrum over the hotpot to retrieve them. If you are terribly British and not yet in the habit of slobbery, finger-licking bone sucking, it is one of those things you need to absorb to live the Persian good-life.

Cut the meat into 2–3cm chunks. Fry the onions, garlic and chillies in a little oil, and then stir in the lamb. Sear the meat, and then add the spices. Add the tomato concasse and a little water, bring to the boil, cover the pan and set to simmer for around half an hour. Then add the sour grape juice, sour grapes, split peas and more water (so that the meat is nicely covered). Carry on cooking for another hour, and then add the tomato paste, turnip and carrot. Season to taste and then simmer for a final half hour.

Serve strewn with the fresh coriander, alongside bowls of pickles or *must-o-khiar* (see p. 50). We recommend that this dish is eaten with brown basmati rather than the white so beloved of Iranians – it is more authentic for Afghan food, generally a lot tastier, and it is just so much better for you. Not that we are trying to nanny you or anything.

به سبک جدید

Rhubarb Stew – *Khoresht-e-Rivas*

'Ooh no!', we hear you cry. Rhubarb is something that many people find at best unpleasant. One is forced to consume it with custard when one is a child. That slimy sharpness can leave a psychological scar, and I have seen grown men weep rather than face a rhubarb crumble.

This recipe may thus be regarded as therapy for rhubarbo-phobes. It is really nice. Trust me. I like Marmite too. My mother would like readers to know that this recipe has her full endorsement, it is her favourite Persian dish.

This combination of mint and parsley is used for a range of casseroles, most commonly celery and cardoon, so I have listed a couple of variations underneath. I have added coriander because I like it. This makes a stew large enough for 4–6 people.

1 skinned chicken
a little butter
1 large onion, chopped
1 teaspoon ground turmeric
½ bottle sour grape juice (or 2 tablespoons lemon juice)
2 dessertspoons fresh or pickled sour grapes (optional)
salt and pepper
1 small bunch mint (or 60g dried mint)
1 small bunch parsley (or 60g dried)
1 small bunch coriander (or 60g dried)
1 large bundle rhubarb, washed and peeled (if large, mature stalks)

Chop your chicken: separate legs from thighs, and halve the breasts, leaving it all on the bone. Melt the butter in a pan, and toss in the onion and turmeric. Once the onion has started to soften, add in the

chicken and seal all over. Add the sour grape juice, sour grapes, salt and pepper, and enough water to cover, bring to the boil and set to simmer. As an alternative to the above, you can just place the chicken, onion, turmeric and seasoning in the pan with the verjuice and water and bring to the boil – but I believe that frying best releases the flavour of the turmeric.

In the meantime sort, wash, drain and chop your herbs (if using dried herbs you will have needed to soak them first). Pour a little oil in a frying-pan, and fry the herbs, stirring constantly so that they do not catch. Cook for around 8 minutes and then add to the casserole. Continue to cook for around half an hour until the chicken is cooked through.

Chop the rhubarb into pieces approximately 3cm long and lower it into the sauce. Cook the whole thing for around another 10 minutes, check the seasoning, and ladle carefully into a serving dish.

Serve with plain basmati rice, yoghurt and fresh raw garlic. And expunge all memories of custard.

Variations on the theme

Celery: you do the same as above, substituting celery for rhubarb. But as celery requires a little more cooking than rhubarb, you need to sauté it gently for 5–10 minutes before adding it to the *khoresht*.

Cardoons: not something you find easily at your nearest CostMore or PriceBooster supermarket, but can be grown easily in an English garden. The plant is a wild cousin of the artichoke; it is the stalks which are eaten. They resemble salsify (which is available if you look hard enough – the canned variety is very easy to use). Just sauté them as I suggest you do the celery above.

Ab-Gusht as an art form

Ab-Gusht, literally 'meat-water' or stock, truly is an art form in the Iranian kitchen. While *gusht* does actually mean meat, the term *ab-gusht* is equally applied to 'chicken water'.

What was historically (and may still be) a way of stretching a few meagre bones into a nourishing meal, is today eaten as a soup and relished as an accompaniment to rice.

Everybody makes it differently, while adhering to a few basic principles, and once you have grounding in what it's all about, you can experiment freely and have a bit of fun.

The one more or less essential ingredient is dried limes, *limoo armani*. If you really can't find them in your local or nearest Middle Eastern store, give our mail-order department a ring. It is worth the effort, and they are lightweight and inexpensive. At a pinch, you can substitute a fresh lemon: give it a rinse, quarter it and pop the whole lot in.

In Iran you can get *ab-gusht* in roadside cafés – it is the Persian equivalent of egg and chips, good lorry-driver fare. It is cooked for several hours, whereupon the meat is stripped out and mashed with the potatoes – the resulting meat patty is served on a plate, with the *ab* served alongside (usually in a baby metal tureen) as a broth. *Lavash* bread is often dunked into the broth. Eaten this way, the dish is called *dizee'*.

Ab-Gusht with Lamb

This is to feed 8 people as a main course. For fewer people, just reduce the quantities. If you are going to make it just as a soup, then you can do it with bones alone.

1 shoulder of lamb, trimmed and chopped on the bone into 2cm cubes
2 medium onions, chopped
8 dried limes, washed and pricked
2 teaspoons ground turmeric
100g chick peas, soaked overnight (or 1 can cooked)
100g white kidney or cannellini beans, soaked overnight (or 1 can)
4 medium potatoes
salt and pepper

Rinse the lamb, and then place in a pan with the chopped onions and dried limes. If you are using dried beans, rinse and add them at this stage as well. Cover with water so that the surface of the liquid is about 5cm above the meat (only 2cm if you are using canned beans). Sprinkle in the turmeric, bring to the boil, and set to simmer; ignore for around an hour and a half. After this, peel and halve the potatoes and lower them in and, if you are using canned beans, add these as well. At this stage, check that the meat is still covered by the stock (add a little boiling water to top it up if necessary), and only now should you add some seasoning to taste. Cook for another half an hour, or until the potatoes are just starting to disintegrate.

Serve with brown basmati – actually I usually serve this with the lentil rice featured in Chapter Seven. Spoon the lamb into the centre of the rice, and serve the *ab* in a bowl separately. This dish needs the company of pickles, yoghurt and bread.

به سبک جدید

Ab-Gusht with Chicken

This is eaten with lots of things – *bogoli pulao, sib pulao* – its simplicity provides the prefect accompaniment to these delicately flavoured rice dishes. Again, it can be eaten as a soup if you are just using bones and scraps of raw chicken or used as a casserole if you are using whole joints. The recipe assumes the latter. It will be enough for 5–6 people.

> *1 chicken, skinned and jointed*
> *1 large onion, chopped*
> *5–6 dried limes*
> *1 teaspoon turmeric*
> *¼ teaspoon saffron, steeped in boiling water*
> *salt and pepper*
> *100g Iranian split peas (or the Indian* chana dall*)*
> *1 can cooked chick peas*
> *75g* kritheraki *(rice-shaped pasta) or pudding rice*
> *1–2 potatoes (optional, but then, as I explained above, all these*
>   *ingredients can be pretty much played around with)*

Wash the chicken and place it in a pan; prick the dried limes and add them to the chicken along with the onion. Pour in enough cold water to cover the meat with around 1cm to spare. Sprinkle in the turmeric and saffron and a starter-offering of salt and pepper, add the split peas and bring to the boil. Once it has boiled, turn the gas down and allow it to simmer for half an hour. At this point add the pasta and the chick peas; peel and halve your spuds if using and lower these in too. Cook the chicken through for another half an hour.

Serve with the rice of your choice, or just dish up in a big bowl and serve with plenty of warm Persian bread. Once again, pickles are a requisite; raw onion, yoghurt and herbs are desirable.

Lubia Chitti – Baked Beans with Cheesy Meatballs

In Iran there is a bit of confusion about bean nomenclature, and I find quite a large number of beans get called *lubia chitti* (literally, 'stripy beans') – in truth the term most probably refers to pinto beans, which are indeed striped, but it also seems to refer more broadly to any beans in sauce. Our baked beans here are made with haricot or navy beans, but we *still* call them *lubia chitti*. Use any bean you like, as long as it is one which withstands slow cooking. This will be enough for about 6 supper guests, although you will have enough beans left over for lunch the next day.

for the beans:
500g navy or haricot beans (soaked overnight)
butter
2 onions, chopped
3 sticks celery, chopped
1 red and 1 green pepper, diced
½ teaspoon cinnamon
½ teaspoon cumin
½ teaspoon smoked paprika
1 teaspoon oregano
1 teaspoon mint
1 tablespoon tomato paste
2 tin crushed tomatoes
2 tablespoons Persepolis patent piquant tomato sauce (see p. 331)
salt and pepper
for the meatballs:
1kg minced lamb
1 grated onion

به سبک جدید

2 grated potatoes
3 teaspoons dried oregano
2 teaspoons dried mint
½ teaspoon cinnamon
½ teaspoon turmeric
100–150g halloumi (or mozzarella) cheese, cut into centimetre cubes

Bring the beans to the boil in unsalted water, cook for about 10 minutes, then drain. Melt the butter in a skillet, and sauté the onions, celery and peppers. When they have softened, add the spices and herbs, stirring well, and then the tomato paste, tinned tomatoes and special sauce. Bring this to the boil, season to taste, then remove from the heat. Layer the beans in an oven dish, and pour the sauce over the top, mixing well. Cover the dish with foil, and bake at gas mark 4/180°C for around an hour and a half.

In the meantime you can get cracking with the meatballs. Make sure that you drain the grated onion and potato before using them; your mixture will otherwise be really mushy. Mix all the ingredients (bar the cheese) together, then with wet hands roll the mixture into little balls no more than 3cm in diameter. Poke a cube of cheese into each one, making sure that it is completely surrounded by meat – the cheese will otherwise just leak out and burn.

After the beans have been cooking for 1 ½ hours, take them out, stir them, and season to taste.

Put the meatballs on to a greased oven tray and cook for 15 minutes on gas mark 5/190°C, turning once. Take them out of the oven. Next, check that the beans have enough liquid (add a dash of boiling water if necessary), and then spoon the meatballs on top of the bean mixture. Re-cover the beans, and put back in the oven for another 30 minutes.

You can serve this dish with rice or jacket potatoes – there are those who need real concentrations of carbohydrate with every meal – but I reckon it's best just with some warm *naan-e-sangak* (or other bread of your choosing), and a vibrant, verdant salad.

غذاهای مخصوص ایرانی

The unmentionables – offal

Offal is hugely popular in Iran. I debated long and hard as to whether to include it in this tome – the modern English are pretty lily-livered, if you'll excuse the pun, when it comes to eating the insides, not to mention the extremities, of animals. But it is so very much ensconced in Iran's cuisine that its omission would have been to offer less than a full picture of the nation's kitchen. Besides, with the success of restaurants such as St John, it would seem that 'real' English food, comprising all these things, is enjoying a bit of a comeback.

The successful cooking of such delicacies as tripe, brains and tongue depends less on fancy ingredients and more on method: which is why I will not be proffering recipes for lamb's feet with a blackcurrant *jus*, or brain and pesto gnocchi. I have simply had a chat with the mother-in-law, her brother Mohsen – himself a consummate chef and passionate about animal unmentionables – and a quick flick through Rosa Montazami's oeuvre (see Bibliography). Just for the record, I have tried, enjoyed and tested all of these recipes, but me and tripe are never going to hit it off (although it seems awfully big in Peckham), so for that particular recipe entire credit is due to Ms Montazami and several chats with my local butcher and his customers. Please note that other than liver, kidney and heart, offal tends to take rather a long time to cook. For this reason, Iranians often resort to pressure cookers. If you have one, feel free to get it out and play.

Tripe — Seer Abi

سیرابی

For 4–6 adventurous souls, you will need:

2kg tripe
vinegar and salt
2 carrots, peeled and roughly chopped
1 stick celery – roughly chopped
4–5 dried limes (or zest of 1 lemon plus juice of 2)
3 medium onions, peeled and roughly chopped
1 bulb garlic, peeled
100ml olive oil 50g ghee or butter
2 teaspoons ground turmeric
2–3 fresh chopped chillies (or 1 teaspoon chilli powder)
1–2 tablespoons flour
100g walnut halves, roughly chopped
1 small bunch parsley, chopped

To enjoy this dish at its optimum, you should begin the process 2 days ahead of when it is required.

The key to doing anything with tripe is to clean it properly. To this effect you should first wash it thoroughly. Then cut it into 4cm squares, place it in a large bowl, immerse it with three parts water to one part vinegar and a handful of salt, cover it and leave overnight to soak. The next day, wash again and clean once more with water, vinegar and salt; then rinse until the water runs clear. Place in a pan, add the carrots, celery, dried limes and two of the onions, together with half the garlic and half the turmeric. Bring to the boil, cover, and cook slowly for 4–5 hours. At the end of this cooking time, remove the tripe and set to one side: strain the stock. Heat the oil and ghee in a pan, and gently fry the

غذاهای مخصوص ایرانی

other onion with the rest of the garlic and the chillies. Once the onion has started to brown, add the rest of the turmeric, and then the flour, stirring constantly. Slowly pour in the strained stock, and put the tripe back in the pan as well. Bring to the boil, season to taste, and then stir in the parsley and walnuts. Allow to simmer for one hour more. You can then dish up if you wish but this dish is one of the few which improve for being left (in the fridge of course) overnight and reheated the next day.

Serve with raw onion and lots of warm Persian bread. Just don't ask me to share it with you.

Caleh-pah-cheh – Lamb's Head and Feet

Lambs are bought by families in Iran to slaughter and cook as an offering or by way of thanks for something – and yes, that does include the return of prodigal sons, as many a Westernized Iranian will tell you upon their first trip home for a while. Professionals are hired to carry out the slaughter, and it is not any crueller than the processes at an abattoir. But it can still be a bit of a shock for the jet-lagged West Londoner in his Armani suit arriving at the family house to find the driveway awash with blood, or ringing with the sound of piteous bleats.

Anyway, the custom of buying a whole lamb has naturally led to some enterprising ways of consuming it. Nothing is allowed to go to waste. Usually some will be given away to the poor, but the head and feet are regarded as a great treat and therefore retained for family use. They are traditionally cooked very slowly through the night and eaten as a breakfast 'fit for shahs'; they are also touted as a hangover remedy.

I am assuming for the purposes of the exercise that you are not actually going to be killing your own sheep on the front lawn, but rather making a trip to the butcher. Nice butchers will sear the furry bits off, and cut through the tendons of the feet, so that all you have to do is give them a quick rinse and cook them. This is what you need for a romantic 'breakfast' for 2 people.

> *1 lamb's head, skinned*
> *2 lamb's feet, de-furred*
> *2 large onions, chopped*
> *2 level teaspoons ground turmeric*
> *3–4 bay leaves*
> *100g dried chick peas, soaked for 6 hours*
> *100g dried cannellini beans, soaked for 6 hours*
> *salt*

غذاهای مخصوص ایرانی

Rinse the head and feet and pop them in a large pan with the onion, bay leaves and turmeric. Cover with plenty of water and bring to the boil. Drain the soaked beans, and add them to the pan. Wrap the lid of the pan in a clean tea towel (it helps absorb any cooking odours), and set to simmer – preferably overnight, but 5 hours will do. Just before serving, add salt to taste.

The eyes, tongue, flesh and brain are all edible, as is the bone marrow, but you can fry the brain separately (see below). Serve with the stock and lots and lots of bread. You will be surprised at how tasty this is (and this is from someone who really doesn't rate meat that highly).

Fried Brains

If you haven't acquired your brain as a by-product of the previous recipe, buy really fresh calves' or lambs' brains from the butcher (1 per person for lamb, half a head per person for a calf, as a rough guide). Soak them in cold water for ten minutes, and then blanch them in boiling water with a dash of lemon juice for 15 minutes. Remove from the water, pat dry, and then cut each brain in half (there is a 'natural' dotted line down the middle for this). Mix a couple of serving-spoons of flour with a teaspoon of turmeric and a teaspoon of salt: coat each piece of meat with the flour, and then fry in butter. Serve with lemon wedges. Again, extraordinarily scrummy.

Tongue à la Mother-in-Law

Oh squeamish ones, you can peek again now – this dish is at least familiar. Pressed tongue is still a regular presence in the British diet.

My mother-in-law usually uses lambs' tongues, and so that is what I have assumed for this recipe. You can use calf's tongue: as a rough guide, 1 calf's tongue, in feedability terms, equates to about 3 lambs' tongues. When we eat this, it tends to be more as a casserole; which suits me, as I am less than thrilled about the appearance of the things (not to cook, but to eat), so when they are heavily disguised I can just dip in and enjoy the flavour of the sauce. In Iran, this dish is a prize item, served to guests with great aplomb. It is another of those dishes which serve to separate the women from the girls (at least in terms of culinary skill). This will be enough for 4 people.

> *about 8 lambs' tongues*
> *1 large onion, chopped*
> *2 bay leaves*
> *black pepper*
> *a handful each of chopped tarragon, mint and parsley*
> *4 cloves garlic (2 quartered, 2 chopped)*
> *salt*
> *a bunch of spring onions, washed and chopped*
> *oil for frying*
> *500g mushrooms, cleaned and quartered*
> *2 dessertspoons tomato purée*

Again, preparation is key. Scrape the tongues to remove any unwanted bits, then wash them and place them in a pan. Cover with water, add the chopped onion, bay leaves, pepper, fresh herbs and the two quartered

cloves of garlic. Bring to the boil, and then turn the heat down and cook for 4–5 hours (until the tongues feel tender when you poke them with a fork). At the end of this cooking time, add salt to taste and bring back to the boil for 10 minutes. Take the meat out, reserving the stock. Whilst they are hot, peel the tongues, and if you serving these as a party piece, slice through each tongue at 2 mm intervals, nearly but not all the way to the base, so that the tongues can be opened out like a fan and guests will easily be able to help themselves to individual slices (if not, just leave them whole). Set them to one side.

Now make the 'sauce'. Fry the spring onions in a little oil. Add the mushrooms, and continue to cook until they are golden brown and all the water content has evaporated. Grind the remaining garlic with a little salt, and add to the mushroom/onion mix, and after 5 further minutes, add the tomato purée, stirring well. Pour in the reserved stock (which you should really strain), and bring to the boil. If you are having the dish informally, just lower the tongues back into the sauce, and when piping hot, serve with hot Persian bread and fresh herbs. If you are showing off, you will need to range your tongues tastefully on a platter, making the partially severed slices clearly apparent. Spoon a little of the sauce over each tongue. Surround with..., well, they usually use piped mashed potato these days, but I prefer rice and the lentil mash on p. 240. The idea is to make the dish look really spectacular, with piles of fresh herbs dotted in between. Serve the remaining sauce in a bowl on the side.

Chicken on a Bed of Prunes and Spinach

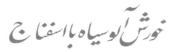

This recipe is based on another *khoresht* from the north-west of Iran, but we have gone all *ash-pazi jadide* (Persian *nouvelle cusine*) with this. Rather than dish up a vat of green casserole, we merely wilt the spinach, toss lightly with the prunes and top it with shredded chicken. The delicious sweet/sour sauce is drizzled over the top. I saw something like this done on Persian daytime television, but I only caught the end bit, so have had to devise my own method. To feed 4 people.

4 chicken breasts, on the bone if possible
1 large onion, chopped
1 knob of green ginger (anomalous to classic Persian cuisine, but all
*   the rage on daytime TV over there), chopped*
4 cloves garlic, chopped
1 teaspoon ground turmeric
2 tablespoons apple (or cider) vinegar
1 teaspoon saffron, steeped in boiling water
1 teaspoon ground cinnamon
500g prunes
2 tablespoons honey
1 tablespoon sugar
1kg fresh spinach, washed
100g nibbed almonds
olive oil, salt and pepper
4 portions basmati rice

Fry the onions, garlic and ginger, and when they start to soften, stir in the chicken and turmeric, together with a light sprinkle of salt and pepper. When the chicken is sealed all over, add 1 litre cold water and

the vinegar, bring to the boil and add half the saffron. Cover the pan and simmer for around 15 minutes or until the chicken is cooked through. Retrieve the chicken breasts and set them aside, and then bubble the sauce gently for another 10 minutes to reduce it.

Take 4 tablespoonsful of this chicken stock and put them into another pan. Stir in the prunes and heat gently for 7–8 minutes. Then add the sugar, cinnamon and honey; stir, and take off the heat.

Cook the basmati rice according to your normal method, and streak the rest of the saffron through it to give variegated colour.

Take the breasts off the bone (which you may now discard) and chop into fine slices. Scoop the prunes out of the spiced syrup and reserve. Pour the reduced chicken stock into the syrup, and heat through.

Heat a drop of olive oil in a frying-pan, and fry the nibbed almonds. Remove them with a slotted spoon and reserve, and then swiftly toss the spinach into the hot oil, stirring constantly. Just as it starts to wilt, throw in the prunes and take off the heat.

Layer a large and splendid serving dish with the rice, followed by the prunes and spinach. Then comes the sliced chicken, and a strewing of nibbed almonds. The sauce should be trailed across the top.

Tamarind Lamb and Mushroom Cobbler

This recipe is based on *khoresht–e-gharch* – mushroom casserole – a perennial favourite in my mother-in-law's family. It has to be said that mushrooms are not one of *the* quintessential Persian ingredients – as you travel east out of Europe you will find that they are used less and less (until you get to the Orient, where they have plenty of indigenous, exotic varieties), so I suspect that the Persian mushroom eating habit was introduced from Europe. This recipe sees the *khoresht* thickened, and topped with a herby, saffron crumble – it should thus be served without rice. Enough for 4 people.

1 onion, chopped
450g lean, boneless lamb – neck fillet, leg or shoulder
½ teaspoon ground cumin
1 teaspoon ground turmeric
1 teaspoon ground cinnamon
1 tablespoon flour
1 tablespoon tamarind concentrate (see note below)
2 tablespoons sour grape juice (or 1 tablespoon lemon juice)
350g mushrooms
salt and pepper
for the cobbler:
90g butter
100g wholemeal flour
100g plain flour
100g grated cheese (optional)
½ teaspoon ground saffron dissolved in boiling water
handful each of fresh chopped coriander, chives and parsley
salt and pepper

غذاهای مخصوص ایرانی

Fry the onion in a little oil. Cut the lamb into 2–3cm cubes, and add it to the softened onion, together with the cumin, cinnamon and turmeric. Seal the meat well, before adding the flour. Stirring constantly, add enough water to cover the meat, cover the pan and set to simmer. You can at this stage transfer it to a casserole dish and cook it in the oven (gas mark 4/180°C), but it is easier to play with and observe on the hob. Cook for one hour, stirring occasionally, and then add the sour grape juice and tamarind paste. Wipe and quarter the mushrooms, and fry these in a knob of butter until the water content has evaporated (5–10 minutes, stirring regularly). Add these to the meat, season to taste, and cook for a further 15 minutes.

Make the crumble topping by cutting the butter into little pieces and rubbing it with your fingertips into the mixed flours (it should resemble breadcrumbs). Add the saffron, herbs, cheese and a sprinkle of seasoning. Transfer the meat to a proper casserole dish (if you haven't already), and strew the crumble on top. Bake at gas mark 5/190°C for around 25 minutes, until the top of the cobbler is lightly browned.

Serve with your choice of potatoes or vegetables.

به سبک جدید

Tamarind

Tamarinds are deeply intriguing little fruits, strongly resembling
something John Wyndham might have created, or perhaps the product
of a space-ship's hydroponics bay. Once you have cracked the outside
pod, you need then to peel off the 'string' inside, and watch out for
the shiny, black alien-spawn pips. Tamarinds come in two varieties
– sweet or sour – both of which are incredibly flavoursome. The sweet
is prepared and eaten just so – its chewy pulp is more like a confection
than a fruit, and it has a similar effect to prunes (if you see what I
mean). The sour can also be eaten *au naturel*, but is mostly made into
a thick, sharp, exotic paste for cooking. You can make your own paste
by steeping a few peeled tamarinds in boiling water and then pressing
it all through a sieve. But the ready-made stuff is available in all Middle
Eastern food stores, and is a great little ingredient to have in your
pantry – use it for thickening and sharpening sauces and soups, or as a
marinade ingredient.

غذاهای مخصوص ایرانی

CHAPTER SIX

FISH

Mullah Nasruddin chanced upon a wise man who was lost, and kindly gave him directions. As the wise man was hungry, he offered to buy the mullah a meal if this latter could also show him a good restaurant in the town. The mullah was delighted to oblige, and took him to the best restaurant in town. When they enquired of the restaurateur what his recommendation would be, they were told to order the fish speciality, which of course they did.

When the two fish dishes arrived, one was much bigger than the other. Without any hesitation the mullah seized the larger one for himself. Startled, the wise man hesitated before querying the mullah's action, saying that it contravened all moral and social norms. The mullah looked surprised, and replied, 'Why, sir, what would you have done?' The wise man naturally answered that he would have claimed the smaller fish for himself. 'Well there you go then, my friend!' cried the mullah, and placed the smaller portion on the wise man's plate.

Fish – *mahi*

Iran only has sea at the top and bottom, and it isn't known for its gushing rivers or profound lakes. So it should come as no surprise to learn that only inhabitants of the Caspian coast to the north and those abutting the Persian Gulf in the south truly know what to do with fish.

But oh! what variety of fish there is for those lucky few. The Caspian is of course famous for being home to the sturgeon (caviar's Mummy) – but the sturgeon has a great number of cousins, and all of them are jolly tasty. And the Gulf is just full of fish.

Many Persians do not like real fish, especially if it smells of fish – so be careful if you are trying to entertain and impress Iranian friends. For the majority of Iranians fish is something that comes white, skinned and filleted, and is fried and eaten with rice, and so that is where we will begin.

Sabzi Pulao Ba Mahi – Herbed Rice with Fried Fish

سبزی پلو با ماهی

You will need per person:
1 side filleted white fish (cod, plaice, haddock or similar)
1 side smoked fish (mackerel is fine)
1 cup rice
1 clove garlic, finely chopped
You will also need:
1 bunch each parsley, coriander and dill
2 bunches chives, or 2 leeks
(or substitute the herbs and chives for 1 bag of dried sabzi pulao *mix)*
1–2 teaspoonsful turmeric
300g firm prawns
1½ tablespoonsful capers, chopped
1 baby tin anchovy fillets, chopped
½ teaspoon ground saffron
butter, flour, oil, salt and pepper
2–3 lemons (at least one of them unwaxed)

غذاهای مخصوص ایرانی

Wash the fresh fish and pat it dry, and then put it in the fridge to chill. An Iranian housewives' trick is to wrap the fish tightly in a clean tea towel – this minimizes fishy smells in the fridge and also absorbs any surplus water from the fish. When my mother-in-law told me that if fish is too wet when you cook it, it tastes of water, I was nothing if not sceptical, but of course most housewives' tales have their basis in fact and this particular one is absolutely true.

Trim, soak, drain and chop the herbs (or if using the dried variety simply soak, scoop them out and squeeze out the excess moisture). Heat some oil in a frying-pan, and fry the garlic without allowing it to turn brown. Toss in the herbs, a handful at a time, stirring constantly. You will need to fry the mixture for around 10 minutes to make sure that all the particles are coated and cooked.

Wash the rice and boil it as per the general rice recipe on p. 200. Drain it and rinse it and sizzle some oil in the bottom of the pan. Add a layer of rice, and let it fry until it starts to catch and then layer the rice and fried herb mixture alternately. Make four or five fumeroles through the rice with the handle of a wooden spoon. Fit a cloth-covered lid on top, cook for 5 minutes on high, and then reduce the heat and allow to cook through for about half an hour. If you are lucky enough to be using a rice cooker, wash your rice as usual and then add the garlic in with the butter right at the beginning. Stir the herbs through the rice just at the end of the cooking process – the rice should end up looking quite green.

In the meantime, sieve some flour on to a clean tray, and sprinkle some salt and the turmeric on top. Mix, and then one by one roll each piece of fresh fish in it so that they are all well coated. Heat some oil in a pan – it should be really hot – and then fry each fillet until it is a proper looking shade of gold: put them in the bottom of the oven to keep warm. Grill the smoked fish, or heat it through in a foil parcel in the oven.

Melt some butter in a pan, and when it is sizzling throw in the prawns, anchovies and capers; fry them gently for around 5 minutes.

Steep the saffron in a very little boiling water, and then add the juice and rind of one unwaxed lemon. Pour this fragrant mixture over the prawns, and then after a further minute take the whole thing off the heat.

Take your rice off the heat, run 2cm of cold water into the sink and stand the pan in it for a few minutes – this will make the sticky *tahdik* (see p. 202) unstick a little and come out looking just so. Even if you are using a rice cooker, turning it off a few minutes before you turn it out aids the process. Turn the rice on to a large serving dish, and then crack the crust in one line through the middle. Pour the saffron prawn mixture in a stripe along the length of the crack. Serve the fish in a separate dish. Eat with fresh herbs, plenty of lemon or sour orange when available, and lashings of posh and piquant Persian pickles. This dish is a staple at the time of the New Year.

The Persian New Year – *Nowrooz*

Although there are plenty of *eid*'s in the Iranian calendar, they are mostly Islamic festivals celebrating things like the end of Ramadan or the end of the *Hajj* (pilgrimages to Mecca). The real let-your-hair-down, boogie-boogie stuff is concentrated into the period of *Nowrooz* (literally New Day), the Persian New Year. Its origins pre-date Islam by at least 2000 years. Originally a Zoroastrian festival (although, as with Saturnalia and Christmas, elements of the newer religion, in this case Islam, have been woven into it) it always falls on the day and at the precise time of the Spring Equinox, so that one year it might be at an inconvenient 5.13 a.m., and the next a rather more civilized 12 noon. At the time of writing, the year is 1386 – the years are worked out using the lunar calendar and dating from Mohammad's flight from Mecca to Medina in AD622.

It starts on the eve of the last Wednesday of the year (*char-shanbeh suri*), when Iranians the world over light a series of small bonfires, which

they then leap over, addressing the flames as they go in an effort to shed their bad deeds or bad luck, purging themselves for another year and taking strength from the fire. The Iranian government are uneasy about allowing such acts of flagrant paganism (quite apart from the obvious health and safety implications), but all efforts to stamp out this ancient rite have failed.

Iranians decorate for the New Year – they prepare a special spread (*sofreh*) of items representing the re-growth and prosperity that they hope will come. There is the *haftsin*, the seven 'S's, seven items beginning with the letter S (well, the Persian equivalent of, that is); you may choose from: *sib* (apple, for health and beauty), *sir* (garlic, to represent the power of medicine), *samenou* (a sweet paste made from wheat sprouts), *sombol* (hyacinth), *sumak* (a red spice to represent the sunrise of the new day), *senjed* (the fruit of the oleander), *serkeh* (vinegar, for age and patience), *sabzeh* (herbs) and *sekeh* (coins). The *sabzeh* is grown from wheat or bean sprouts a couple of weeks before the actual day. They will also have live goldfish to represent prosperity, and shedsful of sweets (to bring sweetness into their lives). The *Nowrooz* table will also be set with painted eggs, mirrors, candles and a copy of the Koran – it is awfully pretty. Iranian shops are usually brightly bedecked for the New Year, a riot of music and dancing and chatter; for the week preceding *Nowrooz*, every day is party day – a visit to an Iranian 'Super' at this time is a good way to sample Persian culture.

On the actual day it is important to start the New Year as you mean to go on, pink and scrubbed, in new clothes, relaxed and happy, with a clear conscience and surrounded by your nearest and dearest. As the clock strikes you hug and congratulate everyone, and then eat some of the vast array of sweetmeats in front of you. Gifts and money are given, especially to children, money being distributed by the elders from the pages of the Koran. Food? Well they enjoy elaborate rice dishes like the recipe for *chirin pulao* on p. 214, usually with chicken, and most importantly, *sabzi pulao ba mahi* (see above). They do have a sort of Father Nowrooz (known as Haji Firouz), traditionally a jolly black man

in a red outfit who plays the *daphf* and dances: sadly, when Iranians in
London tried to recreate this quaint, harmless practice a few years ago,
they got accused of racism and pelted with bad fruit. In Iran there is
then a period of great festivity – businesses and schools close for two
weeks, and the time is spent visiting friends and feasting.

Finally, on the thirteenth day after the New Year, the *sabzeh* (which
should by now have grown quite high) is tied by members of the family
as each one recites their wishes for the coming year, and then tossed
into moving water (again, trying this in the River Thames can raise
some eyebrows). This is a sort of unofficial national picnic day, when it
is believed that the weather is finally clement enough to permit feasting
al fresco. Oh, and in case you were worried, the goldfish are released into
ponds or proper aquariums and live happily ever after.

غذا های محصوص ایرانی

Khoresht Ghaliheh Mahi – Herb and Tamarind Fish Stew

خورش قلیه ماهی

This dish from the south of the country is just the biz. Even people who profess generally not to like fish fall for this one. Just the aroma tends to draw in the crowds. It is an exotic concoction, rich with herbs and spiced as well, a perfect way to prepare some of the chunkier, blander cuts of white fish. This will feed 6 people.

> *1 bunch each parsley, coriander and spring onions*
> *½ bunch fenugreek*
> *oil for frying*
> *1–2 fresh, chopped chillies*
> *2 cloves chopped garlic*
> *½ teaspoon curry powder*
> *1 teaspoon ground turmeric*
> *2 tablespoons tamarind paste (see p. 168)*
> *600ml pint water*
> *6 white fish cutlets – haddock, cod, halibut, etc.*

Trim, wash and drain the herbs in the normal way (see p. 39). Pour a little oil into a large frying-pan, and when it is sizzling, fry the garlic and chillies. Chop the herbs and spring onions, and add them to the frying-pan, stirring constantly. After 6 or 7 minutes, add the spices, and then after another minute or two add the water and the tamarind paste. When the mixture has come to the boil, set to simmer for 10–15 minutes, then whack the heat up again and carefully lower in the fish portions. These will take around 15 minutes to cook through. Serve this *khoresht* with white rice. It doesn't really need anything else, but I usually roast some long, sweet red peppers and serve these as a garnish

به سبک جدید

– they offer a contrast in texture and flavour, and sure-as-goodness look pretty. And red, white and green are of course the Iranian national colours.

A quick word about caviar

This may be another of Iran's most famous exports, but most Iranians don't really rate it very highly (too fishy, I guess, and they find the price of it an insult). After a lot of pollution and over-fishing during the last fifty years, the industry is now (quite rightly) tightly controlled by the Iranian government. It is only sold at official outlets in Iran, which is also a good move as tales of its potential for food-poisoning are justified.

In England it is available from good Persian stores, but it is always best to get a quote first; you also need to decide which grade you want – there is sevruga, 'astra', and beluga – they're all good, but there is a vast difference in price.

Chunky Fish with Split Peas and Sour Grapes

I've had a lot of dishes which resemble this in Spain and Portugal, albeit the tackier, touristy parts. I have been invariably disappointed. They have promised much, but have either lacked depth, been overbearingly tomatoey, the wrong sort of fishy, or, as with so many fish-in-sauce scenarios, woefully overcooked. The best 'cod with tomato sauce' pairing that I've tried was actually at a great fish restaurant in my home conurbation, Southend-on-Sea. If you ever happen to be passing (and, let's face it, only Russian cruise ships and lost sea gulls 'just happen to pass' Southend), check out Fisherman's Wharf by the legendary pier.

The truth is that I have never been entirely sure that tomato and

fish are particularly good bed (plate) fellows. It was only when I turned this classic Persian combination into a sauce fit for fish that I felt comfortable with the whole concept. See what you think – it is very simple. This will make enough for 4 people.

> *2 cloves crushed garlic*
> *1 large onion, chopped*
> *1 red pepper, chopped*
> *4–5 chopped anchovy fillets (optional)*
> *1 teaspoon turmeric*
> *¼ teaspoon ground cumin*
> *1 tablespoon tomato paste*
> *¼ bottle sour grape juice (or dry white wine and the juice of one*
> *lemon)*
> *1 tablespoon pickled or fresh sour grapes (in this recipe you can*
> *substitute pickled capers)*
> *50g Persian yellow split peas (chana dall)*
> *4 smallish potatoes, peeled and halved*
> *4 cutlets of chunky fish – cod, salmon, hake, conger eel*
> *salt and pepper*

Fry your onion, pepper and garlic together; when they soften and start to colour, add the anchovies and spices, stir in the tomato paste, and add the sour grape juice, sour grapes (or capers) and 300ml of water. Add the split peas, bring to the boil, and set to simmer for around half an hour. After this time is up, check there is still enough liquid (add a dash more sour grape juice and water if necessary) and add the potatoes. 10 minutes after that, season the sauce to taste and lower in the fish portions. Bubble away for a further 10 minutes, check the potatoes are cooked through, then serve. This recipe is good with saffroned sauté potatoes, or plain white basmati rice. And as it is so very red, I recommend a green salad as a further accompaniment.

Fish 'Pahlavan' with a Walnut and Tarragon Tarator

ماهی پهلوان در گریل با سس گردو و ترخون

Pahlavan-anything in Iran indicates big, fit for a king (reputedly like the Pahlavi shahs of the country), but it is a particularly common expression in relation to cooked fish. It is my firm belief that it is used in the context of fish on a restaurant menu when either they know not which fish they are serving, or when the chef reserves the right to serve whatsoever fish he jolly well pleases. Most often in the Iranian restaurants of London, *Mahi Pahlavan* is, at least currently, sea bass, although I have been offered grey mullet, sea bream and tilapia under the same name. I would suggest that it best suits Dover sole, but as at the time of writing our cosy but exotic basement restaurant featuring authentic *bazaari* cuisine at affordable prices is still on the drawing board, who am I to comment?

Suffice it to say that in the context of this recipe, you need a largish fillet of fish – and sea bass is as good as any.

Fresh tarragon can be hard to find, so you can substitute a mixture of fresh coriander, parsley and dill if you wish. As my father was a paint chemist, I've always been interested in emulsions, and the idea of this spicy, herby *tarator* is just such fun to play with. But you can equally use the tahini emulsion on p. 227 (which is also known as *tarator* in Arabic countries). For 4 people.

for the *tarator*:
100g fresh white breadcrumbs (from approximately 3 slices of bread)
200g walnuts
1 bunch fresh tarragon (or 2 of those pathetic supermarket packets)
handful fresh parsley

غذاهای مخصوص ایرانی

3–4 cloves garlic, chopped
1 green chilli
2 tablespoons apple (or cider, or red wine) vinegar
2–3 tablespoons cold water
extra virgin olive oil to thicken
salt and pepper
for the fish:
4 medium sea bass, cleaned and filleted
1½ tablespoons flour
1 teaspoon ground turmeric
salt and pepper
oil for frying

First of all make the *tarator*. Make the breadcrumbs by pulling apart about 3 slices of bread and then whizzing them in the blender. Add the walnuts and whizz those as well. Wash and roughly chop the herbs, before adding those to the blender goblet with the garlic and chilli (you'll probably have to do it in two batches). Spoon in the vinegar and water, and give it all another whizz, before trickling in olive oil, very slowly – best use a jug. You need to add enough to make a thick but still just about pourable emulsion – it will continue to thicken in the fridge anyway. Season to taste, and chill until needed.

Now wash and dry your fish fillets. Mix the turmeric with the flour, and some salt and pepper. Dip each fillet in the flour and fry in hot oil until golden on both sides. Serve with the *tarator* drizzled diagonally across it, and some extra lime or lemon wedges on the side.

You can of course forego the flour and frying – simply brush the fish with olive oil and sprinkle it with salt and pepper before grilling for 5–6 minutes. But frying makes it slightly crisper, which makes the sauce work really well.

به سبک جدید

Salmon and Saffron Patties, with Spinach and Rice

These are basically fish *kookoo*, similar to the *kookoo* recipes in Chapter Two. But with the use of fish, the *kookoo* elevates from snack material to a rather elegant dinner component. This would feed 6 people as a summer supper.

for the fish:
3 fresh salmon cutlets (or 2 x 400g cans good quality salmon, drained well)
juice of 1 lemon
3 anchovy fillets, chopped
salt and pepper
9 eggs
1 teaspoon baking powder
2 teaspoons flour
oil for frying
for the spinach:
3 cups basmati rice (or other rice of your choice)
3 bags or bunches of fresh spinach (or 2 packs frozen)
1 large onion, chopped
butter for frying
1 teaspoon turmeric
salt and pepper

If you are using fresh salmon, poach it in a little salted water; when cooked, set aside to cool. Cook the rice according to your normal method. Wash or defrost the spinach. If you are using fresh, cook in

boiling salted water for 2–3 minutes, drain well and then chop roughly. If you are using frozen, defrost and drain thoroughly. Fry the onion in a modicum of butter, and when it has started to colour, add the turmeric. Stir in the rice and the spinach and season to taste.

Back to the fish: remove the skin and any bones from the salmon, and flake it roughly with a fork. Place it in a bowl, and add the lemon juice, anchovies, ½ teaspoon of salt and some black pepper. Beat the eggs with the baking powder and flour, and pour them on to the salmon, mixing well. Heat a little oil in a large frying-pan, and pour the *kookoo* mixture in. Turn down the heat and let it cook through for around 10 minutes, and then put the pan under a hot grill for another 5 minutes to brown the top. Cut the *kookoo* into six wedges, and serve each on a plate with a large spoon of the spinachy rice alongside. You'll need yoghurt, pickled cucumbers, and probably some warm bread, to eat with this.

به سبک جدید

Persepolis Barbecued Tuna

So called because I spend hours in the shop giving out recipe ideas, discussing ingredients and trying to solve culinary conundrums. One such frequent conversation would be subtitled 'other uses for pomegranate paste', and it invariably concludes with my pseudo-reluctant divulgence of my secret fish marinade. This will work equally well for swordfish, conger eel, halibut or salmon. The following is sufficient for a dinner for 4 people.

4 goodly sized tuna steaks
for the marinade:
4 dessertspoons pomegranate paste
1 teaspoon soy sauce
1 teaspoon English mustard
2 cloves garlic, crushed
1 small knob ginger, chopped
2 teaspoons honey
2 dessertspoons olive oil

Nice and simple. Mix all the marinade ingredients together. Add the fish, ensuring that it is well coated. Cover, chill and leave for a couple of hours.

Cook on a really hot barbecue, or under a hot domestic grill, turning once. Three to four minutes per side is sufficient for pinkish tuna, but the Iranians (and many British) would not dream of having pink fish, in which case you should cook it for around 6 minutes per side. Serve with Shirazi salad (p. 115), or pomegranate and cucumber salad.

About pomegranates

Despite being the Rubik Cube of the fruit world, the pomegranate is one of Allah's better inventions. Its luscious juice has been savoured across the millennia; it can be eaten or juiced; and has been used medicinally, in cooking, even as a dye for clothing. And the Persian pomegranate is quite the best in the whole world, far fuller bodied than those from anywhere else. It is a real feelgood fruit – to sup of these is truly to ingest the warmth and fragrance of this most magical of lands.

Firstly, please note that your relationship with this fruit will quickly sour if you fail to wear pomegranate-coloured clothing (or at least an apron) when handling it for any great length of time. A good pomegranate may well be truly ugly on the outside, so do not go for looks: to select a good one you need to go for firmness of skin. Size is not an issue – the smaller ones are often sweeter. Pomegranates last for a few weeks if you keep them in a cool place.

To prepare your pomegranate, cut it open slightly and then pull it apart. Gently crumble the seeds into a bowl, pulling the pith away as you do so. It is best eaten chilled with a spoon, and yes, one generally eats the pips 'n' all. If you want to juice your pomegranate, you need to knead it gently all round so that all of the beads burst. Pummel it with your thumbs, slowly rotating it all the while, until it feels quite liquidized inside. Then make a small incision in the skin and either stick a straw in directly or squeeze the juice into a glass. Great for cocktails.

Pomegranates have cleansing properties, and are full of anti-oxidants: the Prophet Muhammad said, 'Eat the pomegranate for it purges the system of envy and hatred'. Like many red fruits and vegetables, it is good for the kidneys. It also has a cooling effect on the body.

Pomegranates are the fruit of winter (remember Persephone) – in Iran they are very important for *Shab-e-Yalda*, which is the night of the Winter Solstice (21 December). Traditionally, folk would stay up through this longest night with lamps and fires burning brightly to

keep away the dark forces and they would chat and play games and eat pomegranates until dawn broke. They are available from October to March, but you can enjoy them in other forms all year round. Quite apart from the pomegranate paste which we have used on and off throughout these recipes, it creeps into cordial (which we know as grenadine); fruit leather (*lavashak*) which is the boiled and sun-dried fruit paste, a chewy sweet/sour confection much loved in Iran; and juice, the benefits of drinking which have been an Iranian secret for centuries, until some Western marketing team cottoned on to it, so now it's everywhere.

Pomegranate paste/purée/molasses/ketchup (*rob anaar*) is a wondrous ingredient. Many British chefs now use it with great verve and imagination – the divine Nigella and the marvellous Sams Clark to name but three. It works as a ketchup to thicken and sharpen sauces, as the sharp ingredient in a salad dressing, and, or course, as a superb marinade.

Iranian Fish and Chips

Iranian fried fish is normally achieved as in the recipe for *sabzi pulao* at the beginning of this chapter. Fillets of white fish are coated in turmeric-infused flour, pan fried and served with rice. (The rice is usually the main feature.) But the following two or three recipes up the ante, and remove the rice. They were all devised with a view to getting my family-in-law away from their 'rice seven nights as week' compulsion, and on to slightly more adventurous fish consumption. We still eat rice six nights a week. '*Ya, Ali*' (a sort of Persian sigh of resignation, although it has religious connotations).

Haddock Cooked in *Doogh* Batter

ماهی سوخاری دوغی

This is my stab at a sort of 'halal alternative to beer' batter. They love beer (*ab joh* – literally, barley water) in Iran – but of course it is all non-alcoholic and often rather sweet. Made with *doogh*, the fizzy salted yoghurt drink (for the recipe see p. 315) beloved by Iranians in hot weather, this batter achieves wonderful sharp overtones. You can use any fish, but I find that the slightly more robust flavour of haddock does the job very nicely. Enough for 4 people.

> *330ml bottle ready-made* doogh *mixed with 1–2 tablespoons of*
> *thick plain yoghurt, or 330ml sparkling water mixed with 4*
> *tablespoons thick, plain yoghurt and a pinch of mint*
> *4 heaped tablespoons plain flour*
> *salt and pepper*
> *4 large fillets of haddock*
> *1 teaspoon ground saffron steeped in boiling water*

To make the batter, if you are using shop-bought *doogh*, you will need to add a little extra yoghurt as it is rarely thick or sour enough. If you are making your own, gently whisk the water into the yoghurt, add salt and pepper and a little dried mint. Put two of the spoons of flour into a mixing bowl, and slowly beat the *doogh* in until you have a thick batter. Whisk well, and set aside for half an hour. When you are ready to serve, lightly season the other 2 spoons of flour on a plate, and dip each fillet of haddock into it until they are properly coated. Whisk up the batter again, and add the saffron, before dipping each fish fillet into it in turn. As you bring each one out of the batter, allow the surplus to drip away before plunging them into hot oil. Fry the fish until it is golden brown and rises to the surface. Serve with lemon wedges, spiced chips (see p. 191), and a big handful of *sabzi* garnish.

به سبک جدید

Pan Fried Fillet of Mackerel Coated in Hemp and Sesame Crumble

Hemp seed is big in Iran, surprisingly more so than its dodgy cousin hashish. Iranians have recognized its extraordinarily healthy properties for centuries. It is eaten by the handful as a snack, raw or roasted and salted, and it is often married with sesame and blended into breads and wafers. We have been importing the seeds for a number of years. It is gratifying to note that it is finally gaining recognition and its presence on our shelves no longer generates rib-nudging sniggers. It is packed full of Omega 3 and Omega 6 oils, and thus jolly good for the brain, muscles, skin and general mobility.

As the sesame and mackerel in this recipe are also 'super foods', this is a really, really healthy dish. Once more, enough for 4 people.

> *100g hulled sesame seeds*
> *100g slightly crushed raw hemp seeds*
> *150g fine breadcrumbs*
> *handful fresh parsley, washed and finely chopped*
> *2 tablespoons flour*
> *salt and pepper*
> *2 eggs beaten with a dash milk*
> *juice of ½ lemon*
> *2 teaspoons Dijon mustard*
> *4 filleted mackerel*
> *olive oil*

Like any sort of breaded food, the key to success with this is organization. You need two plates, a broad shallow bowl and a nice clear work surface.

Mix the sesame, hemp, breadcrumbs and parsley, and place it on a plate. Season the flour on the second plate. Make the egg-wash in the shallow bowl.

Mix the lemon and the mustard, and brush each fillet with the mixture. Coat each one with flour, and then dip into the egg-wash. As you withdraw them from the egg, allow any surplus to drip before pressing them into the breadcrumb/seed mix. Ensure each fillet is thoroughly coated before wrapping in cling film and chilling (half an hour or so will do).

Pan-fry straight from the fridge in hot oil – about 3 minutes a side should be enough. Serve with extra lemon, herbs and Persian wedges (see next recipe).

Sumac

Sumac is a sour, reddish berry which is ground and used as a spice. It is used all over the Middle East, but extensively in Iran, where it is sprinkled on kebabs. This habit goes back centuries – sumac has slightly anti-septic properties, and so at times when the provenance of meat was not always properly understood, it seemed natural to use it 'to be on the safe side'. In flavour it is somewhere between salt, lemon and paprika. It is, as I write, a very trendy ingredient, cropping up in all sorts of cookbooks; admittedly it is good for marinades and grills in general, but I find it greatly overrated. The berries can be steeped in boiling water and then squeezed to produce a sharp juice, which may then be drunk as a tea to soothe the stomach, or used as an alternative to lemon juice.

Persian Wedges

This is a great way to use up left-over cooked potatoes (especially those baked in their jackets), although my recipe assumes that you are starting from scratch. If you are using left-overs, just cut the potatoes into wedge shapes and then cook them through in the frying-pan – there is clearly no need to cook for very long or to transfer to the oven.

500g firm potatoes (Maris Piper, King Edward)
butter, olive oil and salt
1 large onion, sliced
3–4 cloves garlic, chopped
2 green chillies (or ¼ habanero chilli)
1 dessertspoon ground sumac
1 teaspoon ground turmeric
1 teaspoon ground coriander
½ teaspoon ground cumin
dash olive oil

Wash the potatoes, and cut into wedge shapes. Place in a pan of cold, salted water, bring to the boil, cook for 6–7 minutes, then drain thoroughly. In a large frying-pan, melt a knob of butter and fry the onion, chilli and garlic. Add the spices and a dash of olive oil to the pan, and then the potatoes, stirring so that they become well coated. Now you can either transfer them to an ovenproof dish, cover with foil and cook in the oven on gas mark 6/200°C for about 20 minutes, or you can turn the heat down, cover the pan and continue on the hob for 20 minutes or so. The wedges should be sticky and slightly crisp on the outside, well cooked inside. You can serve them as a starter with a range of dips, or as an accompaniment to main dishes.

Spiced Chips

پیپس تند

I like the principle of non-fried chips, but shop-bought ones, in my hands, turn to a mushed disaster. So I make my own. You can of course used fried chips for this – simply mix the spices and dredge the cooked fries with them prior to serving.

> *3 teaspoons za'atar (see below)*
> *½ teaspoon chilli powder*
> *4 tablespoons healthy oil (I do use olive oil for this, but there are*
> *   many who would find this heinously wasteful, so use rape-seed oil*
> *   or sunflower instead)*
> *500g potatoes (Maris Piper or King Edward)*

Mix the spices with the oil in a shallow bowl. Cut the potatoes into the chip shape of your choice (i.e. thick or thin), and then roll the chips in the spiced oil before scooping them out and spreading them out on a baking tray. Bake on gas mark 6 (200°C) for around 40 minutes, turning once.

Za'atar

Za'atar is an Arabic spice mix used classically as a seasoning for bread – chunky bread is dipped in olive oil and then into the spice. It is also great for marinades and grilling. It consists of 4 parts dried thyme, to 2 parts sumac, to 1 part sesame seeds, with salt to taste. It is readily available in Middle Eastern shops, but easy enough to make yourself.

به سبک جدید

Khanum Sohaila's Stuffed Fish

Khanum (literally, 'lady' or 'wife' – in practice the polite way to address any lady) Sohaila is one of my customers. A pretty and gracious lady from the deep south of Iran, she is also a fabulous cook – she has guests week in, week out. And her speciality is fish. She is very modest, so it took me months of cajoling to coax this recipe out of her – she could not see what all the fuss was about. This should be enough for around 4 people.

> *1 large stuffable fish – a whole, fresh salmon is good*
> *salt and pepper*
> *1 large onion, finely chopped*
> *2 cloves garlic, finely chopped*
> *1 bunch fresh coriander, finely chopped*
> *9–10 pitted fresh dates*
> *1 ½ dessertspoonsful tamarind paste*

Gut and clean the fish, and then pat it dry. Make a few diagonal slashes through the skin on both sides, and season the fish inside and out. Place it on a shallow oven tray. Next, fry the onion and garlic, and once they have softened add the coriander, followed by the dates. Mash the dates into the mixture until it becomes quite fudge-like, and then stir in the tamarind paste. Fill the tummy of your fish, and rub some of the mixture into the slashes on the outside as well. Bake on gas mark 6/200°C for 10 minutes, and then turn down to gas mark 3/170°C for a further 30 minutes. Sohaila serves this with plain white rice; I usually serve it with saffron mash (see below).

You can reverse the sweet and sour of this recipe by replacing the sweetness of the dates with a mixture of a handful each of cooked

rice, chopped walnuts and sour barberries (pre-soaked), and the sour tamarind with sweet grape syrup. This combination is more common as stuffing in the north of the country.

Bonus Recipe – Saffron Mash

Very simple: steep half a teaspoon ground saffron in boiling water, and when it is nearly cool, mix it with some *fromage frais*. Mash your tubers of choice (for fish I usually opt for a mix of sweet potatoes and regular potatoes) with a tiny knob of butter, and then stir in the *fromage frais* and season to taste. You can also add half a teaspoon of ground cardamom to the mash for extra fragrance.

Every customer tells a story

Sohaila and her family, like a lot of my customers, are from Ahwaz in the south of Iran. It is a troubled region, plagued even today by Arab separatists who want independence from Iran. During the Iran/Iraq war the province was decimated, and its people are still paying the price. Many are those who have given birth to deformed children, the result of countless Iraqi incursions with chemical weapons. The same story is true of the Kurds who come into my shop; a naturally happy and kindly people, they are reluctant to discuss their history, personal or national – it is just too painful. Many of them are in the UK with chronic health problems, again brought on by chemical weapon usage.

I also have many Afghan customers. They are philosophical about their plight, so many are the times that their country has been invaded and ransacked. There is a tangible sadness at the back of their gaze which is the only real indication of their usually traumatic tales. They

are a gracious and hard-working people, who invariably speak around five languages.

The Iranians who come into my shop are likewise mostly refugees (although there are of course many wealthy and hard-working Iranians who have been in the country for many years and are pillars of the community). Some come to escape religious or political persecution, some to escape crushing poverty, mostly they come just to make a better and freer life for themselves and their families. In Iran, they were doctors, teachers, engineers, and here they deliver pizzas, or flyers, or clean fish. Many of them are terribly homesick, but realize that they are longing for a half-remembered configuration of land, people and way of life which in truth no longer exists. Iran, more than any other nation I have encountered, exists most strongly in the heart and minds of her children.

From the above you might conclude that I am advocating a free-for-all on the immigration front – this is not the case. But it is hard to remain unmoved and unimpressed by most of the tales we hear, and the humility and tenacity displayed by most 'asylum seekers' deserves respect.

It is 10 a.m. on a Saturday morning, and I am just thinking about opening my shop. There is something dark against one of the shutters, so I creep around the side to investigate. It is a lad of perhaps 16 or 17, and he is asleep. As I actually cannot open my shop without moving him, I shake him gently awake. He looks disorientated and more than a little scared. His name is Mohammed, he is from Shiraz, he has 'just arrived' (I do not ask how). He has not eaten for 3 days, and has barely slept. We give him tea and cookies and try to unravel his tale. In the first of many different versions of his story that he is to tell us that weekend, he says that his parents have died and he is looking for his brother, whom he believes may be in London. I ring around my list of hostels, but until a refugee has visited that immigration

غذاهای مخصوص ایرانی

ziggurat, Lunar House in Croydon, no doors are opened to them; they are stateless. As Croydon doesn't do weekends, we lodge him at a local B&B for two nights, with a food-parcel and written instructions on how to get to the IND (Immigration and Nationality Directorate) on Monday morning. He comes back to the shop on and off during the weekend, and I encourage him to chat to some of our other Iranian customers. Some of them give him money, or their 'phone number – they have nearly all been in this position, they sympathize. Why, Jamshid himself had two nights' sleeping rough in Paris when he first arrived as a 14-year-old fleeing the Iraq war. If this chap's story had not been so inconsistent, we might have taken him in ourselves, but we have no way of ascertaining whether he is refugee or fugitive, and he is not giving much away. In the end he vanishes into Sunday night, and on this occasion, sadly, we do not see him again.

This was not an isolated incident. Peckham, let's be honest, does currently have a lot of transient residents; and so we watch as our customers – young lads, young lovers, families – arrive, settle, consolidate and improve, before moving on to pastures better. A gratifying number keep in touch and continue to shop with us where possible.

Running an ethnic cornershop can be a strange, onerous, humbling and heartbreaking affair. All life passes before your counter during the course of any one week, and there is no such thing as 'just another customer'.

Southern-Style Spiced Fish with Rice

This is another dished from Sohaila's extensive and impressive fish repertoire. Here the rice and fish are layered and steamed together in a classic
pulao (of which more in Chapter Seven). This will feed 4 people.

1 large onion, chopped
2–3 cloves garlic, minced
butter/ghee
200g cleaned squid, cut into rings
200g skinned fish fillet of choice, cut into 4
100g sultanas
50g pine nuts
200g prawns
100g mussels, cooked
40g dill
1 teaspoon turmeric
1 teaspoon garam masala
salt and pepper
4 measures of rice

Fry the onion and garlic in some butter, then add the squid, followed by
the fish fillets. Add the sultanas and pine nuts and, finally, the mussels
and prawns. Stir in the dill and spices, and a little seasoning.

Next blanch the rice in boiling water for 8 minutes; drain. Melt a
little butter in a big pan, sprinkle it with cold water, then spoon a layer
of rice across the bottom. Follow with a layer of the fish, then a layer
of rice, and so on until both rice and fish are finished. Make a few holes
down through the rice, cover the pan lid with a clean tea towel and set
to steam – 40 minutes should do it.

Serve with *must o-khiar* with sultanas (see Chapter One).

CHAPTER SEVEN

اع پلو

CHAPTER SEVEN

RICE

Rice is probably the single most important part of the Persian kitchen. Although in times gone by it was regarded as fare for the rich man (the standard being bread), it really is staple stuff. A mother-in-law's test for a future bride for her son is whether the poor lassie can cook rice to perfection. There are probably thousands of recipes for it.

Rice culture came hard to me – I come from good, basic, Uncle Ben-eating folk, where a spoonful on the side is more than enough and never mind how it tastes. Now I can eat on its own, and I have got to the stage where I can tell particular basmati rices apart just from their fragrance. I am becoming a rice geek.

For the purposes of these recipes I have specified basmati rice, but true Persian rice, although prepared in the same manner, is a sort of cousin-of-basmati. There are a number of varieties, but the one most readily available (in Persian shops in Britain) is *sadri* rice. It has a fabulous fragrance, which is important to Iranians, and holds its shape well. Look out for smoked *sadri* rice – it has an aroma to set you drooling, and a mouth-watering, smoky flavour.

Rice is always washed beforehand – this can be done in a sieve, stirring it gently until the water runs clear, or by running cold water slowly into a pan until it overflows and again runs clear. Iranian rice (and brown basmati) should be soaked in cold salted water for at least an hour before use, but basic Indian or Pakistani basmati rice does not need this.

There are three basic ways of preparing Persian rice (*berenj*, in its raw state), although they all depend on the absorption principle.

199

The first and most basic is known as *chelow* – plain white rice – and I have given the method of preparation for this below. Dishes such as *chelow morgh*, or *chelow kebab* simply mean 'plain rice with chicken' or 'plain rice with kebab'. The second is known as *pulao* – it is prepared in the same way as *chelow*, but is made more of an event by the addition of spices, vegetables or fruit, meat or fish, layered through the rice. Most of the recipes in this chapter are for *pulao*.

A third method is known as *katteh*, and is prepared by absorption; but the rice isn't drained after its initial boiling, and so remains water-logged and cooks into a glutinous lump. Rice prepared this way is very popular in the north of Iran; it is certainly more nutritious and filling, as the nutrients and starch aren't drained away,. It is, shall we say, an acquired taste.

All Iranians aim to get a good *tahdik* (again, basic recipe below) on the bottom of their rice (which will of course be the top of the dish once it is inverted on to a plate), regardless of how they are cooking it. *Tahdik* (literally, 'the bottom of the pan') refers to the golden, sticky crust which is encouraged to form in the bottom of the pan. It can be achieved with practice in a normal saucepan, but for those with a penchant for eating Persian, I would strongly recommend the purchase of a Persian rice cooker, which really does all the hard work for you. They are built to last (my mother-in-law has two which have been working for over 20 years, with the exception of the odd replacement of the removable inner pan), and are readily found in Persian shops in Britain.

Chelow – White Rice

Iranians can eat a lot more rice than most – we English are a tad namby-pamby about portions. As a basic guide, allow one cup of rice per person (a standard rice cup is 180ml). If you are using a rice cooker, measure your soaked, washed rice into the pan, followed by 1 cup of water per person; add 1 teaspoon of butter or ghee and ½ teaspoon of salt per person. Cook according to the instructions for your cooker model. To serve, simply invert a plate over the pan, and turn upside down – the non-stick interiors turn out perfect rice cakes again and again.

Slightly harder is the saucepan method. This assumes you have read the previous pages and that you have thus washed, soaked (if applicable) and drained your rice. Bring a pan of salted water to a rolling boil, tip the rice in, and cook for around 7 minutes. The rice should then be soft outside but still hard inside. Pinching a grain between your thumb and forefinger should determine this. Drain the rice thoroughly in a sieve (as clearly it would pass through a colander). Heat a knob of oil or ghee in the saucepan, and add 2 tablespoons of water. As soon as it starts to sizzle, carefully spoon a layer of rice across the bottom, followed by another and another until all the rice is piled into the pan. Resist the temptation to pour the rice, as this will weigh it down and it will not have the legendary Persian fluffiness. Poke the handle of a spoon or a skewer down through the rice to the bottom of the pan – do this 5–6 times to make steam fumeroles. As soon as the rice starts to steam visibly, wrap the lid of the saucepan in a clean tea towel, and turn the heat down very low. The rice will take about 35 minutes to cook, although it will keep quite happily on that setting for a further 30–40 minutes.

To evict the rice from the pan (and it usually proves a little reluctant to move), sit the bottom of the pan in a couple of inches of water in the sink – the sudden cold will cause the rice to contract from the sides, and you should then be able to turn it on to an inverted plate with ease.

Tahdik with magic

Once you have achieved the above, you will be ready for the *tahdik* masterclass – wherein you will learn how to use assorted secret ingredients at the bottom of the pan to create the perfect crust. The most common variant is to use saffron, sprinkling a little steeped, ground saffron into the sizzling ghee just before you start to layer up the rice. Or there's always:

Tahdik with yoghurt
Mix a spoon of the hot, drained rice with 2 tablespoons of yoghurt and a beaten egg before spreading it into the hot oil – this gives a really tasty, glossy crust.

Tahdik with potato
Peel and thinly slice 2–3 medium, waxy potatoes and lay these in the hot oil, before gently spooning the rice on top.

Tahdik with bread
This is my favourite. Simply lay slices of flat bread in the sizzling oil. Halved pitta will do, or *lavash* bread, or best of all, halved Arabic *khobez* – it is already round and will fit the saucepan. Then pile the rice in as above.

به سبک جدید

Bogoli Pulao – Broad Bean Rice with Dill, Served with Chicken or Lamb

This is such a scrumdiddlyumptious recipe that I would be quite happy to have it two or three times a week. I don't, because that would be both sad and greedy. I will point out the obvious which is that a liking for this dish entirely depends on your standpoint on broad beans, and some people are unaccountably less than fond of them

As with so many Persian dishes, the chicken is just a garnish and a moist vegetarian concoction can easily be substituted. This serves 6.

> *2 x 400g bags frozen broad beans, defrosted (or about 2–3kg fresh)*
> *6 cups basmati rice*
> *butter or ghee*
> *1 cup dried dill*
> *saffron, ground and steeped in water*
> *1 chicken, skinned and washed*
> *1 onion, peeled and chopped*
> *2 level teaspoons turmeric*
> *salt and pepper*
> *6 dried limes*
> *2 medium potatoes, peeled*
> *1 can chick peas, drained*

Firstly, shuck your broad beans. Wash the rice and bring it to the boil in a pan of water. Drain, then melt a little butter or ghee in the pan. Mix the rice with the dill then layer it back into the pan alternating with the broad beans. Poke a few fumeroles down through the mixture to the bottom using the handle of a wooden spoon, and then wrap the lid

in a tea towel and set the *pulao* to cook on a low heat. If you are using a rice cooker, just add the beans in with the rice at the beginning and then stir the dill through just before serving.

Pop the chicken into a saucepan together with the onion, cover with water, sprinkle in the turmeric, a little salt and pepper and bring to the boil. Rinse and prick the dried limes and drop these in too. Set the pan to simmer. After 20 minutes or so cut the potatoes into quarters and lower them into the chicken stock, followed by the chick peas. Cook the chicken for another 20 minutes or until the potatoes are soft. Turn off the rice and allow it to sit for a few moments (you can do the same if you wish), before turning it out on to a serving plate. Crack the *tahdik* or crust which will have formed, and trickle the steeped saffron over the rice, mixing it lightly with a spoon. Dish the chicken and potatoes on to a plate and ladle the citrussy, beany stock into a separate bowl. Serve with raw onion, yoghurt and fresh herbs and, most importantly, *torshi* – this dish really needs pickles as an accompaniment.

Another popular dish in Iran is *sib pulao* or potato rice. It is made in just the same way as the *bogoli* rice, but substituting tiny cubes of potato for the broad beans.

Barberry Rice with Chicken – Zereshk Pulao

This is another really famous dish of Iran. The good news is that it is incredibly easy to prepare. I often cook this on nights when I can't quite be bothered to cook.

It is one of many Persian recipes to feature an ingredient which used to be abundant in England, but with which we have long since forgotten how to cook. The barberry was used in lots of sauces and preserves and grew aplenty in England in Mrs Beeton's times. It is full of vitamin C and aids digestion. Fie upon us for ignoring so much of our culinary heritage. Barberries still grow here – if you know anyone with a bush in their garden, start being very nice to them and they might let you harvest them. But do watch out. The etymology is not entirely clear, but I have no doubt that they were named in part for their barbs. Dried barberries are readily available in Iranian and some general-purpose Middle Eastern shops. Failing that, cranberries are a good alternative.

In this dish as with so many, the rice is the star and the meat mere accompaniment. The chicken recipe I have given is my current favourite with this rice, but you could replace the chicken with chunks of aubergine. These quantities serve 6 people.

for the chicken:
1 large onion, chopped
1 chicken, skinned and jointed
1 teaspoon ground turmeric
1 teaspoon ground cinnamon
1 tablespoon tomato purée
1 teaspoon sugar

1 tablespoon tomato ketchup (optional, but it gives the sauce a really nice glossy look)
¼ bottle sour grape juice (although you could happily use a slosh of wine in its place in this instance)
salt and pepper
for the rice:
150g dried barberries
1 cup basmati rice per person
large knob butter for frying
2–3 teaspoons sugar
¼ teaspoon ground saffron steeped in boiling water

Fry your onion gently in a large pan, and then add the chicken, followed by the spices. When the chicken is sealed, stir in the tomato purée, sugar and ketchup, add the sour grape juice, top up with water and bring to the boil. Set to simmer for around half an hour, prodding occasionally. The sauce should be thick, but make sure that it does not reduce too much – top it up with a little water if necessary. Season to taste.

In the meantime, soak the barberries in cold water – this ensures that they are clean and allows any small stones, barbs or sediment to sink to the bottom. Allow them to sit for about half an hour, and then scoop them out and squeeze the water out. Pick through them one last time for any residual 'barbs'.

Wash and cook your basmati rice/*tahdik* in the usual way. Melt the butter in a frying-pan, and stir in the barberries. Fry for around 7–8 minutes, stirring constantly, before adding the sugar and the steeped saffron. Turn your rice out on to a serving dish, crack the crust and streak the saffrony barberry mixture across the top, mixing it into the rice a little as you go. Serve the chicken in a separate dish, accompanied by baskets of herbs and raw onions.

به سبک جدید

Lubia Pulao with *Khorak-e-Morgh* – Rice and French Beans with Andiwornee Chicken

Lubia pulao is a wonderfully flavoursome way to eat basmati rice – it is a good standby when you are cooking for people who are not used to eating vast quantities of rice (i.e. the English). With regard to the name of this dish, we have used the word *khoresht* (casserole) a lot in this book, but it is more often *khorak* which is served with *pulao*. *Khorak* refers to a simple, much reduced and often thickened sauce in which meat is cooked (see, for example, the previous recipe). *Khoresht* is a more elaborate dish, where the sauce itself is the main feature.

Andiwornee is one of my favourite customers. This old Greek Cypriot lady is about four-feet tall, and only has about five teeth. If her heart is of gold, then her character is priceless. She never fails simultaneously to amaze and cheer all who meet her while she is hold-ing court in the shop. She is well known throughout Peckham for her unstudied wisdom and grace. And she cooks enough to feed an army; she does indeed feed half of the borough, trotting round every day with parcels of *dolmeh* and cakes and *keftethes* (Greek meatballs). I developed Andiwornee chicken around one of her 'recipes'. It was she who told me about the joys of *kritheraki*, rice-shaped pasta which is great on its own but really useful for adding to soups, stews and gravy to add body and texture. She taught me, too, not to be afraid of tomato paste. If it is of a good quality, it may be used with impunity. These quantities are for 6 people.

for the chicken:
50g butter or ghee
1 large onion, diced

1–2 fresh chillies, chopped
1 medium-large chicken, skinned and jointed
1½ teaspoons ground turmeric
1 dessertspoonful tomato paste
1 dessertspoonful tomato ketchup
½ litre good tomato juice or passata
3–4 dried limes
1 cup kritheraki
for the rice:
6 cups basmati rice and 75g ghee or margarine
500g–750g (cooked weight) French beans
1 onion, chopped
150g minced lamb (optional)
salt and pepper
1½ teaspoons cinnamon mixed with a pinch each of ground mace,
nutmeg and coriander
1 dessertspoonful tomato paste

First of all prepare the chicken. Melt the butter in a large pan (add a little oil to stop it catching), and fry the onion and chillies. Toss in the chicken, stirring constantly; when it is sealed add in the turmeric and, after a couple of minutes more, the tomato paste. Add the tomato juice and ketchup, and top up with cold water so that the chicken is covered. Prick the dried limes and drop them in, then set the whole thing to simmer for 15 minutes or so.

In the meantime, wash the rice and either boil it briefly (for saucepan-cooking method see p. 201), or measure it into the rice cooker with the ghee, water and salt. Bring a pan of water to the boil, and cook the French beans for 7–8 minutes, until just cooked. Drain and put aside. Fry the onion, and then toss in the minced lamb, stirring vigorously so that the meat does not clump: season, and stir in the spices, and then add the tomato purée. Mix in the French beans.

Now either layer your rice with the bean mixture if you are using

the saucepan method, or set your rice cooker to cook. If you are using a rice cooker, you should spoon the bean mixture into the rice and mix it thoroughly just as the rice is cooked. Then let it all cook through for another 10 minutes or so.

At this stage (i.e. shortly after you put the rice on) add the *kritheraki* to the chicken, and turn the heat up. Remove the chicken, place it in an ovenproof dish, cover and pop it in the oven on a low heat to keep warm. Allow the sauce to reduce until it is thick and shiny (10 minutes should do the trick).

Turn your rice out the usual way, and crack the *tahdik* from one side to the other with a spoon. Pour a stripe of the chicken sauce from one end to the other. Pour the rest of the juice over the chicken. Serve with *sabzi*, yoghurt, raw onion and garlic and plenty of pickle.

About weddings

Weddings are big the world over. To say that they are big in Iran would be no more than a cliché. However, they are regarded as potentially the most prestigious day in a man or woman's life. Accounts by early travellers such as Sir John Chardin and Joseph Knanishu (see Bibliography) describe incredible feasting and merriment. Chardin was surely the original gourmand, but Knanishu gives lavish (albeit gloriously disapproving and bigoted) descriptions of all aspects of Persian marriage. It is not uncommon still for wedding ceremonies to go on for a week.

In Iran, there are several layers of betrothal or attachment under Islamic law. It is actually possible to get 'married' for an afternoon, a week, or any pre-determined period. This can be done in front of a mullah, but is just as likely to be done by the couple in question themselves through the simple speaking of a few words. A price (dowry) is normally set which is payable to the 'bride' upon the conclusion of her term in favour. I can hear the cynics amongst you drawing breath here

غذاهای مخصوص ایرانی

and muttering about legalized prostitution, but the practice itself is harmless enough, and is seen as a way of sanctifying something beautiful by many modern, young couples. It can also be regarded simply as a form of betrothal, especially in the West, which is why I found myself sitting in the Universal Islamic Institute in Holland Park a number of years ago. My beloved and I had just become engaged in the British sense, and this was the closest we could find in the Iranian sense. The mullah was a charming and benevolent man, with twinkly eyes which belied his austere robes. He was also possessed of a sense of humour. Reader, he married us. He wasn't meant to, but he apparently decided that this was a good match, and spontaneously upgraded the bonding. I caused much mirth when I named my price for separation or dowry – a Persian kitten; the norm is a gold coin or six. More laughter when I went to shake his hand (one doesn't touch mullahs). I am sure that I am still a standing joke at the Institute. Anyway, thirteen years on (Jamshid doesn't like to rush things), we have finally married in the conventional sense, as we did not want this book to be born out of wedlock.

The next level in Iran is the simple, legal marriage. This is performed in front of a registrar in a registry office without too much ceremony, just like a registry office wedding over here. Again, a price is put on the cost of separation. Should the couple divorce, the bride is entitled to compensation of a specified number of gold coins (not kittens), thus reclaiming her dowry.

And then there is the all-singing, all-dancing, no-holds-barred, proper Persian wedding. Again, a mullah will preside, but the traditional 'arousee' is inextricably bound with ancient Zoroastrian rituals and delightfully overlaid with some typically Western conceits. I will describe this at some length because there are lots of Iranians in the West, and if you are lucky you may be asked to a Persian wedding at some stage. It is nice to know what is going on. Also, at the time of writing, the man and I have just gotten hitched, so it's kind of fresh in the mind.

Persian brides dress as meringues, the same as brides the world over, and on this one day in Iran they do not have to be too covered-up. All

به سبک جدید

the world loves to see a wedding, and the authorities are indulgent (or can often be persuaded to be indulgent) about such occasions. The bride will spend hours and hours at a 'wedding parlour' (a big industry in Iran and specialists in this area are in great demand for those living in exile) on the morning of the wedding. Hair is usually straight out of *Dallas*, and make-up is, shall we say, extreme – but then she will have to undergo hours of filming on set. Weddings are usually held in a rented 'salon'. Bride and groom sit next to each other under a canopy, over which female relatives grate sugar (for sweetness). Before them is laid a *sofreh* (a spread cloth) piled with things which will bring them luck, fertility and happiness: eggs (obvious), a needle and thread (to sew shut the mouths of meddlesome relatives – great fun this), bread and cheese (for energy), a pot of honey (which they suck from each others' fingers), sweets (to bring sweetness again), together with lots of flowers. The couple hold a Koran so that they can follow as the mullah recites from it. A mirror is placed facing them so that they can see each other without direct eye contact – the bride should be very demure.

Once the mullah has done his bit, the guests pay their respects and give gifts. These are almost always jewellery for the bride, which is a valid and respected currency and investment in Iranian culture. And then there'll be music and dancing and feasting; and lots and lots of filming (if the film isn't quite right, there'll be endless re-takes; this is a movie that will have to run and run; it will be sent across the Atlantic, and posted on the Internet – Iranians video absolutely everything with an incredibly embarrassing passion).

Newly-weds do go away on honeymoon, but this is usually within Iran itself. Very soon after the ceremony they will be expected to endure visits to the houses of all their relatives to accept felicitations. In Iran it is quite common for the couple to live with the groom's family for at least a while; in the case of poorer families, this is often a permanent arrangement. It need not be a bad thing. I myself live with the in-laws during the week as it is too far to commute to our own house, and I have lived with them in this way on and off for twelve years. Yet I am

not a demure and inexperienced blushing bride. My brother-in-law did acquire just one such, the lovely (*nazzi*, in Persian – it sort of means sweet, in a bridal way) Anahid, and brought her all the way from Iran to live with us – and it works a treat. She is able to learn housekeeping skills and keep up her studies and make friends, whilst not really having any responsibilities. Being a new bride can, by all accounts, be pretty lonely otherwise.

Iranian women generally wear the trousers. This may seem a direct contradiction of everything you know or have read about Iran, but it is the case. Polygamy, although allowed by law, is nowadays extremely rare, and no-one regards women as chattels any more. Women run the house, and often control the family destiny, albeit through secondary channels (i.e. they tell their husbands what to do). If anybody in Jamshid's family wants anything done, they have but to ask mother-in-law. In wider society too, women wield a fair amount of power. They occupy professional and governmental positions and are freely accorded intellectual equality. In reality, of course, actual equality within the constitution is a distant prospect, and in some of the outlying regions and the Arab south of the country, women's rights are still regarded not exactly top priority. Although women have full rights in the divorce courts, custody of any children is always given to the father. The situation for women in Iran is far from ideal, and some would argue that as long as the *hejab* remains compulsory, the country will never move towards equality. But it is not quite as bad as the Western press would have you believe.

Stuffed Quail with *Chirin Pulao* (sweet rice)

There are quails in Iran. I mean, there must be, because they have a word for it, and people know what they are. They're just not very widespread. My research (posh word for asking around) indicates that when they are eaten, they are usually simply grilled with salt. But the idea of having birds and meat in general filled with a glorious fruit and nut mixture is completely authentic. And this gorgeous, sweet (*chirin*) striped rice is an Iranian classic, often eaten on special occasions. Its shiny, multi-coloured components truly resemble jewels. This will serve 4 people.

8 quails, butterflied
1 tablespoonful soy sauce
dash of peanut or sesame oil
2 tablespoons pomegranate paste
a little tomato juice

for both the stuffing and the rice garnish:
200g dried barberries (or cranberries if you really cannot find
    barberries), soaked and drained
200g walnuts, roughly ground
200g raisins, soaked and drained
50g each nibbed pistachios and almonds
3–4 medium carrots, peeled and grated
2 medium onions, peeled and chopped
100g sour orange peel (see note below)

for the rice:
4 cups basmati rice
butter or ghee, salt and pepper
1 teaspoonful ground saffron steeped in a cup of boiling water

3 teaspoons 'rice spice', adveih pulao, which is usually 2 parts cinnamon to 1 part each ground cardamon, rose petals and nutmeg, although recipes vary
100g nabat (Persian rock or crystallized sugar), crushed

Firstly, marinade your birds. Mix together the soy, oil, pomegranate paste, then spoon or rub it all over the skin of the quail, both inside and out. Cover and chill – they are best left for at least a couple of hours. Take half of each of the other ingredients (except the walnuts – use all of these – and the orange peel, which you should reserve entirely for the rice) and mix together. Lay out the eight quail, and spoon a little of the mixture on to the inside of one half of each bird: fold the other half of the quail over the mixture, so that in fact each bird looks complete, and then secure each with a cocktail stick. Place them in a greased oven dish, and trickle a little tomato juice into the dish. Cover with foil, and bake at gas mark 5/180°C for 45 minutes.

Meanwhile prepare the rice. This is easy but requires patience, as the idea is to keep all of its components separate. Which means that you have to prepare them separately. The nibbed nuts should be blanched (separately) in boiling water; the barberries should be fried in a little butter with a dash of sugar; the raisins should be fried in butter until they start to puff up; the carrot, orange peel and onion should be sautéed in a little oil. Cook the basmati according to your normal method, and just before it is cooked, stir through with the liquid saffron and the rice spice.

Now back to your quail. Remove the foil, and trickle a little saffron glaze (melt a knob of butter in 30ml of stock, and add a drizzle of saffron water) over each bird. Put back in the oven to crisp up (a further 10 minutes).

Turn the rice out onto a dish, then literally stripe each of the 'jewels' across the top in pretty little rows (trying to contrast the colours). Right at the last minute, pour a little boiling water over the *nabat* so that it slightly dissolves, and then strew the whole lot over the rice dish – this

makes the whole thing glisten like real gems (with a bit of imagination it does, anyway).

I serve the quails with their saffrony tomato sauce separately – the rice can thus enjoy some of the limelight instead of playing a supporting role.

Some Iranians would serve the 'jewels' mixed into the rice, which makes the whole thing easier to prepare, but not everyone likes all of the ingredients, so serving the dish like this is easier on you, the chef. It also looks more sensational segmented in this way.

Sour oranges

In Iran, both the peel and juice of sour oranges (akin to the Seville oranges so prized for marmalade-making) are used. The juice, known as *ab-naranj*, is used in northern regions in place of *ab-limoo* or lemon juice, to add sharpness to casseroles; the fresh fruits are also excellent when squeezed over fish. But the grated peel, or *halal-e-naranj*, is used all over the country to add an extra dimension to rice dishes. Iranian shops sell a ready-grated, dried version, which may just be rinsed and fried. Or you can make your own. Even if you can't find Seville oranges to use, just pare the skin of a regular orange in very thin striplets, blanch briefly in boiling water (to remove any nasty chemicals), then spread it out and leave it in the airing cupboard (or other warm spot) to dry for a day or two. A special bonus tip from my mother-in-law – oranges are such uplifting fruits that it seems a shame so much of their fragrance is wasted. Next time you peel one, leave the peel on the radiator for a while and before long the whole room should be infused with a waft of citrus.

Lentil Rice with Date Fudge

This is perhaps my favourite of all of the Iranian *pulao*s, especially when served with thick, lamby *ab-gusht* (see p. 152). They are not traditionally served together, but ohmigosh they make a grand combination. But you can serve it with any *khoresht* you like, and the rice works with wet vegetarian concoctions as well (like the lemony recipe on p. 245). Here I insist on brown basmati (which I prefer anyway, but find hard to sell to Iranians who are mostly die-hard white rice eaters) – the slightly nutty flavour of brown and its crunchier texture contrast well with the buttery, squidgy dates. This will be enough for 6 people.

> *6 cups brown basmati rice*
> *250g (uncooked weight) green (or brown) lentils*
> *2 tablespoons ghee*
> *salt*
> *1½ teaspoons ground cardamom*
> *around 24 fresh Iranian dates*
> *butter*
> *½ teaspoon ground saffron, steeped in boiling water*

Firstly, soak your rice in cold water. The secret in cooking brown basmati is in this pre-soaking – brown rice is that little bit more resilient than white, and this gives it a head start. Two hours should do.

Rinse and pick through the lentils. You'd be amazed at how much of the farmyard ends up in a bag of lentils, so always sort and wash them thoroughly. Put them in a pan of cold water, bring to the boil and simmer for 20–30 minutes (until cooked but not mushy). Drain.

Cook the rice according to your normal method. If that is to boil and then steam it, before you put it back in the pan to steam, mix it

به سبک جدید

through with the ground cardamom, and then alternate it with layers of lentils (see the recipe for *bogoli pulao* on p. 154). If using the rice cooker method, cook the rice with the ghee, and then add the lentils and cardamom at the end of cooking.

Pit the dates, then melt a knob of butter in a pan and fry them gently until they become sticky and impossible to work, i.e. like fudge.

Once the rice is cooked, do not let it sit on the heat too long, as brown basmati has a habit of 'catching'. Turn it out and serve it as soon as it is ready. Crack a path through the *tahdik*, and drizzle the saffron across it, mixing it a bit with the surrounding rice. Spoon the dates in small clusters around the edge of the serving dish.

Albaloo Pulao – Sour Cherry Rice

This is a great festive dish, its sweetness adding a degree of opulence. I have suggested making it with lamb here, in the traditional manner, because I think that the cherries perfectly contrast the grease of the lamb. My mother-in-law invariably makes it with chicken, and you could easily layer it up with a moist vegetarian concoction. If you are using a rice cooker, it is best to make the rice by mixing the cherries through at the last minute, and serve the *ab-gusht* (lamb and stock) separately. This would be enough for 4–6 people.

> *½ shoulder of lean lamb, boned (but with the bones retained)*
> *1 onion, chopped*
> *1 teaspoon ground turmeric*
> *salt and pepper*
> *butter or ghee*
> *5 cups basmati rice*

500g fresh sour or morello cherries, stoned and cleaned plus 3
tablespoons sugar or 1 x 400g (net weight) jar of sour cherry jam
1 teaspoon ground saffron steeped on a saucer in boiling water

Cut the lamb into small pieces (2cm 'cubes'). Place in a pan with lamb bones, onion and turmeric, cover with water and bring to the boil. Set to simmer – you need to cook it for about an hour and a quarter. At the end of cooking, season to taste.

While the meat is cooking, wash and soak the rice. After about an hour, drain it and plunge it into boiling water for 6–7 minutes, before draining again.

If you are using fresh sour cherries, cook them gently in a pan with a splash of water and the sugar; 10–15 minutes should see them softened.

Melt a knob of butter or ghee in your rice pan, and as soon as it is spitting hot, sprinkle a generous layer of the parboiled rice over the bottom. Follow with a layer of meat (scoop it from its stock with a slotted spoon so that you do not add too much liquid), more rice, and then a layer of the cherries. Continue until all of the ingredients have been used, all the while being careful not to press the rice down too hard. Poke 5–6 holes down through the rice, and then cover the lid of the saucepan with a tea-towel and set the pan to steam over the gentlest of heats. Leave to cook for around an hour. At the end of this period, plunge the bottom of the pan into a little cold water in the sink: after 5 minutes, you should be able to invert a tray over the pan and turn the rice out on to it – all things being equal you should have the most amazing *tahdik*. Crack the top of the *tahdik* with a spoon and trickle a little saffron on to the cracked bit; in fact, take a spoon of the rice and rub it around the saffron saucer before mixing it back with the rest of the rice – this helps to make sure that you use all of the saffron. The dish will be very moist anyway – but I like to serve this with the rest of the lamb stock, which you can dish up separately in a bowl.

Serve with yoghurt and fresh herbs.

220

CHAPTER EIGHT

سالادها

VEGETABLES AND SALADS

This section of the book will look at the Persian approach to vegetables, and the myriad different ways of preparing them. It includes quite a few actual vegetable and vegetarian dishes, and a range of salads, although some salads have already been touched on and described in other sections of the book.

Street food

The Iranians like their junk food as much as the next man. Neon-lit, plastic-coated burger bars and pizzerias abound in most town centres. In fact, Iranians are obsessed with pizza – they love to eat it and they regard it as a sort of national dish, stopping short of claiming that it was actually a Persian invention. This obsession is nowhere more obvious than in London, where around 60 per cent of independently owned pizza takeaways are under Iranian ownership.

But street food is not the same as takeaway food – it is older and quainter and healthier, and invariably a lot more interesting.

The heart of most Iranian towns is the bazaar. Some, like Tehran and Isfahan, are truly vast, dense and often mysterious – rambling mazes, a town within a town. And it is here that there is the greatest need for street food – simple snacks to nourish weary shoppers or to fortify traders. Street snacks in Iran are nothing if not simple, but it is this very simplicity that intrigues me. I have learnt to take a fresh look at some of the ingredients they use and treat them with great respect. Favourites in the winter months are boiled turnips or beetroot; a perennial feature are the hot-potato vendors; in the spring there are broad beans; and in the summer months you can buy grilled corn. Of course, such foods never taste as good as they do when eaten *in situ*, whether it be in the bitter cold or the sweltering heat, conveyed upon bits of newspaper or in cones of greaseproof. But I have tried below to recreate some of these simple pleasures.

Shalgam – turnips

North of the border (English, that is, not Iranian) 'neeps' have almost iconic status – they were a big part of the staple diet in Scotland, and still play a large and affectionate role in the national cuisine. In England sadly, and I suspect in many other countries, they are just another root crop to lob into hotpots or serve with the Sunday roast. And yet he's a really tasty little chap, the turnip, and extraordinarily good for you. In his excellent book, *Miraculous Plants*, Dr Sohrab Khoshbin waxes lyrical over the healing properties of this humble root (see Chapter Fourteen, 'The Medicinal Pantry', below).

To enjoy them in the Iranian style, buy, if possible, young, baby turnips – big old wrinklies belong to the stockpot or stew.

Top and tail each one, scrub the skins well, and then quarter them. Although the skins are not eaten, leaving them on during the cooking procedure ensures that the vegetables remain intact. Place in a pan, cover with water and bring to the boil. Do not salt the water, as this makes the turnips tough and they will take longer to cook. Simmer for around half an hour, or until a fork penetrates them with ease. Drain and serve with salt and pepper. That's it. They are absolutely delicious. If you're still not convinced, try mashing them with a little butter and a grating of nutmeg.

غذاهای مخصوص ایرانی

Laboo – beetroot

This is awfully good for you as well – beetroot is a great de-toxer, scrubbing the kidneys and waterworks as he goes. And he's such a pretty colour too – who can resist him? I actually developed a strange antipathy to these tubers when I lived with my granny for a while. Four times a year we had the beetroot ritual, wherein a whole sack of the things were cooked and proffered for the Bridge Club luncheon. It was all very Mapp and Lucia, but the smell lingered. Anyway, now I'm back on them again, and I can't wait for them to appear on the vegetable stalls in Rye Lane each spring.

To cook them bazaari-style, top, tail and peel, and cut them into manageable chunks. Cover with water (again, no salt), bring to the boil, then simmer for around an hour and a half. Convention will have you add around 1 dessertspoonful of sugar per kilo of beetroot – this is a matter of taste and, personally, I find most people make them too sweet. Eat with a fork. While not remotely authentic, I rather like them with a big dollop of mascarpone on the side.

Street sweetcorn

As someone who grew up eating sweetcorn smothered in butter, this method of preparation came as something of a revelation.

Grill your corn cobs whole over fire, then skin them and plunge into hot salted water for a few moments. Eat. It's as simple as that. I never thought I would find butter superfluous to my requirements.

Jacket potatoes

I will never forget my first evening at my in-laws' house: for a range of reasons, not all of them food-related. But the meal did make a lasting

impression. The business of eating on the floor, cooking over the fire, and the sheer number of apparent courses: I knew then that I had entered a rather different world. My father-in-law, endowed with four sons, had long since resolved the issues of domestic responsability by appointing different ministers for different duties. Thus he had a minister of offal, who would clean, trim and skewer liver for cooking over the fire; a minister of carrots, who would juice carrots and anything else that would go through the machine; and the baby was minister of potatoes – his job it was to wash, prick and wrap potatoes in foil to cook in the embers. He's grown up now and resigned his ministry a while ago: but we still like to eat potatoes this way.

Once your potato is cooked and crisp, mash the inside with a little salt, the tiniest knoblet of butter and a sprinkling of *golpar*. This latter is the magic ingredient, and until recently I was a little lost as to its name in English. It is in fact the ground seeds of Persian hogwort (*Heracleum persicum*). It is worth visiting or contacting your nearest Persian shop to source this mysterious spice as it has a unique and rather wonderful flavour, although it does admittedly smell like old socks. The whole seeds are used widely in pickle-making in Iran, and ground *golpar* is sprinkled on beans, lentils and potatoes (as it is believed to counteract the flatulence-inducing effects of these foods – see Chapter Fourteen for the full low-down).

Bogoli – broad beans

They really know what to do with broad or fava beans in the Middle East. If you haven't tried Lebanese or Egyptian *fouls medammes* with lashings of lemon and perhaps a dash of tahini, well, we won't go so far as to say that you haven't lived, but you are certainly missing out. Fresh broad beans have a woefully short season, so the beans are often found frozen or dried, either shelled and split to make purée, or whole for salads and the like. The broad beans of street food are fresh, still in the pod.

In our household, when the broad bean season begins, there are often ungainly squabbles over who gets the last serving.

For *bazaari bogoli* (4 people can easily eat 2–3 kg of whole broad beans – by the time they are shelled they don't go very far), bring a large pan of water to the boil (no salt until later as it makes them tough). Wash the bean pods well, and then plunge them into the boiling water. Allow to cook for around 45–60 minutes. Drain and serve still in their pods, accompanied by the salt cellar, a pot of *golpar* (see above) and wedges of lemon. Iranians invariably shuck their beans; personally, I prefer to eat them with the skin on. I also like to serve them with a tahini dip, although this is not an Iranian idea.

Tahini dip

Beat 2 tablespoons of *tahina* (sesame paste) together with 2 cloves of minced garlic, a handful of chopped coriander leaves, the juice of one lemon, salt, pepper and enough water to make it a pouring consistency (it will thicken considerably in the fridge).

Mirza Ghassemi, and Other Nice Things to Do with Aubergines

It is a shame that a lot of vegetarians do not seem to like aubergines, as they really are very versatile, and can easily stand in for meat in a lot of dishes. They are used extensively in Iran; there are all sorts of wonderful regional recipes. In fact, you will find them as a sort of vegetable leitmotif throughout this book.

This particular recipe is to be found across the whole of Iran, although it comes from the north. It is one of those dishes in which it is really easy to overindulge. It is eaten as a starter or a snack, but it has found its way into this section because, for me, it is more about honouring the aubergine than fulfilling a particular food requirement.

> *approximately 1 aubergine per person*
> *1 clove garlic per person*
> *salt and pepper*
> *dash olive oil*
> *¼ teaspoon ground turmeric per person*
> *1 medium tomato per person*
> *1 egg per person*

Heat the oven to gas mark 6/200°C, wash and prick the aubergines, place them in the oven to bake. After 20–30 minutes, fish them out and allow to cool a bit (else you will burn your fingers). Chop off the aubergine 'hats', and semi-peel (in Iran they would do it properly, but as this dish is about flavour and not finesse, I think a little skin enhances it). Chop or mash roughly. Peel and chop the garlic, blend in the salt and fry in a dash of oil. Just as it starts to cook, sprinkle in the turmeric,

followed by the tomato, and finally the aubergine. Continue to fry for a few more minutes, and then crack the eggs into the pan. You can either make little holes in the aubergine mixture and fry the eggs individually, or you can just whisk the eggs into the vegetables. After a minute or two more, serve alongside warm Persian bread. This is another dish that I invariably serve out of the pan. However, please note that had I been Iranian, this would mark me as a peasant.

To bribe small people to eat this, or to persuade obdurate carnivores that this is real food, you can add chopped frankfurters to the dish at the garlic-frying stage.

به سبک جدید

Marinated Aubergines

This is a very versatile dish – it will go to barbecues or buffet parties with you, or just sit in the fridge like a good little snack. It is best to use the baby aubergines widely available in Continental greengrocers in the spring and summer, but you can use quartered regular aubergines instead if you like. Baby aubergines are not as bitter as adults, so they do not need to be salted first.

> *10 baby aubergines, halved lengthways (leave their hats on – it looks pretty in this dish)*
> *10 prunes*
> *1 tablespoon runny honey*
> *2 bay leaves*
> *2 cloves and 1 stick cinnamon*
> *¼ teaspoon chilli powder*
> *2 tablespoons of apple (or cider) vinegar*
> *salt and pepper*
> *olive oil*
> *50g sesame seeds, lightly toasted*

Brush the aubergines with a little olive oil, and grill for around 10 minutes, turning halfway. Halve and pit the prunes. Heat the honey slightly and pour over the prunes, ensuring that they are thoroughly coated. Mix the bay leaves, spices, vinegar, salt and pepper with around 4 tablespoons of olive oil. Add the prunes and sesame seeds, and pour the whole lot over the warm aubergines. Cover, refrigerate, and leave to marinate overnight, turning once.

Marinated Courgettes

سالاد کدو

While we're in marinating mode, raw courgettes are big in Iran at the moment. Since the discovery that they have brilliant effects on cholesterol levels and possibly blood pressure, they are being juiced and crop up in every conceivable salad. Dill is similarly credited with lowering cholesterol. The trouble is, neither ingredient is especially delectable on its own, hence this salad. This marinade stands as a salad in its own right, or you can use it in other salads, or as a garnish for other things.

1kg courgettes
4–5 cloves garlic, chopped
handful fresh dill, chopped
handful fresh coriander, chopped
salt and pepper
juice of 2 lemons
100ml extra virgin olive oil

Slice the courgettes very finely, and place them in a bowl, making sure the slices are all separated. Add the other ingredients, and mix well. Cover and leave overnight, perhaps giving it another quick turn just before you go to bed.

Lettuce with Mint Syrup

This is eaten as a dish all on its own in hot weather in Iran. It is incredibly refreshing. Traditionally, romaine lettuce is used, but I happily substitute the more readily available cos, the leaves of which are great for dipping. Even iceberg will do.

The syrup featured here, *sekanjabin*, is quite versatile – I add it to all sorts of dishes (see the chapter on desserts). It was devised originally as a *shabat* (sherbet), a cordial to have over ice in the summer, but its culinary applications are far more interesting to me. To make the syrup you will need:

> *250ml water*
> *350g sugar*
> *4 tablespoons white wine vinegar*
> *12 sprigs mint*

Place the water in a pan, add the sugar and bring to the boil. Bubble for 10 minutes, remove from the heat and add the vinegar. When it is a bit cooler, add the mint, bottle and chill.

To serve, wash the lettuce of your choice and dissect leaf by leaf. Arrange the leaves like a flower on a plate around a bowl of the *sekanjabin*. If you are using something like iceberg lettuce, you can cut it into 'steaks' and drizzle the syrup over each portion.

Braised Sweet Gem Lettuce with *Sekanjabin*

کاہو کو چک پختہ شدہ در سکنجبین

This is a lovely combination. Sweet gems belie their name as they can actually be fairly bitter, but the bitterness is lost when they are cooked in this way. This makes a fine accompaniment to rich meat dishes. For 4 people as a side dish.

4 sweet gem lettuces
100ml chicken or good vegetable stock
few sprigs mint
2 tablespoons sekanjabin *as in the previous recipe*

Wash the lettuces, removing any mangy bits, but basically leaving whole. Place them in an oven-proof dish, with the sprigs of mint on top, pour the stock over them and drizzle the *sekanjabin* over everything. Cover the dish with foil and bake in the oven (gas mark 4, 180°C) for around 25–30 minutes. The lettuces should be soft enough to welcome advances from a fork. Serve on a bed of fresh lettuce, with the syrupy stock poured over the top.

به سبک جدید

Carrot Salad with Nibbed Pistachios

This is a pretty dish which makes an attractive addition to any *sofreh* (tablecloth/spread of food) or buffet. It also tastes good. I often have it for lunch with some wholemeal pitta or *taftoon* bread. This will make enough for 3–4 people as a light lunch, or a decent bowlful for a buffet table.

> *100g raisins*
> *juice of 2 oranges plus the zest of 1*
> *500g carrots, topped 'n' tailed and peeled*
> *1 teaspoon chopped fresh ginger*
> *50g nibbed pistachios*
> *4 tablespoons olive oil*
> *juice of 1 lemon*
> *sprinkle salt and pepper*
> *1 teaspoon honey*
> *handful chopped coriander*

Steep the raisins in the orange juice for a little while. Grate the carrots, and put in a bowl with the ginger and the nibbed pistachios. Whisk the olive oil, lemon juice, zest, honey, salt and pepper together, and pour over the carrots. Add in the orange juice and raisins, and stir in the coriander.

The patron saint of Middle Eastern food writing, aka Claudia Roden, mentions a similar salad from Morocco which uses just carrots, chopped orange, orange and lemon juice and chopped coriander, and sees it mixed with orange blossom water for a cooling antidote to spicy (as in hot) food. It seems to work.

Extremely Exotic Carrots

This time, the carrots are cooked. They are great alongside rich meats such as duck or gammon or pork. Initially, I evolved this method from Nesta Ramazani's lovely recipe to get the smalls to eat carrots. It failed dismally in this respect (if you've got real children you'll probably understand why, but I'm only a wicked step-mother and I try to make everything fun), but the larger lunchers amongst us loved it.

600g carrots, peeled and cut into slivers
1 large onion, chopped
100g butter
250g pitted fresh (Iranian) dates
100g raisins
2 tablespoons pomegranate paste
100ml good stock
¼ teaspoon ground saffron, dissolved in a tablespoon of boiling water
handful each of nibbed almonds and nibbed pistachios (optional garnish)

Sauté the carrots and onion in the butter, and when both are starting to soften, add the dates and the raisins. After 5 minutes, add the pomegranate paste, stirring well. Add the saffron to the stock, then stir this in as well. Simmer for around 20 minutes – the mixture should be gorgeously syrupy, and the carrots cooked. Strew with nibbed nuts.

To make this more of a suppery dish than a bit on the side, beat 4–5 eggs together and fold them into the carrots just before you want to dish up. As soon as they have set, season to taste and serve with warm bread.

The Iranian cinema

Although not very relevant in a chapter on vegetables, I was thinking pretty food – garnish – arty-farty – art-house – Kiarostami. I have to mention Persian films in this book, because they are a big part of what we do in the shop (selling, not making them).

Persian films, in case you are not a regular at the ICA, are hot. They ooze style and the cinematography is probably the best in the world. The two big directors to look out for are Abbas Kiarostami (*Taste of Cherry*, *The White Balloon*), and the Makhmalbafs, father and daughter (*Blackboards*, *The Apple*, *Osama*). They scoop the pool at awards ceremonies again and again.

It has to be said that this is partly because of the revolution. Pre-1979 Iranian films are good, but not exceptional. Nowadays, they are shown round the clock in crackly black and white on ex-pat TV channels, and are popular for the nostalgia they evoke. There are musicals, and dancing, scantily-clad women, plenty of slapstick comedy, and over-the-top adventures featuring the dashing Behrooz. The first sign of the metaphorical, clever, really watchable stuff to come was a 1960s film called *The Cow*, the story of a man who falls in love with a cow. Sounds silly? It is actually brilliant. You should grab it if you come across a sub-titled version. After the revolution, the women got dramatically re-clad, the dancing stopped, and music was extremely limited. Only the slapstick survived, thanks chiefly to an irrepressible buffoon called Samad, a kind of Persian Norman Wisdom, who remains popular to this day. The directors had to do something exceptional to make their voices heard. So they started making remarkably clever stuff, often with very little story-line and a minimal script, but with such good filming as to make even the story of a little girl losing her pocket money (*The White Balloon*) gripping.

This is not, of course, the whole story. Many Iranians are less than fond of their '*film honarii*' (artistic films) and, of course, such films may be satisfying but not necessarily that entertaining. Hundreds of other

غذاهای مخصوص ایرانی

films come out of Iran every year, from adventure (the Iran/Iraq war is a popular theme), to drama (they love their weepies), to wonderful, gentle comedies. Recent successes have included *Marmolak* (The Lizard), the story of a thief who steals a mullah's clothes (this was banned several times in Iran, but proved so popular that eventually it was shown), and *Barrareh* (which is more a serial than a film), a painfully funny, satirical saga set in a fictional town. The film industry in Iran is now so big that they offer tourists the chance to visit the sets and meet the stars. Whether from what they show or what they don't show, a nation's cinema is a good way of learning a little more about that nation. Take in a Persian film next time the opportunity presents itself and you might be pleasantly surprised.

به سبک جدید

Lubia Chitti – Pinto Bean Salad

When I used to work in a cheap and cheerful, very busy Greek Cypriot restaurant (serving *meze*), I got to the state where the words bean and salad used in the same sentence would induce a slight twitching, if not a rash. Which is a great shame, because some of my favourite things are beans, and I endured several beanless years in recovery. I am happy to state that they are back in my diet with a vengeance, and I am extraordinarily proud of my pulse collection in the shop.

Pinto bean salad is made in Iran, but the recipes I have seen are undoubtedly Westernized, featuring sliced eggs, peas and lots of mayonnaise. In fact, the concept of dressed mixed salad is fairly new to Iran, and recipes in books such as the excellent Rosa Montazami's (Iran's own Mrs Beeton) are less exotic than one would imagine. So this is pinto bean salad as it would have been had it been raised in Iran, if you see what I mean. Without any mayonnaise.

> *250g dried pinto beans*
> *handful each of coriander, parsley and dill*
> *1 bunch spring onions*
> *olive oil*
> *juice of 2 lemons, or some bottled Persian lemon juice (much stronger*
> *than the watery stuff we are accustomed to in Britain)*
> *salt and pepper*

Soak the pinto beans overnight, and cook them in unsalted water for 50–60 minutes, until they are neither crunchy nor mushy. Drain and set aside. Chop the herbs and the spring onions, using the green and white parts of the onions. Whisk the oil and lemon together, and then mix all the ingredients, seasoning to taste. This is good warm or cold.

Spiced Red Lentil Purée

They do lots of nice things with lentils in Iran: in general they are much kinder to them than we are. The lentil has had lots of good PR in recent years and is beginning to slough off the dour vegetarian image it acquired after the 1960s. But it has a way to go before it is enshrined, as it should be, a paragon of nutritional value and culinary versatility. This purée is great. It can be eaten as a snack on its own with a little goats' cheese crumbled on top, or as an unusual accompaniment to a main course.

250g red lentils
1 bunch spring onions, very finely chopped
2 green chillies (or ½ red bell chilli), chopped finely
olive oil for frying
1 ½ teaspoons green cumin seeds
2 teaspoons ground turmeric
1 teaspoon curry powder
2 teaspoons mustard seeds
2 cloves garlic
250ml good vegetable stock
salt

Pick through and wash the lentils. Fry the onions and chilli in a little oil, then add the spices and the garlic, stirring constantly. Add the lentils, and then pour on the vegetable stock. Bring to the boil and cook for around half an hour, topping up with water as required, until the lentils are quite soft and the liquid has all been absorbed. Tip into a bowl and mash, seasoning to taste as you go. Serve as required, garnished with fresh herbs.

به سبک جدید

Everyday Lentils

These are so called because my mother-in-law and I could actually eat them every day. This way of preparing lentils is very common in Iran. Lentils do not need any soaking (I am amazed by the number of people who think they do), so they are great store-cupboard standbys.

250g green (or brown, or Puy) lentils
olive oil for frying (see my note below)
1 large onion, chopped
1 large potato, peeled and diced very small
1 teaspoon curry powder
1 teaspoon ground turmeric
salt and pepper

Pick through and wash your lentils: this is important as lentils and other pulses tend to be packaged with all sorts of little stones. Heat the oil in a saucepan, and then fry the onion until just starting to brown. Add the potato, stirring constantly because it will stick. Stir in the spices, but do not season with salt until the end. Add about 600ml of water (or stock, but it is not necessarily better) to the pan, bring to the boil and set to simmer. Cook for about half an hour, checking occasionally that there is enough fluid: after this time the liquid should just about be absorbed, and the lentils well cooked without being too mushy. Add salt and pepper to taste. Eat surreptitiously in the corner – it is far too tasty to share. You may add a little thick, natural yoghurt if you wish.

Don't forget that you should use only *pure olive oil* for frying, and keep the *extra virgin* for dressing and drizzling. This is because the latter has a very low smoke-point, and will simply burn if you try to cook with it at high temperatures.

Vegetables in Pomegranate Sauce

Have this in hand for unexpected vegetarian visitors. It doesn't take much time, can be made from whatever you have lurking in your fridge or pantry, and is more exciting than lasagna. It also makes a fine lunch or supper dish for omnivores. I serve this in a big bowl with a thin layer of rice at the bottom and plenty of bread alongside for mopping up.

500g fresh, washed spinach (or 1 pack frozen)
200g green or brown lentils
500g root vegetables – potato, sweet potato, parsnip, turnip, swede
    and celeriac are all good – peeled and cut into 2cm cubes
500ml good vegetable stock
butter
2 medium onions, roughly chopped
1 capsicum pepper, chunked
1–2 chopped chillies (optional)
1 stick of celery, chunked
100ml pomegranate paste
salt and pepper

Defrost your spinach, if using frozen. Wash and sort the lentils, and then place in a pan with the cubed root vegetables and the vegetable stock. Bring to the boil, and simmer for around 30 minutes, or until the lentils are cooked. Melt a knob of butter in a frying-pan and sauté the onion, pepper, chillies and celery. Once they are soft and lightly browned, add the spinach, stir until it wilts and then stir the whole lot into the lentil pan. Add the pomegranate paste, and cook through for 10 minutes more. Season as required – a lot of shop-bought stock cubes are overly salty, so you may not need any extra salt at all.

Spinach, Walnut and Tabriz Cheese Salad

This is somewhat of a misnomer. As Europe forbids the import of any milk or animal products from countries outside the Union, we have to make do with pseudo-Tabriz. This is easily done, because in effect it is just a very salty white cheese. The nearest to it that we have found is Bulgarian feta, but in truth any good feta will do the job. This is a rich and impressive salad and makes a good starter.

18–24 walnut halves
100g baby spinach leaves
50g herb leaves – tarragon, parsley and coriander are ideal
50g rocket or watercress
olive oil
2 cloves garlic, chopped
2–3 slices nice bread (I use wholemeal or granary, which a chef
friend of mine says is bizarre – but you get a much nuttier flavour
that way; barberi *or other thick* naan *is good as well)*
100g black olives, pitted
for the dressing:
a good splash of olive oil
2 teaspoons mustard
2 tablespoons apple or tarragon vinegar
50g good feta, crumbled
1 clove chopped garlic
1 teaspoon black olive paste
freshly milled black pepper

Soak the walnuts in cold water, preferably for a few hours. They will swell and become creamier; this process will also allow you to remove

the flaky skin so that the nuts appear almost white. Wash and trim the herbs and leaves, so that just an artistic peeking of stalk is left on each. Leave to drain. Beat all the dressing ingredients together, cover and set aside to let the flavours mingle and get to know each other.

Heat a dash of olive oil in a skillet, and fry the garlic gently. Once it has started to 'catch', take it out and set aside. Cube the bread and fry it in the garlicky oil, turning regularly, until it is nicely browned and crisp. Make sure you do enough to compensate for all the bits you steal as you go: it is impossible to resist.

Finally, toss the leaves in your best salad bowl (or on individual plates). Drain the walnuts and lovingly pat them dry before adding them to the salad along with those glistening olives. Strew the leaves with the still warm, oh-so-fragrant croûtons, and drizzle the cheesy dressing over the top. Now tell me you're not drooling already.

Persian carpets

They are perhaps Iran's most famous export (alongside the oil thing, of course). Whole towns in Iran specialize in their production, each one offering different styles, colours and ways of knotting them together. They have been around for over 2,500 years, although the heyday was during the Safavid period. Designs vary from the Islamic to the great themes of Persian legend, from the abstract to the depiction of real-life scenes.

Amazingly, most Iranians are startlingly well informed about the subject. Carpets (*farsh*) are almost a form of currency over there, an investment. The good ones increase in value as they get older (a fact which I still have trouble absorbing), and so they are often given as wedding gifts.

At the risk of being outcast as a heretic, I sometimes find it hard to see what all the fuss is about. I knew I was in trouble when there were cries of horror when I walked on the in-laws' new carpet in my

shoes and without admiring it sufficiently; I caused further uproar when I suggested that we got a nice artificial rug as 'these woollen things trigger my asthma' (for the record, this effect only lasts a week or so until they settle); and my final sacrilege was to request a plainer carpet for our room (I am a maximalist, but prefer my art on the walls to the floor). But I am coming around to them as an art form in their own right, and have actually seen one or two I quite covet.

It is very easy to be 'had' when buying a Persian carpet (even in Iran). As a rough guide, a real one should have a proper seal of authenticity, and a tag indicating the workshop where it was made. The image on the front of the carpet should also be clearly visible from the back. Unless you have a pet Iranian to help, your best bet in Britain is to visit Kentish Town where there is a whole street of (real Iranian) carpet dealers. They seem to trade with a degree of integrity. Flying models cost slightly more, but have so much cachet; make sure you get the instructions with them though – they can be very temperamental.

غذاهای مخصوص ایرانی

Citrus-infused Vegetable Hotpot

I offer this by way of compensation. I often refer to *ab-gusht* or meat-water, the tasty lamb or chicken stock served with many of the rice dishes. This is *ab-sabzi ja'ht* – 'vegetable-water' – because being a vegetarian or a vegan (or having them to dinner) should never mean having to say you're sorry. This will serve 4 vegetarians as a main course.

> *1 large onion, peeled and chopped*
> *2 sticks celery, washed and cut into 2cm chunks*
> *soya/vegetarian butter*
> *1 teaspoon ground turmeric*
> *1 litre good vegetable stock (optional – you can just use water)*
> *6–7 dried limes (or the zest and juice of 2 fresh limes)*
> *1 tin cooked butter beans (or 100g dried, soaked overnight)*
> *1 tin cooked chick peas (or 100g dried, soaked overnight)*
> *4–5 small potatoes, peeled and halved*
> *2 carrots, scraped and cut into 2cm chunks*
> *1 small head spring greens, or ½ green cabbage, washed & roughly*
>   *chopped*
> *¼ teaspoon ground saffron*
> *handful each of coriander and parsley, washed and chopped*
> *salt and pepper*
> *couple of sprigs of herb for garnish*

Fry the onion and celery in some butter/vegetable equivalent: when soft, stir in the turmeric, and then add the stock and the dried limes and bring to the boil.

If using 'raw' pulses, drain them and add them at this stage – you

will need to let them simmer for around 45 minutes before proceeding with the rest of the recipe.

Sprinkle the saffron into the pan. Add the potatoes and carrots, and then after 15 minutes, the chopped greens, the chopped herbs, and the tinned pulses. Simmer for another 20 minutes or so, until the potatoes and carrots are cooked to the point of disintegration. Season to taste. Garnish with green stuff and serve with one of the fancy rice dishes from Chapter Seven – but to be perfectly honest, it is a lovely dish to have as supper, just with a little warm bread on the side.

غذاهای محصوص ایرانی

CHAPTER NINE

CHAPTER NINE

DESSERTS

The Persians may have a very sweet tooth, but they do not generally serve puddings in the Western sense. They will often follow a meal with fruit and (yet more) tea, or perhaps some sorbet or *bastani* (ice-cream). The desserts I suggest in this chapter, are based on recipes for sweet dishes that are served at other times of the day, or to guests, or for special occasions.

Persian cream cakes

Whilst a lot of Persian sweets are drier than those to which our cloyed Western palates are accustomed, there are a few exceptions

There are three basic models of cream cake to collect, and these are loosely equivalent to profiteroles, roulade and cream puffs. They are all hugely popular in Iran. As these sweets are fairly commonplace in England, we have added our own little twists to the following recipes.

Rose, Raspberry and Almond Roulade

This would be more authentic with mulberries, but they are truly hard to get hold of and raspberries provide a greater degree of sharp contrast.

> *5 eggs, separated*
> *175g castor sugar*
> *50g ground almonds*
> *¼ teaspoon almond essence*
> *25g flaked almonds*
> for the filling:
> *275ml double cream*
> *3 tablespoons rose-water*
> *3 tablespoons rose syrup*
> *25g icing sugar*
> *225g raspberries*
> *castor sugar and rose petals to decorate*

Line a 23cm x 32cm Swiss roll tin with greaseproof paper, cut 2cm larger than the tin. Snip the corners to fit, and oil the paper lightly. Whisk the egg yolks and sugar, and then fold in the ground almonds and the essence. Whisk the egg whites until peaking and then fold them into the yolk mixture. Pour into the tin, and then scatter the almond flakes over its surface. Cook on gas mark 6/200°C for 15 minutes, and then leave to cool.

Prepare the filling – whip the cream until lightly peaking, and then whisk in the rose-water, syrup and icing sugar. Invert the cooled sponge on to a sheet of sugar-dusted greaseproof paper, and pull off the lining paper. Trim the edges if necessary. Spread it with first the cream mixture,

and then the raspberries, and then roll it up and chill. To serve, slice and sprinkle each slice with rose petals. Try not to drool.

Variation: orange, saffron and almond roulade

Steep half a teaspoon of ground saffron in a dash of boiling water and allow to cool.

Make the roulade as above. For the filling, whip 300ml double cream; whisk in the juice and zest of one orange, 25g icing sugar, and then stir in the saffron. Assemble as above.

A rose by any other name

The world is a rose – smell it and pass it to your friends.

Iranian proverb

The cult of the rose is big in Iran. Its exquisite fragrance and flavour are greatly sought after, and the tranquillity of a rose garden is regarded as being as close to paradise as it is possible for a mere mortal to voyage. Persian literature is heavily infused with references to it, and much of our rose knowledge and indeed rose vocabulary stems from Persian garden lore and Persian words.

The flower used to make rose products is the *Gul Mohammadi*, known to us as the Damascene Rose. The petals are dried and used in tea, cordials, ice-cream, and ground into spice mixtures. But it is rose-water which is the industry's biggest product. It is made by steeping rose petals in water, and then distilling that water no less than four times. Beyond its obvious appearances in baking and sweets, it has myriad other uses, and I would recommend that every pantry should have some. Check these out:

❀ Use it as a facial toner: it has very mild astringent properties, and so is great for dry skin.

❀ Put it in a dinky spray bottle and keep it in the fridge – it makes a great facial spritzer in hot weather.

❀ Add a little to warm water and wash your guests' feet with it upon their arrival at your abode (extreme, perhaps, but that is one of the most original and authentic uses of rose-water).

❀ Add it to finger bowls for dinner parties (together with some dried rose petals).

❀ Add a few drops to your ironing water, and come up smelling of roses time and time again.

❀ Add a splash to your ice tray, and offer juices and cocktails with rose-scented ice cubes. If you have dried rose petals, you could throw some of these in as well.

❀ Add a measure to fruit smoothies and shakes: it lends a beguiling fragrance.

Noon Khameii with Lime and Pistachio Cream

نان خامه ای

This is another imported Western idea which has firmly lodged in the nation's culinary heart. For *noon khameii* is none other than profiteroles, without the chocolate. They are usually made alongside the Persian version of roulade, and both are filled with rose-water-infused *crème chantilly*. In the winter months we sell an almost indecent quantity of them. To the English palate they are perhaps slightly disappointing, and so I usually shove some fancy cream inside them to give them a hint of the exotic.

غذا های مخصوص ایرانی

for the choux buns:
50g butter
120ml water
pinch salt
50g plain flour
2 eggs
for the filling:
300ml double cream
juice of 2 limes and zest of 1
50g nibbed pistachios
½ teaspoon ground cardamom
1 tablespoon icing sugar
garnish:
1 tablespoon icing sugar, mixed with ½ teaspoon ground cardamom

Bring the butter, salt and water to the boil in a saucepan, remove from the heat and then add the flour all in one go, beating mightily with a wooden spoon. Beat the eggs, and then fold them into the mixture – it should now resemble a shiny ball of goo.

Preheat the oven to gas mark 5/190°C. Using a dessertspoon, place little dollops of the dough on to a baking tray, leaving a gap in between to allow for expansion during baking. Cook for around 10 minutes, until risen and golden, before cooling on a wire rack.

When cold, pierce each bun with a small knife. Whip the cream until quite stiff, and then fold in the other filling ingredients. Using a teaspoon, fill each bun with cream.

Serve them in a little pile, dredged with the spiced icing sugar.

به سبک جدید

Earl Grey Ice-Cream with Chick Pea Shortbread

In Iran, traditional ice-cream does not come in many flavours but rather in two colours. You can have white (plain) or yellow (saffron), garnished with pistachio slivers. Nor is it usually eaten at the end of a meal – pudding is a Western thing – but rather as a hot-weather treat, or to refresh summer visitors.

However, we like ice-cream lots.

This is a fusion of subtle flavours, but it has to be said that it is the sort of ice-cream, if you're a girl, to make you wiggle. If you're a chap, well, ask your nearest and dearest female to explain. The chick pea bread consists of tiny morsels of fragrant, melt-in-the-mouth sweets. The Western palate can find them very dry, but they go beautifully with ice-cream. They are also a useful standby if you or your guests have a wheat intolerance.

for the ice-cream:
150ml strong Earl Grey tea (either strained, or make with tea bags)
150ml each full fat milk and single cream
1 strip lemon peel
3 egg yolks
110g castor sugar
150ml whipping cream
for the chick pea sweets:
50g castor sugar
110g Iranian chick pea flour (made from roasted chick peas, unlike
    gram flour, which is made from raw ones)
½ teaspoon ground cardamom
50g unsalted butter
crushed, nibbed pistachios

Put the tea, single cream and milk into a pan with the lemon peel and bring it all to a simmer. Whisk the egg yolks and sugar together until they thicken and pale. Remove the milk mixture from the heat (get rid of the lemon peel), whisk it into the egg mix, then put the whole lot back on a gentle heat until it thickens. On no account should you let this boil, otherwise the egg will scramble. Let the mixture cool. By placing a disc of dampened greaseproof paper on the surface of the custard, you will stop a skin forming while it cools. Pour the mixture into a freezer-proof container, cover and freeze until half-frozen. At this stage, scoop it into a bowl, whisk it and then whip the whipping cream, and fold this into the ice-cream. Pop back into the freezer until it is of ice-cream consistency.

On the shortbread front, it has to be said that these sweets are readily available from Iranian shops around the country, so if you are short of time, the answer is on their counters. Otherwise, however, sift the dry ingredients together on a flat, clean surface, then work in the butter with the tips of your fingers. Once the mixture decides to hold together, roll it into little chick pea shapes and place these on a sheet of greaseproof paper on a baking tray (or, if you are a domestic goddess, you can roll it into a flat sheet around a quarter-inch thick, and use pastry cutters to fashion flowers or what you will). Bake for around 10 minutes on gas mark 2/150°C, and then allow to cool. Sprinkle with the crushed pistachio.

Serve the ice-cream scooped on to individual plates surrounded by the little sweets. For extra colour, if you're showing off, streak some rose syrup or jam artistically around the rim of each plate.

به سبک جدید

Stewed Quince with *Bastani* – Clotted Cream Ice-Cream

Bastani, the classic Persian ice-cream, is almost impossible to recreate in this country as it calls for *sahlab*, the extract of an orchid root, and sometimes mastic, or natural gum. These ingredients are occasionally available, but this tome was always meant to be a kitchen-table book rather than a coffee-table book, and so to 'keep it real', we're going to cheat. The following recipe produces a veritable facsimile of a down-town Tehran ice-cream-parlour's finest.

Quinces are not available all year round, so you may substitute cooking apples or even pears if you wish, although nothing beats a quince for sending the potential consumer into paroxysms of pre-prandial, olfactory pleasure. A lot of my Middle Eastern customers buy these ugliest of fruits just for the fragrance they bring into the home. This will feed 4–6 people.

> *450mg full fat milk*
> *5 dessertspoonsful rose-water*
> *180g castor sugar*
> *5 egg yolks*
> *150ml pint slightly frozen clotted cream*
> *few drops vanilla essence*
> *50g nibbed pistachios*
> *4–5 quinces*

Firstly, pour the milk into a saucepan, add two spoonsful of the rose-water and 75g of the sugar. Heat slowly until the sugar has dissolved, but do not allow to boil. Beat the egg yolks with a further 75g of the sugar,

until the mixture thickens and pales. Slowly pour the hot milk on to the egg concoction, beating it all the time. Place the bowl over a pan of simmering water and continue to whisk until the mixture is of coating consistency. Set the bowl aside and leave to cool. Once it is nearly cold, break up and stir in the clotted cream and vanilla essence. Pour into a suitable container and freeze. Churn or beat the mixture after half an hour, and then leave to firm up for an hour or so. This instruction presumes that you do not have an ice-cream machine.

So, on to the quinces. If you have very sensitive skin, be careful with the furry outer coats of these fruits – they can induce itching. Peel and quarter them but do not core them (this is an essential instruction) – the gorgeous, chi-chi pink colour and natural jelling of Mademoiselle Quince comes from her pips. Place in a pan with a cup and a half of cold water, the rest of the rose-water, and the remaining 30g of sugar. Cook on a low heat for around 40 minutes. Allow to cool slightly, and then spoon a few segments and a little syrup into each bowl. Top with a generous scoop of the clotted cream ice-cream and a sprinkling of pistachio slivers.

This ice-cream is also the biz when made with saffron. Dissolve quarter of a teaspoonful of ground saffron in a couple of spoonsful boiling water and add it at the same time as you add the rose-water in the first step.

به سبک جدید

Pomegranate Sorbet with Vodka

Traditional Persian sorbet (*faloodeh*) is made with rose-water and a sort of vermicelli, and it is eaten with lime juice; it has to be said that it tastes quite strange to the uninitiated.

So once again, we've taken Persian ingredients and blended them into an apparently 'authentic', albeit non-existent dish. Vodka, just so you know, is as much an Iranian drink as it is Russian; it is usually consumed in shots as an aperitif, with a dish of salted yoghurt and cucumber.

> *500g castor sugar*
> *300ml water*
> *juice of 2 lemons plus the rind of one*
> *6 tablespoons vodka*
> *4–6 large (Persian if possible) pomegranates (or use half a carton of*
> *   good pomegranate juice and reduce the sugar a little)*
> *about ¼ of a cucumber*
> *a handful of fresh, chopped mint (or mint sauce)*

Place the sugar and water and lemon rind in a pan and heat gently until all the sugar has dissolved. Bring to the boil and cook for 5 minutes, adding the vodka at the last minute. Take off the heat and allow to cool for at least an hour. Scoop out 2 tablespoons of the syrup and put to one side.

Juicing your pomegranates is hard work – each fruit will take you 5 minutes or so – and it may be best to ask someone to help you. The easiest method is to knead each pomegranate gently with your thumbs until it is quite soft all round, prick a hole in the skin and squeeze the juice into a glass. Stir the lemon and pomegranate juice into the cooled syrup, pour into a freezer-proof container and freeze until firm.

Half an hour before you want to serve this refreshing concoction, slice the cucumber thinly (you want about twelve slices) and then make one cut through the radius of each slice. Dip each slice of cucumber in turn into the reserved syrup, followed by a quick romp in the mint. Or just coat each slice in mint sauce. Twist each piece, assemble them on a saucer, and pop them in the freezer. By the time you're ready for your sorbet, these cucumber twizzles should be lightly frosted (although still malleable) – twirl a couple of slices on to each portion.

به سبک جدید

Cinnamon Ice-Cream with *Gaz*

Gaz is one of the most popular Persian sweeties. In essence, it is nougat made with pistachios or almonds and rose-water. It comes in two basic varieties – *logmeh*, which are usually individually wrapped, and *ardi*, literally 'floury', which is usually loose and coated in flour and icing sugar. There is huge competition in Iran between *gaz* men – every town will claim the origin of the confection and maintain that theirs is the best. The packaging for this sweet is an art form in itself – there is an amazing array of pictures and styles available, some of them quite surreal. I am not for one minute going to suggest that we try making our own nougat – it just isn't done. If you cannot find *gaz*, French nougat or Spanish *turrón* will do.

This is not really a Persian recipe – like quite a few of the recipes in this book, it is, rather, based on authentic ingredients and a certain Persian culinary ethos. But I have to say that real Iranians on whom I have tested it absolutely adore it. I suggest you serve it with the 'window wafers' that I describe in the next chapter – but you can buy good enough ready-made waffles in most supermarkets.

250g castor sugar
8 cinnamon quills
600ml milk
6 egg yolks
1 teaspoon ground cinnamon
300ml whipping cream
12 small squares of gaz (or other nougat)
chocolate curls/nibbed pistachios for garnish

Put half the sugar in a pan with two of the cinnamon sticks and the

milk, bring to the boil, remove from the heat and set aside to cool for an hour or so. Whisk the remaining sugar into the egg yolks until your wrist aches and the mixture begins to lighten and thicken. Take the cinnamon bark out of the milk, and reheat the milk carefully. Just before it boils, take it off the heat and pour very slowly on to the egg mixture, beating vigorously all the time. Mix in the ground cinnamon, and chill in the fridge for a few hours – this gives the cinnamon a chance to work its magic and thoroughly infuse the milk. Chop the nougat into tiny pieces (using clean scissors isn't a bad idea). Finally beat in the cream, pour into a freezer-proof container and freeze until it starts to solidify. At this point, whisk it yet again, beat in the nougat pieces and then pop back into the freezer to freeze properly.

Serve garnished with the remaining cinnamon quills, chocolate curls and pistachio slivers. Or dollop on to the *noon pangareii*, 'window wafers', as suggested above.

Persian Winter Fruit Pudding with Saffron and Cardamom Suet

Suet pudding is really, really not Iranian, and I suspect that such a rich and complex creation would be anathema to a Persian chef. Nevertheless this does capture the essence of Persian cuisine, using spices and dried fruits in a manner designed to inject a little warmth into the dark of winter. This is a dream pud, one of those for which it is truly worth holding back on the main course (sorry, but what's a girl to do?). It is based on Sussex Well Pudding, which dates back to around 1800.

250g plain flour
pinch of salt 1 level teaspoon ground cardamom
250g grated suet (vegetarian if you wish)
125g chopped dried fruit of your choice – I use chopped dates, raisins
    and mulberries, but peaches and apricots are good as well
60g candied mixed peel
250g brown sugar
½ teaspoon ground saffron steeped in boiling water
190g butter or margarine

Sieve the flour, salt and cardamom into a bowl, add the suet, fruit and peel, and trickle in enough cold water to make a soft dough. Divide the mixture into two, and roll each half into a thick, flat round. Beat the sugar, saffron and butter together into a ball, and place it on to one of the rounds of dough. Bring up the edges and fold over about 2cm. Damp the edges of the second dough disc, and put it on top of the first round so that the turn-up is covered. Pinch the edges together tightly so that the butter has no way out.

Put into a floured cloth, tie tightly (allowing a bit of room for the pudding to swell), and boil or steam for 3 hours. Alternatively, you can boil in a greased, lidded pudding basin. Half fill a pan with boiling water, sit the basin in it, cover the pan and off you go. This is less fun, but the pud will be easier to turn out once it is cooked. The joy of breaking through the fragrant suet to find all that saffrony butter is as close as it gets to pudding nirvana. Serve with lashings of cream or ice-cream.

Shir Berenj – Rice Pudding Unlike-mother-used-to-make

Rice pudding has to be one of Britain's favourite winter comfort foods. Hot and creamy, with a drizzle of jam or syrup, it is a taste of childhood. Persian rice pudding is quite different, although it occupies the same place in the Iranian culinary heart. *Shir berenj* (literally, rice milk) is fragranced with spices and served chilled – it thus makes for rather a pleasant pudding for summer. This should be enough for 4–6 people.

> *150g pudding rice*
> *1 litre of milk*
> *250g sugar*
> *1 level teaspoon each of ground cardamom and ground cinnamon*
> *2 tablespoons rose-water*
> *splodge of double cream (optional)*
> *few nibbed pistachios for garnish*

Soak the rice in a saucepan in enough water to cover it with 2cm to spare. After half an hour or so, bring to the boil and simmer until most of the water has been absorbed and the rice is becoming soft (about 20 minutes). Add the milk, sugar, spices and rose-water, stirring well. Leave to simmer for 30 minutes, stirring from time to time. Once again, cook until the liquid has more or less all been absorbed. Take off the heat and fold in the cream if required. Pour into one large or several smaller serving dishes, cover and chill. In a throwback to the English variety of rice pudding, I find it quite fun to spoon a dollop of red jam into the bottom of the glasses before pouring the rice on top. But this is entirely up to you. Sprinkle with nibbed pistachios before serving.

Sholeh Zard – Saffron Rice with Sour Cherry Sauce

شله زرد

This is another national favourite, with a particular ritual attached in the making thereof. It is often proffered as *nazr*, a food-offering giving thanks in some way for, most often, the life of a child, and it is also made and given to the poor on an annual basis to commemorate the martyrdom of the Imam Hassan and the mourning month of Moharram (a bit like Lent). My mother-in-law makes great vats of it to give out at the Persian community centre during these times. But its significance in no way detracts from the fact that it is a very tasty little pudding, and with the sour cherry sauce it becomes extremely moreish (on its own it can be very rich). I have given the measurements in this recipe in cups, because that is how I have learned to make it, and it makes the proportions easy to increase or decrease depending how many of the masses you are feeding. Here I give the quantities for 4 people.

1 cup pudding rice
4 cups water
2 cups sugar
1 teaspoon ground saffron dissolved in boiling water
1 tablespoon butter
2 tablespoons rose-water
juice and zest of 1 lime
for the sauce:
200g sour cherries (or morello), washed and pitted
400g sugar
100ml water
ground cinnamon, nibbed pistachios and nibbed almonds to garnish

به سبک جدید

Wash the rice, and put it in a pan with the water. Bring to the boil, and then set to simmer for around 20 minutes, or until the rice is discernibly softened. Add the sugar and saffron, followed by the butter, rose-water, lime zest and juice, stirring all the while. When the mixture has become quite thick, pour into glasses and chill (although I rather like this hot as well – try it and see what you think). When it is cold, dredge with a little cinnamon and sprinkle the nuts prettily over the surface.

To make the sauce, sprinkle the cherries with the sugar and leave to 'sweat' for an hour. This draws out their flavour. Then place it all in a pan with the water, and bring to the boil. Simmer for about 10 minutes. You probably ought to strain it before bottling or using, but I never do. I like the added fruity bits. Serve it hot or cold in a sauce boat alongside the *sholeh zard*.

An acceptable shortcut may be to warm a little sour cherry jam (widely available in Turkish shops as well as Iranian emporiums) and use that as a sauce.

Sour Cherry Soup with Meringue 'Croûtons'

There is something a little avant garde about serving chilled soup, or hot lettuce, or anything which challenges our culinary norms (as long as it isn't gratuitously silly). Iranian cuisine is full of uncontrived contrasts and the unexpected, but it is still with that little frisson of excitement that I proffer this recipe. It is food at its most fun, and makes a delightful light dessert after a rich meal. Meringue is patently not an Iranian speciality, but is popular in modern Iran as it conveniently uses up unwanted egg whites – the yolks are often used solo in rice and in soups. This ought to be the right amount for a dessert for 6 people.

for the meringues:
3 egg whites
175g castor sugar
for the soup:
675g sour cherries
800ml water
100ml rose-water (or kirsch)
3–4 cinnamon quills
200g sugar
1 teaspoon cornflour
to serve:
fresh cream (optional)
nibbed pistachios (optional)

Make the meringues first of all. Whisk the egg whites until they form peaks. Beat in half the sugar until the mixture is stiff, and then fold in the rest. Line a baking tray with silicone paper, and then pipe the meringue mixture in small swirls (3–4cm diameter). You could also

spoon it in random dollops of the same size. Bake for an hour and half on your very lowest oven setting – usually gas mark ¼ /50°C. If you are baking ahead, you can then turn the oven off and leave the meringues in there to harden a little more, or do as my mother does and pop them in the airing cupboard overnight.

Now for the soup. Wash and stone the cherries and remove the detritus. Place in a pan with the water, rose-water, cinnamon and sugar, bring to the boil and simmer for around 20 minutes. Scoop out the cinnamon, and then whizz the rest through a blender before putting back on the heat. Mix a dessertspoon of the cherry stock with the cornflour, and spoon it back into the pan, mixing well. Heat for five minutes more, stirring constantly, and then take off the heat and chill thoroughly.

To serve, ladle the soup into bowls, swirl in some cream as desired, and then float 2–3 croûtons onto each. Two or three slithers of nibbed pistachio on top of each meringue are an optional but very pretty garnish.

Sour cherries

Sour cherries are beloved by all Iranians, and are inserted into the diet in different forms throughout the year. In addition to the obvious jams and cordials, they are dried and eaten with salt, and stirred into rice. Fresh ones are imported in the summer months and so are readily available in Persian and some Middle Eastern shops – but they the most fiendishly fragile of fruits and require great care when handling. To use, it is best firstly to lower them gently into a tub of cold water – it is thus easy to separate the stalks and leaves, which will float to the top. They freeze beautifully, and can be used straight from the freezer. Try dropping some into your favourite cocktail, or using them as an unusual frozen sweet garnish. If you cannot source them, morello cherries are a fair substitute.

Oh-my-God-how-many-relatives-did-we-invite-for-dinner? Pudding

امشب مامان میهمان زیادی داریم

When you feel a flutter of joy inside, water it. And when it bears fruit, offer it to your friends.

Rumi

We English have perhaps lost our childlike delight in ice-cream sundaes. An increasingly sophisticated and health-conscious eating public is no bad thing, but it would be a shame if the knickerbocker glory and banana split of my youth became the quaint pudding anachronisms of the future. So I was delighted when Jamshid's aunt Tahereh first served me her take on them. Since then I have been to many Iranian homes, and invariably it is some sort of jelly/ice-cream configuration which is wheeled out as dessert.

Iranians love jelly and ice-cream. Persian recipe books (the ones actually in Persian that is) are full of creative things to do with jelly and we import for the shop some wonderful 'ready-to-make' jellies – with pomegranate and quince flavours amongst others. As I have nightmares about gelatine, I am not going to tell you how to make a good jelly from scratch, but rather how to assemble a jolly decent dessert for lots of (invariably unexpected) people.

Step One

Make sure that you always have things like ice-cream (2 different colours, preferably), and packet desserts – jelly or Angel Delight – and sauces and toppings in your freezer or pantry; and fruit in your fruit bowl.

به سبک جدید

Step Two

This should be done as soon as you put the 'phone down after Aunt so and so's announcement that they'll 'be there in an hour and of course they don't want to stay for dinner, it would be far too much trouble.'

First of all you should get one of the easy one-pot *khoreshts* from Chapter Five on to cook. Once that is bubbling nicely, make up some jelly (or instant whip) and put it in the freezer to set rapidly.

Step Three

As soon as the washing-up is in the sink, assemble your ingredients. We are going to offer our guests a fully fledged ice-cream parlour. They will leave delighted by the realization of just how much fun you can have with food, and refreshed by this therapeutic dip into kiddieville.

In a range of pretty dishes, assemble as many of the following as possible:

dry ingredients:
chopped/nibbed nuts (pistachios are great)
dried fruit – chopped apricots, raisins, sultanas, chopped dates, figs
crumbled cookies or crushed cereal
silly sweeties – jelly drops, liquorice allsorts, smarties etc.
wet ingredients:
alcohol of choice – Kahlua, Amaretto, Midori or other liqueurs all
     work well (assuming guests are non-Muslims, non-children)
chocolate, butterscotch or fruit sauce
honey, date or carob syrup
canned fruit – cherries, sliced peaches, mandarins, Greek canned figs
and the jelly/whip
last minute:
whipped cream
tubs of ice-cream
fresh fruit – anything you like, just make sure you cut it into
     manageable slices/chunks

Step Four

Tell your guests to dive in. None but the most organized household has a row of glistening ice-cream coupes in their sideboards, so I usually use a mix of drinking glasses. It may be best to do the first one for them:

Swirl a little sauce around the inside of the glass, bit of fruit and jelly in the bottom, and then layer away to your heart's content. The secret to success is having enough serving spoons. If the idea of this free-for-all sugar scrum alarms you (as it most certainly would an Iranian housewife), well, you can do it all for them in the sanitized surroundings of your kitchen, but they won't enjoy it nearly as much.

On unexpected guests

A kinsman from the countryside came to visit Mullah Nasruddin bearing the gift of a duck. Nasruddin was very pleased, had it cooked, and sat down to enjoy a fine meal with his relative. Presently there was a knock at the door, and a friend of the relative strolled in; he was followed by another friend, and then a friend of the friend. The duck was swiftly finished.

The next day further friends of friends turned up on and off during the day to enjoy the Mullah's hospitality, until the mild-mannered Mullah could bear it no more. He sat his guests in a row, and gave them each a bowl of water, meeting their quizzical gazes with the explanation that 'this is the soup of the soup of the duck that the friend of your friend brought'.

In Britain, we plan to entertain, we choose our guests, we devise a menu, we state a time of arrival and often surreptitiously hint at a time for departure. And then, after a suitable interval, we expect a return invitation. Every man's home is his castle, and the drawbridge is kept pretty much raised during unscheduled visiting hours.

Iranian society has a quality about it which is possibly best described

به سبک جدید

as 'contrived spontaneity'. Iranian doors are always open. Invitations are never refused and guests are never turned away. Entertaining visitors is in fact often initiated by the visitors themselves, who will present a very minor reason for visiting; the intended host will then engage them in an exchange laced with *taruf*, which at the very least will result in the guests staying for a meal, but quite often staying the night as well. Even though the Mullah's guests in the tale above were amazingly *pourou* (pushy), he was unable to turn them away outright. The guest will always protest that he must leave, that he couldn't possibly stay for dinner, let alone anything further – but both the host and the hosted know that this is a game with a foregone conclusion. Hence every Iranian home keeps rolls of spare bedding, extra slippers, and piles of baggy Kurdish house trousers. Guests can and do make themselves totally comfortable and, without any compunction, become quite assimilated into the household. The prosaic concerns of the English hostess – not enough beds, who to put next to whom at the dinner table, who can 'bunk up' with whom at night, not enough matching hand-towels, one short on the Dartington crystal, and 'deary-me it's raining, what on earth are we going to do with them all day?' – would not even figure in the Iranian equation of hospitality. Iranians are very happy to eat on the floor, and likewise to sleep on bed-rolls in rows on the floor. And even if the television of a Persian household is nearly always on and loud, they entertain themselves with even louder chatter (perish the thought that the telly gets turned down), games (backgammon and cards) and storytelling. If they do stray towards bored, they will often undertake little projects for you (not necessarily of your choice). Every Iranian man fancies himself as a *mohandes*, or engineer, and so feels compelled to fix, fiddle and re-organize things (the Iranian's spiritual home in the diaspora is Ikea). Lady guests vary from the saintly (once, three days after a particular lady guest had departed, I found all my mending had been done), to the alarming (try a haircut against one's will because it would be rude to say no). To an outsider, it feels like utter chaos, and to the unaccustomed hostess, it often involves crisis management. But

the sense of achievement after successfully hosting your first three-day house-party for 30 offers a pretty big high.

Iranians entertain as happily and naturally as they breathe, and at times they can leave the Westerner feeling pusillanimous, inadequate and plain mean. To summarize, an Iranian home is not about the décor, and even poor cooking can be excused (as long as there is enough food), it is just about warmth and love.

به سبک جدید

Rose Sorbet with Tongue Wafers

Traditional Iranian sorbet, *faloodeh*, is a very strange dish for the uninitiated, a very delicately flavoured water ice, oh-so-lightly infused with
rose-water and bound with vermicelli. Iranians usually pour a little lime
juice on top, and eat it neither between courses nor as a sweet but purely
as a summer refresher. Our ice-cream manufacturer, Mr Moghadam,
uses broken Chinese rice noodles when he makes his *faloodeh*, so if you
want to be very authentic, you could break some into this sorbet at the
egg-white stage. Personally, I loathe the vermicelli thing.

The tongue wafers or *zabun* are Iran's favourite *chirinee* – and they
couldn't be simpler. They are a light puff pastry with a coconut glaze.

for the sorbet:
175g sugar
425ml water
juice of 1 lemon
110g rose petals (you can use fresh, but dried are readily available
    and easier)
2 tablespoons rose-water
pink colouring (optional)
2 egg whites
for the wafers:
250g pack frozen puff pastry (defrosted)
100g icing sugar
1 tablespoon coconut milk or water
½ teaspoon vanilla essence
1 tablespoon rose-water
2 tablespoons desiccated coconut
1 tablespoon finely chopped pistachios

غذا های مخصوص ایرانی

Heat the sugar and water together until the sugar has dissolved, and then add the lemon juice. Bring to the boil and simmer for 5 minutes. Next put the rose petals in a bowl (reserving a few for garnish), and pour the syrup over them, stirring well before setting aside to cool. Once cold, put the mixture through the blender, and then add the rose-water and the colouring if using. Pour into a freezable container, cover and place in the freezer. Just before it sets, bring it out and give it a good stir. Beat the egg whites until stiff, and fold these into the mixture, and then re-cover and freeze until solid.

To make the *zabun*, roll out the puff pastry to a thickness of about 5–10mm, and cut into 'tongue' shapes of around 3cm width, and 6–7cm length. Cut a slit of 3cm through the length of each. Beat the icing sugar with the milk, rose-water and vanilla essence. Brush each tongue with the glaze, and then place them on a baking tray with a gap of a couple of centimetres between each one. Cook on gas mark 6/200°C for around 10 minutes or until risen and nicely coloured. Mix the desiccated coconut and chopped pistachio on a plate, and while the 'tongues' are still hot and sticky, dip the top of each briefly into the mixture so that a little clings to each. Put on a wire rack to cool.

Bring the sorbet out of the freezer a little before you want to serve it – this is not a soft-scoop recipe. Serve two scoops of sorbet per person, garnish with a *zabun*, and sprinkle with the remaining rose petals.

Persimmons Filled with Spiced Cheese

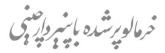

As for so many people, my first time with a persimmon was rough. It took me years of avoidance and fear before I ventured down that road again. For the uninitiated, let me explain. There are two types of persimmon, and the meltiest-in-the-mouth one (usually found in Persian/Middle Eastern shops) has, until it is ripe, a mouth-numbing skin which feels like a nasty case of anaphylaxis. The first contact is not easily forgotten. The other type (the one you will usually see in the supermarkets) is quite safe. If the skin is tough, you can just peel it and eat it: but you will not scale the peaks of taste euphoria. I have to say that thanks to my general re-education in the fruit department by my family-in-law, I have now become a persimmon hog. The first case of the season which we import is mine, all mine. Once these tongue-tingling monsters are ripe, they taste like ambrosia (I haven't actually tasted real ambrosia, you have to understand, but they are awfully like a custard of the same name). The secret is to wait until the skin becomes so soft it looks ripe to explode. The pulp is great in salsas and ice-creams, but I enjoy them most using this very simple recipe.

To summarize, whichever variety you use for this dish, make sure they are very soft and ripe. This will serve 6 people.

6 large ripe persimmons (or 12 small)
¼ teaspoon allspice
½ teaspoon each of ground cinnamon and ground ginger
¼ teaspoon ground cardamom
1 level tablespoon icing sugar, sieved
zest of 1 lemon
250ml fromage frais
1 dessertspoon each nibbed pistachios and almonds

Wash the fruit gently, and then carefully cut off its 'hats', retaining them as lids. Scoop out the soft pulpy centre of each fruit, and either chop it very finely or whizz it in the blender. Mix in the spices, icing sugar and lemon zest, and then fold the whole thing into the fromage frais. Finally, stir in the nuts and then spoon the mixture back into the hollowed-out persimmon skins. Set the fruity hats back on top, cover them and chill very well. If you are in a hurry, pop them in the freezer for half an hour.

Other weird fruit and weird fruit lore

Among the other weird seasonal stuff we import, there are some which I feel compelled to mention, not by way of evolving them into a recipe, but simply because if you see them in a Persian shop, you will know about them. Most Iranian produce is organic although, as there is currently no reciprocal arrangement with Iran, we are not allowed officially to call it thus. It comes in all higgledy-piggledy, unsorted and often very ugly. The seasons for these fruits are woefully short. If you see it, buy it – it probably won't be there next week.

Summer fruit to look out for includes:

❀ Rose apples: tiny, rose-scented apples. Two or three mouthfuls and they've gone; so fragile that they bruise even when you look at them.
❀ Baby pears: no more than 5–6cm long with a delectable fragrance.
❀ Squashed peaches: sweet and juicy and, well, flat.
❀ *Khaysi*: God's own apricots, imbued with the taste of honey and full of juice – the softer and uglier they get, the more divine the flavour.
❀ *Kharbozeh*: Iranian melons with the texture of cucumber and a memorable honied sweetness. There are two types – one is yellow

به سبک جدید

and shaped like a rugby ball, its hard skin protecting it against life's harder knocks and the other, from the northern town of Mashhad, is striped green, with a soft skin. This is the juicier of the two.

And then there's water-melon...

There is a wonderful tale of how Mullah Nasruddin went to market one day and bought a great quantity of victuals for his family. His friends were amazed to see him setting off for home astride his donkey, struggling to carry two water-melons, one in each hand. When they asked him why he did not strap these to the creature's back, he replied that he thought that the donkey had enough to bear, what with his own weight and the weight of his other purchases, and so the least he could do was to carry the fruit himself.

Suffice to say that this fruit occupies a prominent part in the nation's affections. Whilst it is rarely imported from Iran (we usually sell melon from Cyprus, which I think probably the best available in Britain), it is hugely popular. Uunless you are into 'mud, glorious mud', there is nothing quite like it for cooling the blood. At the first sign of a heatwave, Iranians tuck in to this most refreshing of Allah's creations – and do they eat a lot of it. It has practically no calories, and slips down very easily. The British tend to be conservative about consumption of healthy stuff (although we eat rubbish in great quantity), so in case you are a relative newcomer to water-melon, here are a few melon enhancing ideas with which to play:

* ❁ make a salad of cubed water-melon, feta or goat's cheese, mint and black olives;
* ❁ make water-melon gazpacho by blending de-seeded melon, and then adding chopped chilli, salt and pepper and chilling well: serve with croûtons of finely diced red onion, ditto red pepper, ditto cucumber; add ice cubes if desired;

❀ make a water-melon salsa with diced vegetables of your choice, raspberry or apple vinegar and chilli – serve with grilled or cold meats or smoked fish;

❀ purée the de-seeded flesh in a blender; add rose-water, a sprinkle of sugar and lots of ice for a great summer smoothie.

Orange Sorbet with Sweet Minted Lettuce

This is one classy pudding. It cleans the palate like nothing else I have ever tasted and leaves you feeling invigorated, even after an indecently heavy meal. For 4 people you will need:

900ml orange juice
3 tablespoons honey
5 tablespoons lemon juice
1 tablespoon orange zest
1 teaspoon lemon zest
handful fresh chopped mint (and a few whole sprigs for garnish)
handful fresh chopped sweet basil
8 tablespoons sekanjabin *syrup (see p. 232)*
8 pretty romaine or cos lettuce leaves, washed and dried

Heat about a third of the orange juice with the honey until the latter is quite dissolved. Add it to the rest of the orange juice in a freezer-proof container, and stir in the lemon juice, zest and herbs. Once it is quite cool, cover it and freeze, bringing it out for a good churn after half an hour. It is a good idea to bring it out of the freezer 10 minutes before you wish to consume it.

To serve, place two converging lettuce leaves on each plate, and range a couple of scoops of the sorbet in the middle of the plate. Drizzle a spoon of the syrup over each leaf, and then garnish the sorbet with mint sprigs.

نارنج

غذاهای مخصوص ایرانی

CHAPTER TEN

منجات

CAKES AND BISCUITS

Tea-time

This phrase is a misnomer in the context of this book, as in Iran every time is tea-time. It truly is the national drink and Iranians leave us British standing when it comes to both consumption and proper handling of this revered beverage. It is drunk heavily sweetened to accompany bread and cheese for breakfast; it is consumed as a thirst quencher throughout the day; served to guests on their arrival anywhere; and quaffed after lunch and evening meals. Most homes and businesses keep a samovar on the go throughout the day ever-ready to issue yet another cup (see Chapter Twelve).

This section, then, is dedicated, if not to vicarage tea-parties at ten to three, at least to the sort of sweetmeats which go rather nicely with a cup of *chai*. Anytime.

And this is an area where the Persians excel. One of our biggest selling products on the import front is *chirinee* (literally just 'sweets'), which has come to refer to a specific range of perhaps twenty to thirty pastries and cookies. It is difficult bringing them from Tehran three times a week, but they are phenomenally popular: it seems that nothing else so conjures the flavour of home.

Khastegari – Persian match-making

Among the people of Persia, 'the marrying of their children is considered a sacred duty...an unmarried man is considered the most wretched of

283

beings. He is compared to a bird sitting on top of a bush and not knowing where to fly,' writes Joseph Knanishu (*About Persia and its People*, 1899). Things haven't really changed that much, and even methods of match-making remain delightfully old-fashioned. Let's just get this straight, we are not talking about arranged marriages here, but rather facilitated betrothals. The parents of a young lad or lady in Iran will still today be on constant lookout for a suitable partner for them. They will usually look to friends of the family, or even distant family itself. As soon as a likely match is determined, the couple are introduced to each other informally (although it is quite often the youngsters who have initiated the pairing), and if everything seems hunky-dory, the family of the young man goes *khastegari* to ask the bride's family to give her hand in marriage. This is an extremely formal and difficult occasion, with a lot of pride at stake on the part of the groom, and a lot of blushing to be done by the bride. But what fun! Quite often, the answer is no. In cases where it is simply the groom's family who have taken a shine to a particular girl without her previous acquaintance, or there is more than one suitor involved, things can get quite complicated.

A lot of young Iranian men living 'in exile' are happy to return to Iran when it comes to trying to find themselves a partner. It can be very hard trying to find a mate in the competitive, fast-moving Western world, whereas in Iran they will be treated seriously and with respect, and a certain graciousness pertains to the affair. Their contact with the Western world will ensure them a good match – although Iranians are very scathing about life in the West, they are still quick to recognize the advantages that life there would have for their offspring. The only drawback with this arrangement is that a young bride is then often whisked off to the States or Britain with barely a smattering of English, after a whirlwind 'romance' which leaves her in the hands of a man she may fancy, but barely know. It is an awfully big adventure.

I have to say that as a routinely liberated 'Western' female, I whole-heartedly approve of this match-making. It is gentle, sporting, and carried out with great care and consideration. Relationships founded

غذاهای مخصوص ایرانی

this way prove to be durable and the couples involved are invariably compatible. And it means that no-one needs to be 'left on the shelf' – there is someone for everyone.

It is on occasions like this, the *khastegari*, that standards of hospitality are of the utmost importance – if the bride to be is 'in' on the purpose of the visit she will be very anxious to impress her mother-in-law to be, who in turn will watch her like a hawk. Usually the event is in the afternoon, but it could equally be in the evening. At the very least, fruit and tea and sweets will be served.

به سبک جدید

Noon Pangareii – Window Wafers

These are basically Persian waffles. Waffles with holes in, like a window.
Except they are much lighter and more fragrant than the Belgian-style
asking-to-be-covered-in-cream job. And they are very pretty. In Iran
there are special, patent window-effect moulds which are like French
waffle irons – pretty shapes on the end of a metal rod. But you can
improvise with a slotted metal serving spoon, or even a slotted metal
kitchen slice – just make sure that whatever you use has a fairly long
handle so you don't burn yourself.

In Iran they are made with starch, but cornflour is more readily
available and easier to work with.

> *120g cornflour*
> *1 tablespoon rose-water*
> *4 egg yolks, beaten*
> *1½ tablespoons plain flour*
> *175ml milk*
> *few drops vanilla essence*
> *75g icing sugar*
> *1 level teaspoonful ground cardamom*
> *oil for deep frying*

Pop the cornflour into a bowl, and stir in the rose-water and milk. Add
the egg yolks, flour and vanilla essence. Whisk so that a smooth batter
is achieved. Drop a droplet of batter into the oil to make sure it is hot
enough – it should sizzle and solidify immediately. Heat the waffle iron
(or other suitable metal implement) in the oil, and then dip it into the
batter (making sure that it is not completely coated otherwise your
wafer will simply not slip off it when cooked) and plunge it back into

the oil again. As they cook the 'windows' should slip easily off the iron, and you can then turn them over. Once they are golden in colour, remove the waffles from the oil and drain them on kitchen paper. Repeat this exercise until all the batter mix has been used up. When they are all cooked and cooled, sieve the icing sugar and cardamom together. Arrange the wafers on a plate, and dredge the top with the spiced icing sugar.

In Iran these cakes are served as a tea-time confection, but they are such a fun shape that the cleverer cooks among you will, I am sure, find a way of incorporating them into some sort of ice-cream dessert.

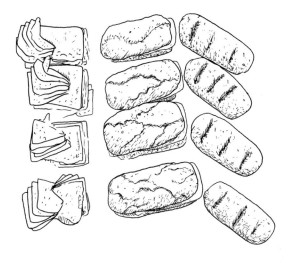

به سبک جدید

Saffron Cookies

Chirinee Keshmeshee (raisin sweets, usually with saffron) are one of the best selling biscuits that we import – they are very light melt-in-the-mouth-oh-alright-then-I'll-just-have-one-more type of cookies. Try as I might, I have been unable to recreate exactly the same product here. Shortcomings of this sort are usually ascribable to fats and oils used, or the water – the words bad, workman and tools spring to mind – but I have devised this recipe as a fair approximation of the down-town Tehran thing. Some of my 'inspiration' comes from an old Essex recipe – Essex and Iranian cuisine actually have quite a lot in common. Both regions feature the barberry, extensive use of saffron, and heavy use of fruits. Trust me on this. I admit it – I *am* an Essex girl.

> *75g butter*
> *350g self-raising flour*
> *75g castor sugar*
> *50g raisins*
> *½ teaspoon caraway seeds*
> *1 egg*
> *150ml milk*
> *few strands saffron, and some ground and steeped in boiling water*

Firstly rub the butter into the flour with the tips of your fingers. Then stir in the sugar, raisins and caraway seeds. Whisk the egg, saffron strands and cooled saffron water into the milk, and gradually stir the liquid into the flour mixture to make a firm dough. Roll the dough out and cut out circles with a pastry cutter. Place on greased trays, then brush each with a little milk. Bake at gas mark 6/200°C for 15–20 minutes; they should look a really pretty shade of golden yellow. Allow to cool on racks.

The story of *Zoolbia-e-Bamya*
Iran's favourite cakes

Let's face it – it is the cakes that draw most people into Persepolis. Nearly everyone knows about *baklava* and her naughty Middle Eastern cousins. They go by different names in different places, but every land east of the Hellespont and west of the Hindus has them. There you are, strolling along minding everybody else's business in true eastern style, when suddenly you'll spot them, winking at you from some alluring pâtisserie window and that's it, you're smitten. These brazen little numbers are the undoing of many a waistband and diet. I am afraid that we too leave them lurking in full public view to tempt the weak and ensnare the willing. The Persian cookies and pastries which we import twice-weekly are barely more virtuous. And recently we have started stocking Persian cream cakes.

These may all evoke an 'ooh!', but rarely an 'ooh-er'. No, to elicit *that* reaction, and for the height of depravity, we need to look to *zoolbia-va-bamya* – Persian honey cakes. Little balls of batter made with yoghurt, deep fried and drenched in syrupy honey: six squillion calories, but scrumptious. The *zoolbia* part of it comes in the form of cobweb-shaped threads, and clearly either lent its name to or took its name from the *djelabi* so popular in Indian cuisine. *Bamya* are fluted, dumpy little fingers, just like ladies fingers (okra), which are also called *bamya* in Farsi. But enough of the etymology, very few people are actually aware of the origin of the sweets themselves. So, if you're sitting comfortably.

Once upon a chai glass, when Persepolis was still a New Town, and long before the Greek hoodlum Alexander came along and spoilt everything, there was a noble vizier called Feridun, whose honour it was to wait upon the ruler of the day, the great King Darius XXV. The two had actually played together as children and remained close, despite the differences in their status and the fact that Darius had a bigger horse, more slaves, more maidens

The Simorgh.

in his entourage, an entourage in the first place, more money, oh, and half the known world at his feet. Feridun was a tad envious. But he was not as vindictive as those scheming courtiers of other genie tales, and resigned himself to a life of modest comfort and moderate recognition.

In time, Darius acquired a Mrs Darius, and Feridun found himself a Mrs Feridun, and they started to think about producing little baby ancient Persians. Thus King Darius brought forth Prince Jamshid, a blonde and blue-eyed darling of a child, bright beyond his years and a fine and fitting heir. If a mite precocious. And the Feriduns gave birth to Zhaleh, a girl. Now I'd like to report that Zhaleh was the cutest little blossom, with ringlets and a rosebud mouth, a bundle of sheer joy for her folks. But that would not, alas, be true. She was a bright and happy child, but there was no way she would win Miss Nowrooz 513BC (or any other year, for that matter). She was plump, plain, and just so clumsy. 'Nice personality' got you even less far then than it does now. Still, just as their fathers had been close before them, Jamshid and Zhaleh played together. They were both fiery and imaginative

little souls, and whilst they did not have *doctors and nurses*, or *cowboys and indians* then, they did have that mountain of a hero, *Rostam*, and that fabled feathered wonder, the *Simorgh*. As they recreated these legends of old, the pair forged an extraordinary understanding – they became inseparable, soulmates. And Zhaleh also became rather attached to her alter-ego, the Simorgh. When no-one else was listening, she would address the bird, and adopted it as her imaginary friend.

Now when Zhaleh was just four, her parents begat another child, a girl as pretty and graceful as Zhaleh was plain and gawky. And they called her Ziba, which means beautiful. By the time Ziba was four, she had already established herself firmly in the limelight; by the time she was six she had become a proper little *khanum*. Zhaleh had a good and pure heart and loved her sister unconditionally, but the behaviour of those around them made her very sad. She barely saw her beloved Jamshid as he was busy with trainee kingly duties and his parents, whilst they had been happy to entertain the young Zhaleh, were now trying to find him a more refined set of playmates. So at the grand old age of ten, she was on the shelf, neglected by her friend and, if not unloved, at least irrelevant to her family. This was really not the glorious, heroic existence of which she had dreamt. She decided to go and look for it elsewhere. One autumn morning before the sun had even stirred, let alone risen, she bundled up some *barberi naan*, cheese and fresh dates (which she had bought at the original Persepolis corner shop the previous day), and off she went. She was sad to leave as she knew her mother would find it hard to run the hut without her.

It was actually three weeks before anyone noticed Zhaleh had gone. Her mother noticed that there was rather a lot of washing-up in the sink. There was a small investigation, and a few tears were shed. It got a brief mention in the *Shiraz Evening Herald*, and there was a wee article about the dangers of letting kids read too

much epic poetry in *Persepolitan* magazine. And that was it, not another ripple. But no-one had told Jamshid.

Unknown to Zhaleh, she was being watched. While the Simorgh was a bit ruffled to find herself dismissed as a fable, she had nevertheless grown fond of her little protegée. So when Zhaleh decided to run away, the big bird followed her, swooping and soaring high and invisible above the clouds. By day, she guided the child, flapping her huge wings until the clouds, the breeze, everything moved in the direction she thought that Zhaleh should take: and by night she stood invisible guard over the sleeping maiden.

Thus it was that our heroine was surreptitiously wafted to Kermanshah and the doorstep of the home of the great Samadi, a wise and wealthy, ageing (and conveniently childless) philanthropist. This gentleman took one look at the bright and curious, if somewhat bedraggled little girl, and took her in. No amount of prompting would persuade Zhaleh to divulge her story, but as the days, then weeks, then months went by, she made herself so useful that she became quite a fixture, and people stopped asking about her past. Her mornings were spent either helping the housekeeper, chatting and giggling and doing girl-stuff or, joy of joys, with the chef, mixing and stirring, tasting and adjusting, and assimilating all the knowledge she could. The afternoons were spent with Aga Samadi, sometimes playing, sometimes chatting, always learning. And in the evenings, the house filled with people. On the one hand, there were intellectuals, artists and mystics laughing and debating and, on the other, the poor and needy, gathering for a feast of goodwill and good food. There were times when she would go quiet and think far-away thoughts of her very own Rostam, but then with a little 'Tut', she would swiftly pull herself together. Life was good. They thought she was pretty. They tolerated the clumsiness. And she felt relevant.

As she grew, she was increasingly drawn to the kitchen. Chef was getting older, and he was only too delighted to have such a

SOON THE DEMAND FOR HER COOKING
WAS SO GREAT THAT SHE HAD TAKEN
ON A TEAM OF STAFF OF HER OWN
AND ONE BY ONE SHE TRAINED
THEM AND SET TREM UP
IN BAKERIES AROUND THE
PROVINCE...

young and fragrant apprentice. By the time Zhaleh was fifteen, she was more or less running the kitchen. She had a sure touch with herbs and spices, and had even planted her own herb garden in one of the courtyards of the house. Her kebab-nights became a highlight of the Kermanshah social calendar. But it was with bread and baking that her real ability lay. Her fingers possessed such a magic, a deftness, that even as she kneaded dough or stirred batter, the aroma was mouth-watering. Soon the demand for her cooking was so great that she had taken on a team of staff of her own, and one by one she trained them and set them up in bakeries around the province, each with their own fleet of delivery donkeys.

All the while the Simorgh kept an eye on her, biding her time. And for her part, Zhaleh still talked to her imaginary fluffy friend;

the thought that there might be a powerful feathery godmother looking out for her gave her a warm glow inside, even if it was a ridiculous idea. She was dismissive of the fact that she sometimes seemed to feel the brush of feathers against her cheek, or hear a flapping sound just behind her when the winds were high. 'Too much daydreaming,' they'd said when she was a little girl. Maybe they were right.

One evening, as she was whisking some experimental sour batter for omelettes, she accidentally dropped some in the hot oil sizzling over the fire in the kitchen. Crossly, she reached for a spoon to scoop it out, and as she did so she noticed it had started to assume the prettiest colour and had risen to the surface. As she lifted it from the oil, she rather daftly reached to touch it, and recoiled in pain, dropping the little golden blob into her preserving syrup. This was becoming very irritating. Cooling her seared fingers in a pitcher of water, she reached for a clean spoon and fished out the now dripping batter-ball. How pert and appetizing it looked. No-one was watching her, so she crammed the whole thing into her mouth, and ohmigosh it was good! Swiftly she repeated the exercise, and soon she had cooked off a whole batch of these novel sweets. As she worked, she thought of Jamshid, and wondered where he was – and with whom. Surely by now they had found him a proper little princess to provide a suitable consort. Maybe he was actually married, with children. The thought was too awful to bear and she found herself drifting off into the fantasy world she had recently begun to create, a world in which Rostam forsook all that was being laid before him and ran off in search of his childhood sweetheart. As she gazed out at the night sky and the moon, she thought she saw some of the stars twinkling just that little bit brighter. Surely she was imagining things.

Overhead, the Simorgh circled slowly. Her friends on the night-sky management sub-committee steering group had

come through for her. The stars were ranged perfectly for her purposes.

Zhaleh turned back to the tray of glistening confections she had just created, and started to fill the piping bag with the last of the mixture. The moonlight streamed over her shoulder, and a bird called mysteriously in the scented night air. As she bent over the cooking pot once again, she saw that same configuration of stars reflected in the now-still oil. This time, she knew she was not imagining it. Furthermore, they were twinkling in a weird but vaguely familiar sequence, one after the other. What did this mean? She grasped the piping bag and began to trace out the pattern they had formed, moving from one reflected star to another as each grew brighter in turn. Again and again she piped out this pattern, until she had finished the mixture. Now she had a whole tray of wispy little shapes, joined dots leading A to B, seeker to the finder, the soured to the sweet, and...... Suddenly she recalled where she had seen the shape before: Persepolis to Kermanshah. The map of her exodus from the capital and her subsequent journey was forever etched somewhere in her cortical pathways. She had cooked up a map, the route home, the path which her beloved should follow on his quest to reclaim his lost love. 'Zud bier!' she exclaimed (although in the thick Kermanshah accent which she had acquired it came out more as 'Zoolbia'), 'Come soon!' She nestled each one of the blobs which she had first produced like fingers (*bamya*) on top of each one of the little maps, pointing the way, beckoning. Zhaleh smiled broadly and cooed a gentle thank you into the whispering, fluttering shape of the night outside.

She rushed a tray of the new delicacies up to Aga Samadi, who still had a few of his cronies from the Hamadan debating league lingering over their *chai*. They agreed that there was no debate – the cakes were the bestest thing that they had ever tasted. The old man raised an eyebrow at her flushed cheeks

He just knew that she was out there somewhere...

and calm radiance, but said nothing. None of his wisdom or worldly experience had prepared him for the conundrum that was a teenage girl. Zhaleh had slimmed down and grown up, and her kindness and serenity imbued her with a grace and beauty that were a talking-point the length of the bazaar. Heads turned and knees shook as she went on her daily rounds. All Aga Samadi knew was that he was glad of the instinct that made him take her in all those years before.

The next morning, Zhaleh called a meeting of her branch manageresses, and soon the whole chain had gone into producing the new sweets. The names *Zoolbia* and *Bamya* stuck and Zhaleh let just the whisper of a rumour escape that the whole thing was based on a treasure map. The good folks of the town could not get enough of the cakes and queued from early in the morning

to secure their daily portions. It was not long before the whole province, nay the whole country, were talking about the baking sensation of Kermanshah.

Meanwhile, back at the palace, Jamshid had grown in stature, had legs like the sturdy mountain rowan, hair all wild like the mane of Rasht, and a chest and arms as strong as the greatest heroes of old. If not yet a mountain of a man, he was at least a goodly sized hillock, and quite the most eligible bachelor in Persepolitan parts. Hordes of swooning maidens gathered where he roamed, and the court was busy with gossip as to whom he would choose as his trainee queen. Now nearly twenty, he was indeed a fine young chap, although mark my words he had been a right so-and-so as a young teenager, joy-riding camels and smoking behind the spear-maker's shed like a good-un. In latter years, he had come to rue his selfishness at not going to look for his truest friend, funny little Zhaleh, and not a day went by when he did not beat himself up over it. He knew that she was out there somewhere. Then he'd sigh a deep princely sigh, and pull himself together. His parents often wondered about these occasional flashes of whimsy on his part, but they were busy preparing to hand over to him and could not afford to have any doubts (they'd bought into a little time-share luxury tent complex in the north and were looking forward to an equable retirement).

Now most fairy tales would have the hero coerced against his better judgement into selecting some hot but brainless chick of the right breeding. This is no exception. Jamshid was dragged from hunt ball to polo-match and introduced to a hundred suitable fillies of appropriate stock. He grew so bored of the whole caboodle that his eyes would glaze at the merest flash of skirt, and the faintest hint of an inane giggle would send him out of the room. Even Ziba was paraded before him. She may not have had the breeding, but she had gone from being precocious to scheming mega-psycho-hellbitchdom and had insinuated herself

به سبک جدید

well at court. Jamshid was taken with her drop-dead-gorgeous looks, but her 'drop-dead-bitch' looks were something else. She was not in the running.

One day, as he was out carousing with some mates from the polo academy, he saw a swelling throng around his favourite kebab stall. Fearing a fight and mindful of his role as chief example-setter and protector of the meek, he rushed forward, drawing his sword, only to find that the attraction was a pile of mutant-looking cakes, cold ones in fact, although they were selling like hot ones. The sky darkened fleetingly as a large bird, no, surely a flock of birds, swept ominously overhead. When the citizens saw that it was no less than the heir to the throne who had joined them, they parted, bowing and scraping, as the stall-holder thrust a pack of the delicacies into the prince's hands. Intrigued, Jamshid ripped off the wrapper and sampled one each of the *zoolbia* and *bamya* (for that is what they were). Clearly impressed, he questioned the stall-holder as to their provenance, only to learn that they were really a bit of a mystery, but that rumour had it that it was a lover's map to guide her lost partner to her. He smiled at this child-like notion, and moved off with his chums, having nevertheless purchased two or three more trays of the mysterious confection.

Later that night, while attending the autumn coming-out ball, and after rather a lot of ruby-red Shiraz, he surveyed the bevy of beautiful, brainless debutantes and rose to his feet and motioned for silence. Then, swaying slightly but in fine voice, he proceeded to tell his parents and the assembled guests that the woman of his dreams was the girl who'd shared his dreams when he was a boy. There were gasps. Jamshid had never given any outward sign of pining for his playmate. If Zhaleh could not be found, then the only woman he would consider marrying was the creator of the *zoolbia* and *bamya* which he had tasted in the market that very day. By his albeit unfocussed reckoning, only a lady of virtue, dedicated to domestic matters, could produce food

غذاهای مخصوص ایرانی

of such technical brilliance; only a kind and warm soul could give the world a morsel so sweet and comforting; and only a creature of profound imagination and learning could create such a perfect marketing campaign. With that he swirled around and, colliding only briefly with the wall, exited left pursued by his startled friends.

The following morning, after several Bloody Maryams (why so surprised? the Persians invented vodka as well as wine), he set out on his quest. He shrugged off the protests of parents, courtiers and even the royal astrologer and vowed to journey alone. The *muralazzi* (muck was spread on walls then rather than on paper) were banned from following him. With a plentiful supply of *zoolbia* to guide him, he began to trace Zhaleh's steps of all those years ago.

His journey was smoothed of course by the legions of wee Persian folk (don't scoff – before the fairy population was decimated by widespread disbelief in the latter part of the twentieth century, the little people were very much part of everyday life), who'd been put on their best behaviour by our friendly Simorgh. The big bird observed his progress from a distance, smiling in a beaky sort of way in anticipation of a job well done.

Before Jamshid actually entered Kermanshah, the Simorgh had one last task to perform. That was to talk to the venerable Samadi, whom she had effectively set up with the task of raising Zhaleh. The old man should be warned, so that he could control the reunion, and he would surely be tickled by the whole story. As twenty-foot-long birds weren't common even then, she appeared to him in a dream. Aga Samadi could not have been more delighted at the prospect of such a perfect ending for what, on the whole, he considered to be a fairly badly written fairy tale. (He would agree to appear in a sequel only if he had a speaking part and was allowed to demonstrate his party trick involving the drinking horn and a camel.)

You'll get all misty if I describe the wondrous reunion between our bird-crossed lovers, the tears of joy that were shed, the luscious banquets and feasting which ensued, the years of happy marriage, the five children (plus two dogs and some truly cute Persian cats), the peace and prosperity which reigned over the land for the next century. As the credits begin to roll on this rosy scene, a few footnotes.

Ziba was cross at first at her sister's good fortune, but then went on the road with a girl-band called the Saffron Sisters. Later she married a renowned polo player, Davoud Becamian.

Feridun was to have had a bigger role in the original story, but he proved too pompous. He and the Missus settled down to a happy retirement out of the spotlight.

The Simorgh finally put in an appearance at the nuptials of Jamshid and Zhaleh. It was, after all, the wedding that legends are made of. And for a while the country felt young and indomitable again. Next time you feel a breeze behind you or hear a gentle rustling from above, you'll know she's out there, helping, fixing stuff, and that you are not alone.

Oh, I nearly forgot, the *zoolbia* and *bamya*. After her marriage, Zhaleh had little time to cook, and she passed the whole business on to the poor people of the land. Like *Big Issue*, all the profits went to the deserving. This wonderful notion did not survive for very long, but fortunately the recipe did At Persepolis we briefly revived the whole philanthropic concept. By selling this story alongside the sweets, we tried to help a modern day Simorgh in the guise of Camilla Batmanghelidjh and her Kids Company charity. Admittedly we didn't sell many stories, but they have been the beneficiaries of our nobler charitable efforts ever since.

غذاهای مخصوص ایرانی

Persepolis...the legend lives on. In Peckham.

Kids Company is a children's charity run by a very nice Persian lady called Camilla Batmanghelidjh. Put simply, she has taken it upon herself to help the most desperate, destitute and disenchanted youngsters in Peckham, Camberwell and Brixton, giving them hope, shelter and love. She does this using a unique formula of child-involvement, one-to-one counselling and tuition; and an all-embracing energy and compassion which dazzle all who meet her. She has an equally energetic and caring team of staff (some 38 of them now), and works not only directly with local kids, but through schools nationwide. The government is so impressed by her creation that they are looking at the possibility of creating similar networks elsewhere. That is not to say that Kids Company is getting anything like enough support. They were recently evicted from the railway arches in Camberwell where they had set up, and they are always grateful for every single penny which is raised for them.

به سبک جدید

Zoolbia and *Bamyeh* – Deep-fried Batter Cakes

زولبیا و بامیه

They use slightly different batters in fact, and so I have written them out as two distinct recipes (with another for the syrup). But they are rarely served apart.

Whilst I am a fairly hard-working girl, in truth I do not actually have time to sit up all night talking to the Simorgh and making cakes for our little emporium and so we buy ours from the very helpful Mr Amini, whose recipes you will find below.

> for the syrup:
> *1kg sugar*
> *500ml water*
> *2 tablespoons lemon juice*
> *4 tablespoons rose-water*

Place the sugar and the water in a saucepan, bring to the boil and simmer until the sugar has dissolved. Add the lemon juice, cook for a few minutes more and then take off the heat. Stir in the rose-water and then set aside.

> for the *bamya*:
> *200g plain flour*
> *200ml water*
> *2 tablespoons oil*
> *2 eggs*
> *oil for frying*

The first bit is like making profiteroles. Boil the water and oil together, and then stir in the flour, beating mightily as you go. Take the mixture off

the heat, and beat in the eggs. The resulting paste should be gloriously malleable and shiny.

Heat the oil to a temperature of around 190°C if using a deep-fat fryer, or until it looks hot if shallow-frying. If you are shallow-frying, you will still need at least 3cm of oil.

Spoon the mixture into a piping bag with a broad, crenellated nozzle and pipe into the hot oil in 2cm dollops. The resulting sausage shapes should indeed look like *bamya* or fingers. When they are cooked (i.e. golden brown), scoop them out with a slotted spoon and dip each one into the syrup before placing on a plate to cool.

> and for the *zoolbia*:
> *500g potato starch*
> *50g flour*
> *½ teaspoon bi-carbonate of soda*
> *½ teaspoon ground saffron (steeped in water)*
> *500g tub yoghurt*
> *125ml sour cream (optional, an extra 125g yoghurt will do)*
> *oil for frying*

Place the potato starch in a bowl, and then sieve the flour and the bi-carb on top. Mix gently. Blend the saffron with the yoghurt (and the sour cream if using), and whisk vigorously into the flour mixture. Cover and allow to rest for a while (an hour is good).

Heat the oil (as for the *bamya*, above). Spoon the mixture into a piping bag with a thin nozzle, and pipe spiral shapes into the oil (each should be about 5cm in diameter, although this is largely a matter of choice – I just happen to find this size easy to work with). Just as you reach the centre of each spiral, trail a little back out to the outside of the spiral so that all the strands are connected. Cook for less than a minute before turning with a spatula. As each swirl becomes golden brown, lift it out and plunge it into the syrup. Retrieve, and arrange prettily with the *bamya* snuggled alongside. Serve with lots of tea.

Saffron Fudge – *Sohan Assali*

This is pure evil, a sticky, greasy, utterly addictive confection that must in part account for the large number of Iranians studying dentistry. One in ten of our Iranian customers at Persepolis are dentists. I do not know how this compares with the figures in the rest of London, but it is a worrying trend. It is widely available in Iranian shops, but is actually very easy to make.

> *175g butter*
> *200g sugar*
> *2 tablespoons honey*
> *200g nibbed almonds*
> *100g nibbed pistachios*
> *2 teaspoons ground saffron, dissolved in a drop of boiling water*

Melt the butter in a saucepan, and then add the sugar and honey. Heat gently until the sugar melts, and then add the nibbed almonds. Stir occasionally until the almonds just start to change colour. Add the saffron, stir one last time and then take off the heat and set to cool. Once it is warm rather than hot, spoon on to a sheet of greased greaseproof paper. Traditionally, *sohan* is made in rounds of around 18cm, but for home use you may wish to make smaller ones. Whatever the shape, the mixture should be pressed into a thin layer (between 5mm and 10mm in depth), and then the nibbed pistachios can be sprinkled liberally on top. Leave it to cool completely (but not in the fridge), and then peel off the greaseproof paper. Store in a biscuit tin rather than a plastic container, as *sohan* 'sweats'. Serve with tea. Probably best to clean your teeth afterwards.

Persian *Baklava*

باقلوا ایرانی

Persian *baklava* is quite different from that of other nations. Every Arab and Balkan country has its own version – the combination of buttery pastry, honey and nuts is a kind of marriage made in Heaven (albeit a three-way one). I had a serious (Lebanese) *baklava* habit for the first couple of years that the shop was open but fortunately, in the case of sweetmeats you *can* have too much of a good thing.

But The Persian Version (this sounds like a Robert Ludlum novel) contains less butter and sugar and is instead infused with rose-water and cardamom, and sometimes saffron, and tastes overridingly of almond; in fact so strong is the almond flavour that it is reminiscent of marzipan. It is so rich that you cannot really eat it as a dessert, but rather as a tantalizing morsel to have with tea or coffee. It is astonishingly sticky, so unless you dislike your tea guests, serve with serviettes.

for the pastry:
6 sheets filo pastry
100g pulverized walnuts
200g granulated sugar
3 tablespoons melted, unsalted butter
1½ teaspoons ground cardamom
300g ground almonds
for the syrup:
200g sugar
6 tablespoons water
2 tablespoons rose-water
1 tablespoon honey
pinch ground saffron, steeped in boiling water (optional)
ground pistachios for garnish

به سبک جدید

Only very clever people with lots of time on their hands make their own filo pastry, so we assume that you will be using frozen filo. This stuff is very temperamental. Once you have extricated your 6 sheets, put the remaining pastry straight back in the freezer, and look after those 6 sheets by keeping them wrapped in a damp (clean) tea-towel until you're ready.

Mix the walnuts with 50g of the sugar, 1 spoon of the butter and ½ teaspoon of the cardamom. Mix the almonds with the remaining sugar, butter and cardamom.

Grease a large oven dish with a bit of butter and then ease one sheet of the filo across it, gently pushing it into the corners. Brush this sheet with a little oil or butter, and then lower another sheet on top. Spread the walnut mixture over this, and then another two layers of the pastry, brushing with oil between each layer. Next comes the almond mix. Spread it as evenly as you can, and then layer on the last two sheets of filo. Brush the top with more oil, and then with a sharp knife score through the pastry in lines 2cm apart. Next, score through the pastry diagonally to create small diamond shapes. Then flick a little water over the surface of the pastry (to stop it burning) before popping it in a pre-heated oven (gas mark 5/190°C) for half an hour.

Now make the syrup. Heat the sugar and water together for 10 minutes, then add the rose-water and the honey. After a couple more minutes, take it off the heat and stir in the saffron. When the *baklava* is cooked, remove it from the oven and drizzle the syrup all over it. Garnish with the ground pistachios, and leave to get quite cold (although it is also lovely eaten hot with ice-cream).

Almond is the most traditional filling, but you can substitute pistachios, more walnuts, cashews or any other nut of your choice.

Coconut and Walnut *Couloucheh*

These are popular and easy to make. They are basically macaroons, although that wonderful word *couloucheh* just means cookie. Given that children have to be allowed in the kitchen from time to time lest they turn into takeaway-junkies unable to boil an egg, these two are good 'My Fun To Cook Persian' standbys: simple, not too messy and good on what I call culinary magic (wherein a pile of unprepossessing goo turns into something surprisingly edible). They are often made together, which makes sense as one uses the egg yolks, and the other the whites.

The first recipe, for walnut *couloucheh*, known as *nan gurduee*, is straight out of Rosa Montazami's book; the second, for *narghili*, is courtesy of our baker in Tehran.

for the walnut cookies:
6 egg yolks
6 dessertspoons sugar
½ teaspoon vanilla essence
300g finely chopped (but not pulverized) walnuts

for the coconut cookies:
3 egg whites
300g sugar
250g shredded coconut
2 tablespoons potato starch
½ teaspoon vanilla essence

To make the walnut cookies, all you do is to whisk the egg yolks, sugar and essence together until the mixture turns very pale, then beat in the walnuts. Place a sheet of baking parchment on a baking tray, and spoon

2–3cm balls of the mixture 4–5 cm apart. Cook at gas mark 2/150°C for 20 minutes, and then place on a wire tray to cool.

For the coconut cookies, whisk the egg whites and half the sugar until stiff; fold in the rest of the sugar and the other ingredients. Line a baking tray with a sheet of baking parchment, and spread out the mixture in 3cm blobs 3–4cm apart. Bake on gas mark 2/150°C for 20 minutes, then place on a wire tray to cool.

Halwa

حلوا

Halwa is but the Arabic word for 'sweet', and every town, let alone each nation, across the Arab world seems to have a different understanding of the word, or a different recipe to fit it. It can be anything from sponge-cake to nougat – so travellers should be careful what they order. Of course in Europe we normally associate *halva* with the rich sesame confection made popular by the Greeks and Turks. This is available and popular in Iran, where it is known as *halwa konjedi*. But the simple word *halwa* in Iran implies a very different dish, a sweetened, roux-based paste offered usually upon the death of a loved-one or at a time of collective religious mourning (during the holy month of Moharram for example). It is always served with tea. I find it quite horrid, but as *all* Iranian women make it from time to time and it is so deeply embedded in their culture, it is not possible to omit it from a Persian cookery book. This is my mother-in-law's recipe.

> *250g sugar*
> *125ml water*
> *50ml rose-water*

½ teaspoon saffron steeped in boiling water or 2 teaspoons cocoa
   powder
250g butter or ghee
about 200g plain flour
nibbed pistachios or almonds (optional garnish)

Firstly, make the syrup by boiling the water and sugar together, then adding the rose-water and saffron if you have chosen to use that rather than cocoa. Heat the butter in a saucepan, and beat in the flour until the mixture is quite dry but will still form into a ball. Add the cocoa if that is your chosen flavour, then slowly pour in the syrup, stirring constantly, until you end up with a smooth paste. Press the paste (while still hot) into a thin layer on a plate (or several plates), and run some pretty patterns across the surface with a fork before sprinkling with nibbed nuts. Chill well. Either cut the *halwa* into bite-sized pieces, or serve with teaspoons so that people can help themselves as they drink their tea.

Mourning in Iran

Mourning is a visible and tangible part of Iranian society, and for the natives of a land which tries to sweep such inconvenient matters as death under the carpet, the 'in your face' grieving of an Iranian recently bereaved, or of a whole town during Moharram, the religious month of mourning, can be a shock. The martyrdom of so many during the Iran/Iraq conflict brought the dying business into sharper focus, but as Shi'ia Islam encourages laments for the departed, and the art-house face of Iran is generally that of black-chadored women, the overall impression is that of a fairly mournful country. This is actually not the case – the grieving process in Iran has a set framework and set conventions designed to curtail rather than extend the matter. The initial cathartic outpouring of grief (like many Middle Easterners, Iranians wail; it is

heart-rending and frightening to behold) lasts until the burial (within 24 hours). After a week, a wake (usually involving a meal) is held to which members of the family and neighbours will be invited. After 40 days, a graveside vigil of a few hours is observed, wherein it is supposed that one officially bids farewell to the departed and then, after a year, another gathering is held to commemorate the life of the deceased. This latter (at least amongst the wealthier Iranians) is quite often in the form of a meal offered for the less fortunate. Black is worn for a year by close relatives of the deceased, although the mothers of martyrs and widows of the older generation will commit to a lifetime of wearing black. After this year, the official mourning stops; a close relative will buy you a gift of coloured clothing to 'lead' you out of your grief. But it is not unusual for the bereaved to continue to make *halwa* every Friday, the holy day, or on anniversaries of a person's death by way of *fateh*, food eaten in remembrance. Iranian customers often bring in *halwa* or buy a box of dates from our shop, which they then leave on the counter for all customers to share. This is also a *fateh*.

Goosh-e-Fil – Elephants' Ears

I should here recount the little-known 1002nd tale of Scheherezade, wherein Allah forgot to give the elephant any ears and so the simple country maid Afsaneh, feeling sorry for the beast, fashioned some out of dough. Allah finally realized his omission, and was impressed by the elephant's forbearance; in recognition of this he gave the creature bigger and better ears than all others, not only for to hear, but to fan his great bulk and wave away pestilent flies. And Afsaneh, as a reward for her perspicacity, was deemed to be friend to all the animals; her fame

spread far and wide, and for her success at taming the wildest creatures, she came to the attention of the then Prince of Persia. They of course fell in love and opened a wildlife reserve and lived happily ever after, because that is what they do in fairy tales. The tale is commemorated both in the name and the shape of these puffy, triangular pastries.

Goosh-e-fil may either be dusted with spiced sugar or drenched in syrup.

> *3 sheets of filo pastry*
> *oil for frying*
> for the syrup:
> *100g sugar*
> *3 tablespoons water*
> *1 tablespoons rose-water*
> *1 dessertspoon honey*
> for the spiced dusting:
> *50g icing sugar*
> *1 level teaspoon ground cardamom*

Spread the first sheet of filo out on a clean surface; brush it with oil, place the second on top, and repeat with the third. Cut the pastry into triangular shapes (of perhaps 4cm sides), and crimp them at the edges. Drop into hot oil and fry until golden. Remove from the oil, and place on a wire rack to cool and drain.

To make the syrup, boil the water and sugar together, and then add the rose-water and honey. Drizzle over the elephants' ears while both the pastry and the syrup are still warm.

To make the drier *goosh-e-fil*, sieve the icing sugar and cardamom together, and dredge the pastry once it is quite cold.

به سبک جدید

The poet Ferdowsi.

CHAPTER ELEVEN

نوشیدنی ها

CHAPTER ELEVEN

DRINKS

The highest heaven is a fountain of kindness, a fountain of justice; beneath it flow four streams brimming with wisdom, the stream of milk, of eternal honey, of wine, and of water that flows away, the Tigris.

Rumi

So yes, they do drink a lot of other stuff besides the ubiquitous tea.

The Persians invented wine and vodka. The same creativity clearly came into play after the advent of Islam. To replace the wine so beloved of Khayam and Hafez, a huge range of *sharbat*s (sherbet or syrup) was evolved – fruits boiled and strained and bottled when in season, and then drunk with water or milk over ice. The Persians have a very good range of hot-weather drinks with all sorts of medicinal benefits.

Doogh

Kebabs are particularly good washed down with *doogh*, a salted, minted, *pétillant* yoghurt drink. This drink is utterly reviled by most first-timers; in fact it takes persistence to acquire a liking for the stuff, but it really is very moreish when you've overcome the initial shock to the taste buds. It is a wonderful drink for hot weather, as the water quenches, the yoghurt cools, and the salt replaces that lost through perspiration. Live yoghurt was traditionally consumed in Iran before proper hygiene was fully understood as it was known to have beneficial effects on the gut: it is still eaten widely and many housewives make their own.

Commercially, many companies use bicarbonate of soda to make the 'fizz', but there are several easier ways to make *doogh* at home. If you have a soda-stream machine this will help you achieve a very smooth drink, but using soda or sparkling mineral water is just fine. Use a very thick and creamy yoghurt, preferably live (no particular reason – its just better for you, that's all); a 500g tub will combine with 1 litre of liquid, although everyone has different preferences. Whisk the yoghurt and water together with 2 teaspoonsful salt and two teaspoonsful dried mint, or, better still, pennyroyal (a sort of poor man's mint, more like dust than dried leaves, but great for this drink). Garnish with fresh sprigs of mint (although making the actual drink with fresh mint can be a mistake as it quickly turns bitter, and does not infuse its flavour as well). Always serve over lots of ice. Rather nice with vodka.

Sharbat – Sherbets

These cordials were phased into the Iranian diet over a matter of centuries as their beloved wine was phased out. Even the name, *sharbat,* is but a couple of twisted letters away from *sharab*, the Farsi word for wine.

In fact alcohol never left the Iranian culture – it just hides its face. I should point out that it remains strictly illegal, with the death penalty in place for serial abusers. But home-made wine is quite the norm, and most upper-middle-class households in Iran are happy to offer guests wine or smuggled spirits (for which you can usually read Johnnie Walker whisky). There is a much-told urban legend that has it that when the state vodka distillery was razed to the ground, several million more were spawned. Home distilling of potato or rice vodka is common,

sometimes, of course, with disastrous results. Lack of proper knowledge can and does lead to blindness and death.

Anyway, back to our cordials. They are simply a great way to enjoy fruit. Most Iranian housewives that I have encountered make their own as a matter of course and as they are so easy to prepare, I really think that it is one kitchen habit we British could do with acquiring. I mean, have you tasted supermarket orange or any other squash recently? I accidentally had some not so long ago and was on my asthma inhaler for around half an hour thereafter. In Iran these *sharbat*s are diluted with water and served over lots of ice in hot weather. They are versatile drinks to have in your larder, as you can also use them in cocktails and as ice-cream sauces. You can of course make them with hot water as fruity winter-time cheerers.

As a general rule, use a non-stick or enamel pan for these cordials. Metallic pans can affect the flavour. You should sterilize your bottles first by pouring boiling water into them then emptying them out. Common sense dictates that once you have started on a sealed bottle, you should keep it in the fridge.

Mint and Cucumber Syrup

> As vinegar becomes more acid, sugar must grow sweeter.
>
> Rumi

I have already outlined the recipe for *sekanjabin*, mint syrup, in Chapters Nine and Ten, as it is mostly used in a culinary context. But I just love this variation – it is sooooo refreshing. And as Mr Rumi observes, very 'balanced' (see the section on *sardi/garmi* at the end).

To make the basic syrup you will need:

500ml water
700g sugar
8 tablespoons white vinegar
half bunch mint, roughly chopped
cucumber

Place the water in a pan, add the sugar and bring to the boil. Bubble for 10 minutes, remove from the heat and add the vinegar.

When it is a bit cooler, add the mint, a little extra water, and half to three-quarters of a cucumber, grated. Put in the freezer until nearly solid. Serve like a frappé – crush it into a glass, and dilute with a splash more water. Garnish with slices of cucumber and sprigs of mint.

Persian poetry

Apart from the fact that I am a girl and most girls dig poetry anyway, the reason that there are so many little snippets of poetry in this book is because the Iranians are widely credited with having invented the

stuff. It helps of course that Farsi is such a passionate and expressive language, while even in translation the great works can send shivers of appreciation down the spine.

During those heady, golden years (actually from around AD1000 to 1500) such a volume of equally heady, golden words was produced as to gush over into the literature of countries the world over. Thanks to great Victorian translators such as Fitzgerald, the works of Hafez and Omar Khayam have long been popular in England, and their influence profound. Here, perhaps, a special mention for Hafez (although in truth he was a bit of a lush). He occupies a unique place in the nation's heart as he wrote a *divan* – a poetical horoscope – to which people refer even today. The idea is that you ponder your problems and allow his book of verse to fall open, whereupon his lines, properly interpreted, will give you the answer you seek. (I know it sounds like something out of *Jackie* magazine, but it's very impressive.) In recent times, Rumi has become the darling of the literati (even Madonna agreed to speak on a recording of his verse), with his touchy-feely, ecstatic poems. But we (as a public at large) still know woefully little about this poetic goldmine. Very few people, for example, have ever heard of Ferdowsi, and yet in Iran he occupies the literary throne held in Britain by Shakespeare. For it was Ferdowsi who recorded the whole of Persian legend and the whole succession of Kings, and he did it in Persian, rather than Arabic, the scholastic language of the day. It took him 30 years, and he died in poverty, but he is fêted as a hero in his homeland now. And then there is Attar, whose *Conference of the Birds* is one of the greatest treatises on Sufism ever written; and Sa'adi (author of the famous *Gulistan*, or *Rose Garden*), whose wise words on equality are actually featured on a plaque at the United Nations: 'The children of Adam are limbs of one another and in their creation come from one substance. When the world gives pain to one member, the other members find no rest. Thou who are indifferent to the sufferings of others do not deserve to be called a man.'

To this day in Iran, poetry is enshrined in the hearts of the people as a viable means of expression; it is not confined to the gifted few.

A vast number of my customers are quite happy to admit that they write poetry; my mother-in-law writes poetry. There are a growing number of Persian jazz poets, and after a degree of struggle following the revolution, many Persian women poets are now making their voices heard. This is very much a living, vibrant genre in Iran

Lemon or Lime Cordial – *Sharbat Ab-Limoo*

This is a classic. I serve it in sugar-frosted glasses. My mother-in-law uses Persian bottled lime juice, which is very strong and pure having merely been pasteurized – but I prefer to use fresh.

> *750ml water*
> *600g sugar*
> *250ml lemon (or lime) juice (about 10 lemons or 14 limes)*
> *zest of 1 lemon*

Heat the water and sugar together in a pan until the latter is all dissolved. Add the lemon (or lime) and zest, and heat gently for around 10 minutes more. Leave to cool, bottle and seal.

Variations

To make *Sharbat Portoogahl* – orange cordial – use the same recipe, but replace half of the lemon juice with orange juice.

Another famous cordial, especially good in the winter, is *beh-limoo* – quince and lemon – you can make a really soothing hot toddy with this. Make it as above, adding 2 peeled, cored and diced quinces to the mixture along with the lemon. Cook gently for 25–30 minutes, and then

strain and squeeze through muslin or a clean tea-towel before bottling and chilling in the normal way.

Handy housewives' hint

My grandmother used to use citrus peel to seal bottles – a cleverly cut disc of zest (no pith) floated on the surface seems absolutely to prevent any unwanted 'must' forming. So now you know.

Rose Cordial

شربت گل سرخ

My favourite. I drink it with ice-cold milk, like the Greek *driandafilou*, but it is more usually diluted with water in Iran.

500g sugar
300ml water
50ml lemon juice
few drops pink food colour (optional)
150ml rose-water
25g rose petals (optional, but pretty)

Boil the sugar and water together. When the sugar has dissolved, add the lemon, colouring and rose-water and leave on the heat for another 5–10 minutes. Set aside. When it is nearly cool, stir in the rose petals, bottle and chill. This syrup and the following recipe are great as ice-cream sauces.

به سبک جدید

Sour Cherry Cordial – *Sharbat Albaloo*

The most famous of the lot. Morello cherries are ready substitutes for sour cherries.

> *1kg sour cherries*
> *500ml water*
> *2kg sugar*
> *1 teaspoon vanilla essence*

Stone and pick through the cherries, and wash them well.

Boil the water and sugar gently together; when the sugar has dissolved, add the cherries and bubble away for around 15 minutes. Strain through muslin (or a clean, non-fluffy tea-towel), stir in the vanilla essence and leave to cool. Bottle and seal.

Tea – *Chai*

Chai is not a type of tea, nor even a brand, as certain clever marketing campaigns would have you believe. It is just the eastern word for tea. Tea in Iran is quite a different affair from our own homogenized blends which we tend to drink with milk.

Surprisingly, black tea entered Iran fairly late in the proceedings. Before the nineteenth century, coffee was the beverage of choice. Green tea was consumed, but it was nowhere near as popular in Iran as in neighbouring countries such as Afghanistan. Black tea seems to have passed from its Chinese source to the Russians, and it was they who brought it to Iran. It swiftly took root, both literally on the shores of the Caspian, and metaphorically in the hearts of the people. Tea

is now consumed all day, every day, in every town and household of Iran, by everybody. It is the first thing you are offered when you visit someone's home, and it is consumed extensively in bazaar and office alike as part of the language of business. Nearly all workplaces and households have a samovar at their disposal, wherein water is heated in a large boiler (usually electric these days, although formerly reliant on a central coal chimney). Tea is made in a pot, which is rested on top of the samovar – the rising steam keeps the tea hot. The idea is that a little thick, strong brew is poured from the teapot into an *estekhan*, or tea glass, which is then topped up with water from a tap on the samovar, resulting in a mellow golden colour (as Persians drink black tea, it is essential to dilute it thus, as it would otherwise be unbearably strong). Assuming that water levels are topped up from time to time, and fresh tea leaves occasionally replace the stewed ones, the samovar can thus be kept running all day.

There are of course lots of different blends of tea. Apart from the homegrown variety, which is insufficient to cover home consumption, the favoured tea is from Ceylon. It is either consumed plain, or flavoured with Earl Grey or cardamom. There are occasional variations – sometimes jasmine, cinnamon or mint are mixed with the tea leaves or, more popularly, saffron (which is said to make you laugh: I believe it works).

To Make Persian Tea

Actually, there is nothing to it. You will need 1 heaped teaspoon of your tea leaves of choice per 2 tea drinkers. Put the tea in your pot (a teapot with a built-in strainer or tea receptacle is ideal), and then pour boiling water over the leaves. Try and keep the pot hot – in Iran quite often they will use a patent tea-stand with a candle underneath it. Steep for around 5 minutes, and then half-fill the relevant number of tea glasses with the brew, before topping them up with boiling water. Serve

with Persian sugar polyhedrons (a bit like cubes, only more interesting) which are strangely resistant to instant melting, although I assure you that they are water-soluble, or *nabat* (rock sugar). Sugar is rarely added to the tea, but rather the sugar is held on the tongue and the tea then drunk through it. Tea can also be served with fresh dates, *noghl* (sugar-coated nuts), or your choice of sweets. If you are offering a second round, just top the pot up with some more boiling water. As the tea gets progressively more stewed, you will need to add more and more water, and thus less and less black tea.

The tea house

To me, the most exciting thing about the Persian tea culture is the tea house or *chai khaneh*. Of course, these were originally *khaveh khaneh*, coffee houses, but they happily switched brew when public tastes changed. In the tea-house you can see a huge and varied slice of Persian life and legend, for it is there that traditionally men would gather to meet, smoke, drink tea, and listen to a bard recite the tales of old – usually from the *Shahnameh*, or 'Book of Kings'. This book was originally 'written' by Ferdowsi in the twelfth century AD, but in truth it is a collection of Persian legends which have been around since the dawn of time, and which, until Ferdowsi's monumental work, were transmitted orally. Although the practice is less widespread now, there are still *chai khanehs* in two or three of the larger Iranian cities – Tehran, Isfahan and Shiraz – where recitals still take place.

Turkish (Persian) Coffee

Coffee is still drunk in Iran, but it is an occasional after-dinner tipple, or perhaps consumed on a rare outing to an up-market Tehran café.

When Iranians do drink coffee, it is not often the spiced, bitter blend brought by the Arabs (although in the mostly Arab south of the country they are naturally partial to the stuff), but rather the thick, rich Turkish or Greek-style blend, brewed up in a little pot on the stove and drunk with a glass of water on the side. As I am asked for instructions on how to make this about three times a day, I felt that it should be included in any book of the shop. And there is an art to it. You should try to use a Greek coffee pot, which is like a '1-cup-sized' saucepan with a tiny base, tall sides and a long handle; a very small regular pan would do at a pinch. If you do not have baby coffee cups, just use a normal teacup, and half fill it.

You will need, per person:

> *1 (small, Turkish style) coffee cup*
> *1 heaped teaspoon Greek or Turkish coffee*
> *sugar as required*

Measure 1 cup of cold water per person into a Greek coffee pot. Add one teaspoon of coffee per person. Plain coffee obviously requires nothing further, but if you like your coffee sweet, add 1 teaspoon sugar per person; if you like it very sweet, add 2 per person You will either have to agree on the degree of sweetness required, or repeat the exercise separately for each person. Mix the water, coffee and sugar gently with a long handled teaspoon, and then put it on the stove. The flame shouldn't be too high, but should just lick the outside of the pot (if you are using electric, put it on a very hot ring). It doesn't need constant stirring, but do not leave it unattended. If the coffee is allowed to boil over, or boils, subsides and then boils again, it will not be palatable. It takes just a few minutes to cook; the coffee will froth up the side of the

pan – just as it reaches the rim, take it off the stove, and straight away pour it carefully into warmed cups. And do serve it with that water on the side – the coffee can be very cloying, not to mention palpitation-inducing.

Hubbly-bubbly smoking (*gallyun*)

The water-pipe (*gallyun* in Iran, *shisheh* in Arab countries, or *narghileh* in Turkey) is very much part of everyday life in Iran (which is not the same as saying that everyone smokes it everyday). It is regarded as a normal part of socializing and, in addition to being available in most restaurants and cafes, most households possess a pipe of sorts, some of them extraordinarily quaint and elaborate heirlooms. Although it is Egypt and Turkey which have popularized this hobby (and it is in most cases a hobby rather than a habit), it is Iran who gave it to the rest of the world. The very words *shishe* and *narghileh* are from the Iranian words meaning 'glass' and 'coconut' respectively – the 'glass' obviously being the base of the pipe, while the 'coconut' refers to the Indian origins of water-pipes, where they were first made out of coconut shells.

It is not entirely harmless, because lighting anything and then inhaling it cannot be good for you, but it is less damaging than cigarette smoking – the nicotine content is minimal, it is non-addictive (that is, if you are not a reformed cigarette smoker – if you are, make no mistake, the *gallyun* is a slippery slope) and, for practical reasons, it is impossible to smoke more than one or two a day.

The principle is simple. A little tobacco is spooned into the head of the pipe, and a disc of lit charcoal placed on top. The bottom is filled with water (or milk/coke/vodka/what you will). The act of inhaling through the attached hose causes air to be drawn across the charcoal, which then heats the tobacco. Bubbled through water this gives a cool, mellow smoke. In Iran they traditionally used a strong, dry tobacco, which they would then soak in water and squeeze before smoking; this

is still popular, but it is the Egyptian idea of fruit molasses (most often apple-flavoured) which has really taken this country by storm.

به سبک جدید

Which is probably the best place to mention drugs

Drugs are illegal in Iran, and the penalty for drug trafficking is death. But the sad truth is that in a society ill at ease with itself, and in a time of growing unrest and lack of direction amongst the young, drug use has never been more widespread. Marijuana is popular, but there is a vast and increasing problem with heroin usage.

Opium, on the other hand, is nothing new, but its use is, if anything, perhaps on the decline. It may not be legal, but it is *socially* acceptable in Iran. It is generally recognized as a hobby for older men (by which they mean over 40) to pursue as the young run greater risks of addiction. Used occasionally and in company, it is actually considered beneficial to health, as it lowers blood pressure and eats cholesterol. The truth is of course that even mature men can and do become addicted, and although formerly it was only the rich who could afford it, there are now somehow great numbers of ageing opium addicts from all social strata in the country. It is on the decline simply because the government has finally been forced to recognize the problem and set up widespread rehabilitation programmes.

CHAPTER TWELVE

اچار و مربا

PICKLES AND PRESERVES

They'll pickle anything in Iran; and if they cannot pickle it, then they'll preserve it. My mother-in-law brings back all sorts of funny pickles from her home town of Kermanshah, where wild herbs and vegetables and fruit grow with reckless abandon on the surrounding mountainsides – half the stuff in these jars I am still trying to identify!

Of course, pickling, preserving and bottling are arts for which the average British housewife/husband has little time these days. Everything seems to be available all of the time, and so there is no need to preserve the best of a season for sampling later in the year. But we are missing out. Pickles are really big in Iran, and every household has its own batch of recipes. And it's actually a great hobby – one can play endlessly with the spices and ingredients. Here are just a few of our favourites.

Persepolis Patent Piquant Tomato Sauce

Tomatoes are big in Iran, and so are tomato products. A vast number of families, in addition to making their own pickles and relishes, sun-dry and make their own tomato purée and from that, a whole range of sauces. At certain times of the year, an aerial view of many Persian villages would yield a sea of red – tomatoes spread out on the rooftops to dry. Sadly we lack the climate (or the flat roofs) to try this at home, but we can still make our own tomato sauce.

Now I have to admit that I don't always have this lurking in my cupboards – I am as happy to cheat as the next woman, and admit to such culinary crimes as using tomato juice or soup when I need some volume of tasty sauce. But I like to do things properly when I can, and it is good to know the provenance of your food; even if it is psychological, one instinctively feels better when one eats home-grown or home-made produce. I find that this recipe, added to tinned tomatoes and purée, makes for a luscious sauce and is a great 'home-made additive' for many dishes. I have used it in the meatball and bean recipe in Chapter Five for example.

The recipe will make quite a large quantity.

3kg ripe tomatoes
3 onions, chopped finely
1 litre spiced vinegar (see below)
1 teaspoon chilli powder
4 tablespoons sugar
2 level tablespoons cornflour
4 teaspoons mustard powder

Chop the tomatoes, and add them, together with the onions, to the spiced vinegar. Stir in the chilli powder and sugar, bring to the boil and set to simmer for around an hour. Then push the whole lot through a sieve, and return it to the heat. Mix the mustard and cornflour into a paste using a little extra vinegar, and stir this into the tomato mixture. Stir constantly until the mixture thickens. Fill a few jars with boiling water to sterilize them, and then empty them and fill them with the sauce. Seal well, and label 'made by clever clogs', with the date. The sauce should keep for a good few months – I haven't actually tested it beyond this time.

For this recipe I suggest you make your own spiced vinegar, as follows:

1 dessertspoon slightly cracked black peppercorns
1 teaspoon ground allspice
1 dessertspoon slightly cracked coriander seeds
1 teaspoon mustard seeds
2 blades mace
1 chopped bell chilli (or 2–3 green ones)
6 cloves
4 bayleaves
1 knob of fresh ginger, chopped
1 teaspoon salt
and the vinegar, of course (1 litre) – I always use apple vinegar for
*   extra fruity kick, but malt vinegar is fine*

All you do is to boil all of the above in the vinegar for about 5 minutes, and lo, it is ready for use. Chill and bottle it if you do not need it all at once. Purists would have you strain it before use.

Barberry Jelly

Barberries still grow in England, although they are not nearly as common as they were at the turn of the last century. They are readily available on the shelves of Iranian supermarkets, which are in turn readily available on the shelves of most big towns these days.

Barberries are desperately sour. They are also very good for you – full of vitamin C and a good aid to digestion. They really are unbearable in their raw state, but Iranians use them in a range of dishes which render them positively delectable, in stews and jewelled rice for instance (see p. 206). They also boil them down to make one of the most popular flavours of *lavashak* or fruit leather.

They are such a useful ingredient, however, and generate such culinary thrills wherever they roam, that I have found this jelly a good store-cupboard standby. It can be used as a jam, as a relish with rich meats, or ladled into a pastry case and passed off as a tart.

> *1kg barberries*
> *450ml water*
> *225g granulated sugar for every 300ml of juice created*

Pick over the barberries, removing any barbs, then put them in to soak so that any natural sediment sinks out. After half an hour or so, scoop the berries out and put into a heavy-bottomed jam-type pan with the water. Boil until the berries are all mushy and then strain the whole lot through a piece of muslin. Measure the resulting juice and add the requisite amount of sugar, return to the pan and simmer gently until the sugar has dissolved. Then bring to the boil and bubble away until the mixture is of a consistency that will set on a saucer. Pour into clean jars, and when cool cover with a circle of greaseproof paper and seal.

Jars, corner shops and saving the planet

I have a theory about the planet. I think that it can be saved if we all do our little bit. And I think that the corner shop should lead the way, flying the banner both for smaller enterprises and grander designs.

At Persepolis we currently have a jar bank and a carrier bag bank: customers are welcome to deposit and withdraw as they wish. Our goods are packed in simple bags, and once they are open, it is hard to keep them without spilling stuff all over the place. Customers were asking us to pack them in jars, but this seemed wasteful and extravagant, hence the jar bank. Recycling carrier bags just makes sense. Having a stash of them on the wall also averts the need for me to glare at the freeloaders who go shopping at the local 'Savapacket-but-we'll-get-the-costs-back-elsewhere' supermarket (who charge for their carrier bags), then come into my shop to get boxes and bags because they know that I am too nice to say no. The point is that if every shop recycles stuff that is relevant to them, e.g. tool shops can have nail and second-hand tool banks, clothes shops should have coathanger banks, timber yards should have firewood banks, there'd be a lot less waste on the streets.

The same applies to charitable efforts. Most shops have a collection box on the counter, but by actively pricing goods at 99p/£1.99 etc. and indicating the collection pot, you are more or less guaranteed to collect a penny from every customer. Furthermore, shops can organize collections pertaining to the goods that they sell, i.e. toy shops should obviously collect second-hand toys for charity, bookshops should do the same with books. The list is endless. End of rant.

Jo-Jo's Chutney

Iranians like chutney, but most of their pickles are of the sour and salted variety. Only in the south and east of the country do they make anything resembling chutney, and I have been unable to find any written recipes for this. Yet there are certain Persian dishes which cry out for chutney as an accompaniment (kebabs and the spicier casseroles). So I turned to Jo-Jo.

Jo-Jo was my grandmother. She was a wonderful cook, master of all the culinary arts of old England, although I don't actually ever remember her making bread. She was a dab hand with all that stuff that we are slowly and collectively forgetting – brawn and pickles and jams and puddings and tripe – the list is a long one. A lot of the same skills are employed in the Persian kitchen, and so much of that which I learnt by osmosis when I lived with her is now coming into play. Her chutney recipe was much fêted and she was fiendishly secretive about it. I was lucky enough to inherit her recipe books and finally found the paper grail on a scrap bearing the wonderful axiom 'AGE AND TREACHERY WILL ALWAYS OVERCOME YOUTH AND SKILL'. As I am not competing with the ladies who lunch, or submitting my efforts for general appraisal at the bazaar, I have decided to do away with the treachery and finally share her recipe with the rest of the world.

This will make enough to go round the family.

1kg dried apricots (Iranian chopped apricots are best)
2kg cooking apples, peeled and cored
2 litres wine or cider vinegar
1kg onions, chopped
1kg raisins
2 teaspoons ground ginger

2 teaspoons salt
2 teaspoons cayenne
6 teaspoons English mustard
3kg soft brown sugar

Soak the apricots overnight in the vinegar. The next day, pour them both into a large pan and bring them to the boil. Add the other ingredients, except the sugar. Bubble away for 15 minutes, and then throw in the sugar. Simmer for around half an hour more, stirring regularly, until the onion and raisins are all soft and mushy. Set another large pan with water to boil, and one by one dip the jars which you are planning to use into the boiling water to warm and sterilize them. Pour the chutney into the hot jars and seal them straight away. This chutney is effectively ready to eat straight away, but reaches peak scrumminess after around 6 weeks.

Persepolis Special *Torshi*

Torshi in Farsi just means sour pickle; but is often used as a generic term for pickles. *Shoor* specifically refers to ingredients preserved predominantly in brine. And *liteh* usually implies a type of finely minced, spicy *torshi*.

There are certain things that men are good at. Frying eggs for example: I don't know any women who can fry a really good egg (and don't all write in – I am sure there really are legions of you). Breakfast generally I tend to leave to my very capable other half. It is a joy to watch the degree of organization that he applies to the matter: serried rows of perfectly trimmed sausages, golden toast, succulent, sizzled

به سبک جدید

mushrooms and those perfect eggs. I think men's success in certain aspects of the culinary arts stems from their scientific approach – they think things through rationally without being intimidated by the bigger picture. Which is why it is Jamshid who took on the process of making the special pickle we sell in our shop. The whole business of vats of this and that, the logistics of it all, made me feel that I needed a lie down in a darkened room. Fret not; on a domestic scale it is nothing like as intimidating. Anyway, this is very much his recipe. It works really well, and *Takht-e-Jamshid torshi* has become quite famous.

2 cauliflowers, washed and trimmed and separated into small florets
1kg carrots, peeled and chopped into 1 cm rounds
2 onions, roughly chopped
1 head celery, washed and cut into 2 cm lengths
3–4 hot green chillies, chopped
500g baby cucumbers, chopped into 1–2 cm rounds
6–8 cloves garlic, quartered lengthwise
2 teaspoons whole golpar seeds (if available; see page 226)
1 teaspoon whole dill seeds
2 level teaspoons ground turmeric
2 litres of salted, boiled water
1 litre malt vinegar
1 bunch fresh spring garlic (or 200g dried, soaked for 24 hours),
    optional

It couldn't be easier: just mix all the ingredients and ladle into sterilized jars or a suitable plastic barrel and seal well. Your pickle should be ready after about one month.

Hafte-Bijar Pickle

ترشی هفته بیجار

For this recipe I have to thank Mr Moghadam, who makes wonderfully syrupy and exotic pickles in Park Royal. The name has a rather sweet Iranian folk tale attached to it, which I have endeavoured to summarize below.

The story goes that once upon a hubble-bubble, in olden Bijar, a little village near Tabriz, a beautiful maiden, the daughter of the town's apothecary, fell in love with a handsome young soldier of the Princes' guard (actually, I really don't know if either of them were that attractive, but you kind of have to assume these things in fairyland). Their love was plain for all to see, and their respective families readily agreed to their betrothal. At about this time, the king sent his two sons on a diplomatic mission to a neighbouring state and clearly that meant that their personal regiment was to go too. The young couple set their wedding for the day the princes' convoy was due to get back and bade a tearful, if somewhat theatrical, farewell. On the day of their scheduled return, the bride, her family and friends waited and waited...but in vain. No soldier. Sobbing she fled to the palace to find out what had befallen her beloved, to discover that only one prince and half the regiment had returned, with a sorry tale of how they had been set upon by bandits and their comrades and the older of the king's heirs slain before their very eyes. The king was distraught, the palace in shock. The maiden slumped to the ground in despair, and dragged herself home. For seven days and seven nights (i.e. one *hafteh*, or week) she wept and wailed and her friends were starting to be concerned for her health. On the eighth day, one of her fiancé's former comrades came

به سبک جدید

tiptoeing to her gate and, whispering for fear of being heard, told her what had really happened. How the younger prince, consumed with jealousy and ambition, had poisoned his brother together with the guards closest to him, and threatened to kill all the rest if they ever mentioned the matter. They had been left to die in the mountains. He would show her where, as his conscience would not rest until he had buried his friend. She knew then that she had to discover his fate for herself; so she scribbled a quick note for her folks, gathered two skins for water and some food, and off they set. For seven days and seven nights they voyaged through strange and diverse terrain. As she went, to distract herself, she gathered new and interesting herbs to give to her father upon her return, pressing them down in the spare water-skin. By night, she cried herself to sleep, without even realizing that her tears were running down into the skin containing the herbs. When they reached the spot where the foul deed had been committed, she quickly spotted the bodies of seven of the soldiers, surrounding the prince. Cradling the limp form of her own true love in her arms, she noticed immediately that his body was neither stiff nor cold. 'Can it be?' she cried, and bade her companion to pass her the water bottle. Grabbing one of the skins, he rushed to her side, and they coaxed a little of the liquid to the fallen soldier's lips. Spluttering and muttering and heaving, he immediately came to. What foul, magical potion had thus released him from the stasis into which he had been plunged? Why, of course, it was the gathered herbs suspended in the brine of her tears. Suppressing the joy the young lovers felt at their reunion, they quickly ministered to the prince and other soldiers, and mounted a triumphant march on their home city. The city had never seen such a celebration; for seven days and seven nights the young couple were wed in style and fêted as heroes. The feckless younger prince was forgiven, but he and his perfidious troupe were banished. The miraculous herbs that

had restored the prince to life are used to this day in healing, but the miracle itself is commemorated in the form of the pickle, *hafte-bijar*.

These days there are rather more than seven herbs in it, and we don't generally recommend that you pickle it in your own tears, but the principle of layers of herbs in salted vinegar is the same.

a large handful each of: spinach; dill; tarragon; coriander; mint;
*   parsley; fenugreek; basil; radish leaves*
4–5 sticks celery
2 leeks
salt and black pepper corns, lightly crushed
dried oregano
5–6 cloves garlic
white wine vinegar

Sort through, wash, dry and chop the herbs, celery and leeks, keeping them all separate, and then layer them into clean, dry jars, trying to range the colours from the darkest at the bottom to the lightest on top. Add ½ teaspoon of oregano to each jar, together with 1–2 cloves garlic, 1 level teaspoon of cracked peppercorns and 1 teaspoon of salt, and then fill each jar with vinegar and seal. Ready after a month; best after 7 weeks.

Aubergine Preserve

Because we don't preserve and bottle as much as we used to in England, our knowledge of jams is mostly a supermarket range of homogenized 'stuff to spread on toast', the most exotic being the occasional jar of marmalade or something with alcohol in it that we buy distant uncles at Christmas. Which is a shame, as we are missing out on a huge range of sweet preserved vegetables and fruits, like the recipe below. It is not a jam, although it is prepared in much the same way, but rather whole produce in syrup, eaten quite often on its own with tea or coffee, or as a sweet with cream or ice-cream.

The fact that aubergines are spongy means that they work well as a jam, readily absorbing the spiced syrup. This recipe really does demand baby aubergines, which are available in the ethnic shops of most towns and cities now. If you really cannot find any, you can use cubed regular aubergines, but you will need to dredge them with salt and leave them for an hour before rinsing well and proceeding with the method below.

1kg baby aubergines
800g sugar
750ml water
3–4 cardamom pods
½ teaspoon ground ginger
3 tablespoons rose-water
juice of ½ lemon

Remove any nasty, spiky bits from the tops of the aubergines. I try to resist cutting their little hats off altogether as I think that these are a nice feature of the jam. Peel half or three-quarters of the skin away

in strips. Do not peel them altogether as the skin helps the vegetables retain their integrity. Now drop the aubergines into a pan of boiling water, and simmer for 15 minutes.

In the meantime, boil the sugar and water together until the sugar has dissolved. Add the spices, rose-water and lemon juice. Drain the aubergines, pressing them gently to get rid of as much water as possible, and then lower them into the syrup. Simmer together for about an hour, and then take off the heat and allow to cool. Spoon the aubergines into sterilized jars, and top up each jar with the syrup.

به سبک جدید

Date Pickle – *Torshi-ye-Khormah*

This is a little treasure, as it is a pickle without vinegar or brine. I use it hot and cold as a garnish to meats and rice dishes, in sandwiches, even as a stuffing for fish. Bizarrely it is particularly nice with fried eggs. It is in fact a recipe one of my customers gave me pursuant to several months' discussion about the multifarious uses of dates, but I think it is largely ascribable to Rosa Montazami.

1kg Iranian dates (soft, fresh)
½ kg ground sumac
1 teaspoon salt
½ teaspoon ground black pepper
1 teaspoon cinnamon
1 teaspoon allspice
½ kg tamarind concentrate (p. 168)
juice of 3 lemons
1 teaspoon chopped garlic (optional; usually, I leave it out)

Stone the dates and chop them roughly. Mix the spices, tamarind and lemon juice together (and garlic, if using), then stir in the dates. Pack into clean, dry jars or airtight plastic tubs. This should be ready after about a week, but is at its gooiest best after about a month.

Garlic Pickle – *Torshi Seer*

ترشی سیر

This is one of a number of Persian pickles which should have a 'best after' date on it. 'Vintage' garlic pickle is prized in Iran and sold at a higher price, much the same as a good wine. Although simple to make, with but three ingredients, the effect is synergistic: the garlic softens the vinegar and the vinegar softens the garlic, until they are transformed into a syrupy, garlicky jam. So if you can, make this pickle and then lay it down for a long time. This will make about 1 big jar full.

> *10 whole garlic bulbs*
> *10 teaspoons salt*
> *750ml brown malt vinegar*

Boil the vinegar and salt together and set aside to cool.

Pull any flaky protuberances off the garlic and pack into a large, sterilized jar. When the vinegar is more or less cool, pour over the garlic so that it is covered, and seal the jar. Don't forget to mark the date of pickling on the label. Then go and hide it from yourself for a few years.

Variation

You probably spotted that we didn't peel the garlic in the recipe above. This is because the skin becomes so soft that it is perfectly edible. But for a pickle that will be ready next month rather than next decade, you can split the garlic into individual cloves, peel it and use white vinegar instead of the brown. Made this way, the *torshi seer* will be ready in about 6 weeks. This is a particularly useful pickle to have in your pantry, as the cloves of garlic thus preserved are great for marinades and salad dressings.

به سبک جدید

Pickled Cucumbers – *Khiar Shoor*

This is probably *the* most popular Iranian pickle. These posh, pert and piquant gherkins are nothing short of addictive. In Iran they are a regular visitor to the dinner-table, sliced into sandwiches, chopped into salads, and enjoyed as an any-time snack. But please note, they bear about as much resemblance to the fish-and-chip shop staple as Pinner to Peckham. They are salty, often eye-wateringly spicy, crunchy, and traditionally very small. In the summer, baby cucumbers can be found in Middle Eastern shops and many supermarkets, so get pickling.

2–3 sterilized jars
1kg baby cucumbers (about 3–6cm in length)
3–4 sprigs fresh tarragon
4–5 thin, hot chillies
4–5 cloves garlic
1 litre water with 4 tablespoons salt
2 tablespoons white vinegar

Wash and drain the cucumbers, tarragon and chillies, and peel the cloves of garlic. Boil the water and salt, take it off the heat and add the vinegar. Distribute the cucumbers, chillies, garlic and tarragon evenly between the jars, cover with the cooled brine and seal. This delicacy will be ready after one month, but reaches perfection after two.

Bandari Marinated Olives

Iranians grow, use and love olives, but have barely enough for home consumption, and so we are able to import but a few cases a year. You can make this lovely Persian marinade with any good, preferably fat, green olives.

For 1kg olives you will need:

3–4 cloves garlic, minced
1 dessertspoon dried dill, or 1 handful fresh dill weed, chopped
1 handful fresh parsley, chopped
1 handful fresh coriander, chopped
3–4 chopped green chillies
1 lemon, washed and cut into quarter-slices (i.e. cut the lemon into 4
*   wedges, and then finely slice the wedges)*
2 tablespoons extra virgin olive oil
2 tablespoons lemon juice

Cut a cross in the top of each olive, and then mix with all the other ingredients. Cover, refrigerate and leave for at least 24 hours. Enjoy with herbs, cheese, yoghurt and hot Persian bread.

Sour Cherry Jam with Vodka

This (without the vodka) is Iran's favourite jam; the Turks love it too;
in fact it is popular throughout the Middle East. The vodka gives it
that little bit of extra oomph, and makes it a nice Christmas conserve.
You can substitute kirsch or even gin, or just use a little rose-water for
a non-alcoholic version.

> *2kg sour or morello cherries*
> *250ml water*
> *200ml unsweetened cranberry or redcurrant juice*
> *2kg sugar*
> *juice of 2 lemons*
> *2 measures of vodka, or 2 tablespoons rose-water*

Stone the cherries, retaining the stones and all of the juice (work over
a clean tray). Try to leave the fruit as intact as possible. Crack the
stones. Put a handful of kernels to one side. Boil the rest in the water
for about 5 minutes. Strain the water into a heavy-bottomed pan, add
the fruit juice and sugar, and boil until all the sugar has dissolved. Add
the cherries and reserved kernels, and then bring to the boil again and
simmer for 15 minutes. Add the lemon juice, and simmer for another
5 minutes. Scoop out the cherries, then boil the remaining juice until
quite syrupy. When thick, return the cherries to the pan together with
the vodka or rose-water, cook for a final minute, and take off the heat.
Once it has cooled a little, ladle into hot, sterilized jars and seal.

Quince Jam with Cardamom

مربای به باهل

I have elsewhere in the book waxed lyrical about the joys of this fragrant fellow. I get over-excited during the far-too-short quince season, but this jam offers a way of enjoying the fruit all the year round.

2kg quinces
1 litre water (see method)
2kg sugar
12 cardamom pods, lightly cracked

Wash, peel and core the quinces, reserving all the 'rubbish'. Cover the quinces with water to stop them from discolouring, and then boil the discarded bits in a little water for around an hour. Strain the water into a heavy-bottomed pan, and then throw the core and pips and peel away. Make the fluid level up to 1 litre with cold water.

Slice the quinces thinly, and lower them into the stock with the sugar. Add the cardamoms and bring to the boil. When all the sugar has dissolved, set to simmer for around an hour and a half. At the end of this time, allow the fruit to cool for a while before pouring into warm sterilized jars and sealing. Really good with ice-cream.

به سبک جدید

Carrot Jam with Pistachio and Almond

I'm not really a jammy person, but I do love this one. Not only has it a Saturday-afternoon-in-front-of-the-telly-with-muffins quality to it, it's a great standby to have in your pantry. I use it for all sorts of things, but it's quite a good shortcut for making a half-decent sweet and sour sauce, or for adding to fried onions for a crisp, caramelized vegetable topping.

Technically, this is more of a 'conserve', as the stars of the jam, i.e. the carrots, are cooked in sugar right from the beginning rather than the sugar being added later on. The Persians don't differentiate and neither will we.

> *2kg carrots*
> *1½ kg sugar (special preserving sugar is best)*
> *120g orange peel (see p. 216)*
> *100g each nibbed pistachios and nibbed almonds*
> *2 tablespoonsful rose-water*
> *1 dessertspoonful lemon juice*
> *1 teaspoon ground cardamon*

Peel and julienne (i.e. cut into very thin strips) the carrots. Place the sugar in 600ml of water (a copper pan is best for this, but any solid-bottomed pan will do), and bring to the boil. Simmer for around 10 minutes, and then add the carrots and orange peel. Again, simmer for around 10 minutes or until the syrup starts to thicken, then add the rest of the ingredients. Another 5 minutes on the heat should do it. If you want to get technical, or already have a jam thermometer, the jam should reach 110°C/220°F and should set when dropped on a cool saucer. You can either pour the mixture into warm sterilized jars when it is still

hot, or wait for it to be completely cold and do it then. Any which way, cover with waxed paper and seal straight away. Don't forget to label your jars. How many times have you thrown away strange-looking substances lurking at the back of the pantry because you simply couldn't remember what they were? Anyway, this is part of the fun of jam making.

That's all there is to it. And it gets so much interest that you'll be producing it for the village fête by this time next year.

CHAPTER THIRTEEN

وص ایرانی

CHAPTER THIRTEEN

THE PECKHAM
INFLUENCE

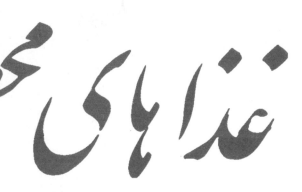

This chapter celebrates the joys of being a shopkeeper and having customers. These recipes are an amalgamation of ideas and conversations with my neighbours, customers and fellow local shopkeepers. One of the pleasures of living in multi-cultural London is to be able to walk along any high street and pick up weird and wonderful ingredients. A lot of our favourite recipes were originally ingredient-driven, derived from having purchased a particular product on spec. and needing to devise something to do with it. I have been careful, however, to make sure that none of the ingredients are so outlandish as not to be either widely available or easily substituted by something else.

Our shop is in Peckham and it would be a shame if we did not learn from our neighbours' rich culinary traditions. There are so many different nationalities living all jumbled up together that fusion is a daily reality here, not just a stylized way of cooking. A walk along Rye Lane, browsing in the many food shops, quickly transports the adventurous cook. What country shall we visit with tonight's dinner?

There has been a lobby of local worthies attempting to get the volume of music blared out by some of the shops permanently turned down – it is a shame because this polyphony only adds to the charm. In some of my favourite lines of poetry, Rumi wrote:

> There is a community of the spirit.
> Join it and feel the delight
> Of walking in the noisy street,

355

And *being* the noise.

Drink all your passion and be a disgrace.

Close both eyes and see with the other eye.

Open your hands if you want to be held.

Sit down in this circle...

He would have loved Peckham. In amongst the reggae beat-boxes you can hear Bollywood hits, bhangra, Afghan laments, Koranic recitals, Chinese pop and, of course, Iranian music. On a good day, with a following wind, I imagine the inhabitants of each shop doing a little jig in the style of their homeland. Whirling Kashmiri butchers flash their knives; gyrating West Indian greengrocers juggle yams and bread fruit; Kurdish fishmongers treat us to some wild folk-dancing (they must keep drums under their counter – don't all fish-mongers?); and Nigerian barbers give us something magnificent and tribal. There is enough material in Peckham for a Gershwin-style extravaganza.

Peckham has not enjoyed the most salubrious reputation. The Pooters in *The Diary of a Nobody* enjoyed the odd jaunt over here, but that was over a hundred years ago, when the area was still faintly genteel. After the Second World War, when much of Southwark was levelled by bombing, the area was rebuilt in an ugly and poorly planned manner; the emphasis was on low-cost/high-density. From the Fifties onwards, when immigration began to escalate, this type of housing was much in demand, so it was natural that many refugees and immigrants were offered accommodation here. Country after country dispatched wave after wave of migrants; layer after layer of displaced and insecure souls thus came to jostle together in Peckham. Surprisingly, the town has not suffered the same racial tensions or anti-police riots that other, similar districts have, but a general lack of education and a feeling of deprivation over many years left the area with some very needy people. Until a few years ago, it was, yes, a little rough. It is still not a bed of roses: there is still far too much gang-on-gang crime, and there are too many less-than-friendly-looking teenagers hanging around,

but an intense programme of regeneration is starting to work. We have a huge pool of artistic talent in Peckham. Even the squatters are gifted. Leave a building empty for long enough, and a colony of artists will break in and redecorate. Hopefully the area will keep its sense of being on the edge and avoid gentrification. It is such a wonderfully friendly area; people smile at each other in the street, look out for each other, and there is a real warmth. Because there are so many different nationalities crammed in together, those differences become irrelevant. It is with ease that I ask somebody where they are from, and about their 'back home' lands – questions that elsewhere, perhaps, would cause offence.

You should come by sometime; you stand to be pleasantly surprised by our little urban village.

به سبک جدید

Suya Chelow with Jerk Chicken

This dish, as so many in this book, evolved through crisis cuisine
– unexpected guests, no time to shop, that sort of thing. Our shop
is located opposite the Suya Spot, a famous and excellent Jamaican
takeaway serving eye-wateringly hot food. While this recipe has nothing
to do with them, the concept was certainly inspired by their proximity.
If you cannot find jerk sauce, it is easy to make. Chop thyme, salt and
chillies and mix with a little peanut oil. This will serve 6 people.

peanut oil
1½ tablespoons pomegranate paste
1½ tablespoons bottled brown sauce
2 tablespoons jerk sauce
6 whole breasts of chicken
5 cups rice – we use basmati
1 large onion, chopped
2 cloves garlic, chopped
1 tin coconut milk
275ml vegetable stock
1 can gungko peas (brown lentils make a good substitute, as do aduki
*   beans)*
flour mixed with 2 teaspoons turmeric for coating
salt
tomato juice
½ bunch coriander, washed and chopped

While leaving the skin on the wings of your chicken breasts, skin the
rest. Separate the wings, then take the breasts themselves off the bone
and butterfly them: i.e. rest them flat on a surface and cut nearly all the

way through each one horizontally. You should then be able to open each one out to resemble a butterfly. Mix together 1 tablespoonful peanut oil, the pomegranate paste, brown sauce and jerk sauce. Place the breasts and wings in a flat dish, and pour over the marinade, turning the chicken so that it is all coated. Cover and pop it in the fridge for half an hour or so.

Plunge the rice into boiling water for 5 minutes; drain. Heat some peanut oil in a large pan, and fry the onion and garlic. Add the rice, stirring vigorously, then measure in the coconut milk and vegetable stock. Altogether you want about 5 cups of fluid, so make up the balance with cold water. Drain the beans and stir them into the rice. Seal the pan by covering the lid with a tea towel. Once the stuff's bubbling, reduce the heat. The rice will need around 40 minutes to cook through and absorb all the moisture.

Heat the oven to 200°C/gas mark 6. Take the chicken breasts out of the marinade, and shake off the excess fluid. Scoop the wings out, put in an ovenproof dish, and pop them in the oven for 20 minutes. They can be doled out as an appetizer. Sieve some flour together with the turmeric and a pinch of salt on to a tray, and coat each of the chicken breasts. Fry them in very hot oil. Once you are sure that they are cooked through, keep hot. Pour the marinade into a pan, add a little tomato juice or tomato concasse and heat through gently. Check the rice is cooked, take off the heat and stir the coriander through it. You will not get good *tahdik* with this recipe, so spoon the rice on to a platter, lay the chicken on top, and stripe the sauce across it. Eat with a pomegranate and cucumber salad; you will need it to take some of that Jamaican heat away.

به سبک جدید

Plantain and Sweet Potato Slosh

My grandmother (who preferred to be known as my sister – it's a long story) was an adventurous eater, but only really liked proper food with visible edges. Anything that was in too much sauce was deemed 'slosh' and thus largely inedible. She would have hated this dish. Oddly enough, most Iranians to whom I have served it actually seem to like it (and they are really *not* adventurous eaters). It is extremely comforting and extraordinarily filling.

I serve it alongside barbecue food; it is pleasingly starchy. Generally speaking, there are never enough carbohydrates at barbecues. I mean to say there is never enough garlic bread to go round and, unless the hosts are Persian or similar (or using this book), the rice is always poorly cooked and the jacket potatoes burnt or soggy. For someone like me, who in truth doesn't like large lumps of meat, that doesn't leave much to eat. Imaginative, starchy side-dishes are therefore always welcome. The addition of bread 'scoops' offers a useful proxy for barbecue cutlery, inevitably lost in the herbacious border

You can also curry this up and have it for supper with a little salsa on the side. The recipe will do for 4 people as a side-dish.

1 tin coconut milk
4–5 green cardamom pods
¼ teaspoon ground saffron, steeped in boiling water
a pinch of salt and pepper
1 large sweet potato
2 'red' plantains (the ones that look really bruised and blackened)
oil for frying (peanut oil if you can get it)
1 sheet lavash *bread (or any other flat bread)*
1 onion, chopped very finely

1 clove garlic, minced
handful of chopped coriander or parsley (just for the colour)

First of all you warm the coconut milk and add the cardamom pods, saffron and seasoning. Simmer oh-so-gently for 10 minutes, and then remove from the heat. Remove the cardamom pods with a slotted spoon.

Peel your sweet potato, cut it into 1½–2cm cubes and drop it straight away into some cold water to prevent it discolouring. Bring to the boil, simmer for 5 minutes, and drain. Peel the plantain and cut it into 1½cm slices. Heat 2–3 tablespoonsful of the oil in a deep frying-pan, toss in the sweet potato, then add the plantain. Stir constantly or it will stick horribly. Once the vegetables start to brown a little (3–4 minutes), pour in the coconut-saffron concoction, turn the heat way down low, and cook through for around 10 minutes or until the potato is well cooked, without falling apart. If it looks at all dry, add a little water.

Cut the *lavash* bread into 3–4cm 'squares'. Heat some oil in a skillet and fry these until they are crisp and golden. Drain on a sheet of kitchen paper, and season lightly. Then fry the onion and garlic until this too is crisp and browned. At the last minute, mix in the coriander or parsley. Serve the 'slosh' in the pan if you like, with the *lavash* scoops ranged around the edge, and the crisp garnish streaked across the top.

به سبک جدید

Greek Lemon Chicken with Dill

In my experience, this is one of those I'm-really-full-but-I'm-going-to-keep-eating-'til-I-pop dishes. In truth it doesn't sound very exciting, but wait until they have their first few mouthfuls. This will serve 4 people.

> *butter*
> *1 large onion, peeled and sliced*
> *2 medium to large carrots, peeled and cut into chunky sticks*
> *5–6 sticks celery, washed and again cut into chunky sticks*
> *1 chicken, skinned and chopped into eight pieces (and this is one recipe*
> *   where a really nice free range, organic bird would up the ante)*
> *2 level teaspoonsful dried basil*
> *2 level teaspoonsful dried dill*
> *1 level teaspoonful ground turmeric*
> *4–5 dried limes, or the juice and zest of one large fresh lemon*
> *300g black-eyed beans*
> *handful fresh chopped parsley*
> *salt and pepper and olive oil*

Heat a little butter (or olive oil, but butter is better) in a pan, and sauté the onion, carrots and celery. Add the chicken joints, and stir until the chicken is sealed. Mix in the herbs and the turmeric, and then add enough water to cover the chicken. Next in are the dried limes (or lemon), and then bring it to the boil, and set to simmer for around 40 minutes.

In the meantime, place the black-eyed beans in a pan, cover with cold water, and bring to the boil. You may need to skim off any scum which appears. After about half an hour, check the beans – they should

be cooked but not mushy. Drain them and shoot about half into the casserole (see below to learn the fate of the other half). Serve with basmati rice, either plain or with dill.

The other half of the beans, if it is not a bit twee – like mothers and daughters in matching outfits – I usually make into a salad as accompaniment. Allow the beans to cool, drizzle with extra virgin olive oil and lemon juice, add some salt and pepper and chopped vegetables such as spring onions, celery, carrot or peppers, plus *lots* of fresh chopped coriander or parsley.

به سبک جدید

Afghan-style Spiced Meatballs with Tortilla Wraps and Avocado and Kiwi Salsa

I first made these small, spicy meatballs one night when mother-in-law was away. The family were dubious and awfully happy to have the chef-in-residence back the next day. I was pretty miffed until I worked out that they are quite hot and Iranians are not used to such 'in your face' spiciness. But chilli addiction is a slippery slope – the more you use the things, the more you crave them – and this dish (together with all things spicy) is now well established among the family favourites. This serves 6 people as a main course.

for the meatballs
1½ kg minced lamb
1½ teaspoons ground coriander
1 level teaspoon ground cumin
1 level teaspoon chilli powder
1½ teaspoons ground cinnamon
1 level teaspoon ground turmeric
4–5 cloves minced garlic
1–2 eggs
100g breadcrumbs
about 1½ level teaspoons salt
1 tin chopped tomatoes
for the salsa
3 small avocados
3 kiwis
4 spring onions
½ cucumber

غذاهای مخصوص ایرانی

1 green pepper
handful each of fresh coriander and fresh mint, chopped
juice of two limes, and the zest of one
1 tablespoon olive oil
salt and pepper
for the wraps
12 tortilla-style wraps (Turkish durum *bread is good as well)*
some thick creamy yoghurt

Mix and pound all the meatball ingredients together except the chopped tomatoes. The more you knead the better. The warmth of your hands will melt the fat of the lamb a little, which will make the ingredients bind together and ensure the flavours are properly mixed. Cover and refrigerate to firm up.

Now make the salsa. Salsa is by definition sauce but in this context is salad chopped so finely you may use it in place of sauce. Chop the ingredients 'real small', add the oil and lime juice, stir well, cover and chill.

To make the meatballs, which in truth are egg-shaped rather than spherical (so they will not roll out of the wraps), grease a large, shallow ovenproof dish, then with wet hands roll the meat mixture into 'sausages' around 5cm long and 2cm diameter. They will shrink a bit in cooking so you can place them fairly close together. Cover the dish with foil and place in a hot oven (gas mark 6/200°C) for about 20 minutes. Remove the dish from the oven, turn the meatballs over and drizzle the tomatoes over the top – the tomatoes serve to deglaze the tray and form a sauce of sorts. Re-cover, reduce the temperature to gas mark 4/180°C, and put the dish back in the oven for another 20 minutes.

To assemble (although I would recommend letting people make their own at the table), spread the wraps with a layer of yoghurt, followed by a thin layer of salsa (don't take this latter all the way to the edge otherwise it will be hard to eat with any dignity). Spoon a couple of the meatballs on to each wrap (ranged in a line lengthways), and roll.

Serve with chunky chips or jacket-potato wedges.

به سبک جدید

Somali-style *Molohiya* (Melokhia)

I like recipes that are passed by word of mouth and so when I want to try something new I usually try to talk to my customers, among whom are many Somalis. The ladies are well-mannered, graceful and modest, without exception startlingly beautiful, and generally a pleasure to have in the shop. As ambassadors of their nation, they do a sterling service. As they are also rather shy, it took a bit of persuasion for them to open up and talk about what they do in the kitchen. I was determined to find out what it is that they do with all the (frozen or dried) *molohiya* that they buy. *Molohiya* is an unprepossessing leaf, in appearance somewhere between nettle and spinach. It is not just eaten in Somalia, of course – it is a staple in Egypt, and a favourite in Turkey and the Lebanon. (It is not, however, even mentioned in Iranian cookery books, nor do any Iranians of my acquaintance seem to know of it.) When you cook it, it turns into the most amazing green gloop, like a slimy entity from a bad 1960s sci-fi flick. It is a strange vegetable.

Anyway, this polyglot dish stems from those conversations. I have put the pastry lid on it to give it 'ooh' (or even 'aah') factor – the idea of breaking through the lid to find all this bubbling green stuff underneath is quite fun. This should feed 6 people.

1 skinned chicken
2 large onions
5–6 cloves garlic
salt and pepper
2 turnips, peeled and quartered
2 cups rice (long grain or basmati)
dash of vinegar
200g dried molohiya, *or 1½ kg fresh, or 500g frozen*

1 teaspoon cayenne pepper
2 teaspoons ground coriander
a dash of oil and a knob of butter
a small pack of puff pastry (defrost but do not allow to dry out)

Wash the chicken and put into a large pan. Chop one of the onions, and roughly chop two of the cloves of garlic. Add these to the pan with some salt and pepper and the turnips. Cover with water, bring to the boil and set to simmer for an hour. When the meat is falling off the bones, remove it from the stock, strip off the flesh and set to one side. Strain the stock and pour it back into the pan.

Cook the rice in the usual way. Peel and cut the other onion into wedges, and marinate in vinegar.

If you are using dried *molohiya* (which is the easiest to source – fresh is hard to find), crush it roughly with your hands, put in a bowl and pour some boiling water over it. The leaves will start to swell immediately, and should be ready for use after 20 minutes. Fresh *molohiya* just needs to be washed and chopped, and frozen just needs defrosting.

Bring the chicken stock back to the boil; add the *molohiya*. Allow to bubble for around 30 minutes (only 10 minutes if you are using fresh or frozen leaves), stirring regularly. The leaves should be suspended in the sauce as if in an emulsion. Chop the rest of the garlic and fry it in butter in a skillet, stirring constantly. When it starts to colour, add the cayenne and the coriander and a bit of salt; mulch it all into a paste, then add it to the *molohiya*. Check the seasoning at this stage.

Heat the oven to gas mark 6/200°C. Roll out the pastry quite thinly. For serving, you can use either a large casserole, or (preferably) 6 individual oven dishes. If you are using the latter, you need to invert one of them over the pastry and cut round it, repeating the exercise five more times until you have six 'lids' for your *molohiya*.

Next we layer everything up. Spoon a thin layer of rice into the bottom of each dish, layer the chicken meat over this, and then ladle the *molohiya* sauce on top. (You can serve any left-over rice, chicken

and *molohiya* in separate bowls.) Grease the edge of the dish(es), and stretch your pastry lids across the top. Bake for around 15 minutes until the pastry is puffed and golden.

Serve with the vinegary onion wedges that you marinated at the outset. Not sure why, but it's a tradition in Somalia. And Peckham.

On the joys of shopkeeping

Robert Browning, at an address not far removed from our own, wrote:

> Because a man has shop to mind
> In time and place, since flesh must live,
> Needs spirit lack all life behind,
> All stray thoughts, fancies fugitive?
> All loves except what trade can give?
> I want to know a butcher paints,
> A baker rhymes for his pursuit,
> Candlestick-maker much acquaints
> His soul with song, or, haply mute,
> Blows out his brains upon the flute.

Britain is meant to be a nation of shopkeepers: there is nothing quite like it for focussing, strengthening the character and generally engaging with the world. Everyone should be a shopkeeper for a day.

A good shop is the ultimate in creative outlets. Shopkeeping offers fantastic opportunities to express oneself, from the business of playing with the shop window to ranging goodies on shelvies. Bored? Rearrange all your books according to the colour of their spines, or poster the ceiling, or anthropomorphize every product with its own little cartoon. It is my belief that the shopkeeper has a duty to make his shop as attractive as possible – there is no excuse for shoddiness or ugliness.

غذاهای مخصوص ایرانی

Furthermore, shopkeeping is the flipside of showbusiness – you are putting on a show for your customers. The counter is a proscenium arch. At the risk of sounding like Pollyanna, everyday is a new day, and offers a new and challenging audience to entertain. What better than that customers come not only to buy your products, but because they enjoy the experience of shopping in your establishment.

But it is a two way exchange. For the counter also acts as a confessional. More check-in than check-out. A shopkeeper's hat confers on the wearer the sometimes-less-than-desirable position of agony aunt or therapist. Quite apart from running, inevitably, an improvised community centre for homesick Iranians, we get an amazing string of people with problems through the door. Some are comical, some are deeply sad, some are embarrassing, and some we can actually solve. One is led occasionally to question 'Care in the Community' – there are some (albeit harmless) scary people out there. We have one gent who comes in who is patently at least five different people, and visibly switches personality in front of us; another (street drinker) comes in to the shop and laughs just like the laughing policeman – it is alarmingly infectious. But even this contributes to the tapestry that is a shop. For what is a shop other than a whole catalogue of stray thoughts and fancies fugitive?

به سبک جدید

Salt Cod with Iranian Herbs and Beans

Salt cod seems to be available in every shop in Peckham, although not in Persepolis. There is some use of smoked and dried fish in Iranian cuisine, so it seemed wasteful not to make the most of this ingredient. Having lived in a fishing port in Spain, I sort of fell into this recipe. I wasn't sure how to cook *bacalao*, and so I asked the local restaurateurs; this then is roughly their feedback. Now suitably Iranianized. You can have it as a main course with rice, but I think it makes a better soup. This is enough for 4 people.

400g dried salt cod (24-hour soaking period needed)
250g dried or 1 can cooked chick peas
2 onions
1 teaspoon ground turmeric
2–3 cloves garlic, chopped
2.5 litres water
600g fresh spinach
1 small bunch fresh or 30g dried fenugreek leaf (soak for 20 minutes before use)
1 handful fresh parsley
1 handful fresh or 1 teaspoon dried tarragon
olive oil, salt and pepper
to garnish:
1 onion, very finely chopped
100g–150g baby prawns or shrimps
½ teaspoon saffron steeped in a little boiling water
juice of half a lemon

As specified above, soak the salt cod for 24 hours, changing the water once during that period. If using dried chick peas, you need to soak these overnight as well.

To make the soup, chop the onion and fry it in a little olive oil. When it is starting to brown, stir in the garlic and turmeric. Add the water, and the dried chick peas, bring to the boil, and simmer for 1 hour (unnecessary if you are using canned chick peas).

In the meantime, prepare the herbs and spinach. Throw away the stalks, wash the herbs well, and drain before chopping. Fry them in a little oil for around 5 minutes, stirring constantly, and then add these to the bubbling chick pea water.

Flake the salt fish, removing the skin and any bones. Fry this gently in the same pan as you used for the herbs, and after a few minutes lower this into the soup as well. Season to taste, cover the pan, and simmer for another 15 minutes.

To prepare the garnish, fry the onion in a little butter or oil until crisp, add the prawns and when they are well coated, tip the saffron and lemon juice in too.

Ladle the soup into a tureen with the garnish swirled across the top. Serve extra lemon wedges and some warm bread.

به سبک جدید

Spiced Red Snapper with Saffron Polenta

Peckham has a wealth of good fish shops, and you can buy myriad strange fish with pretty colours and exotic names. I thought at first the fishmongers (mainly Pakistani or Indian) were fairly monosyllabic, and found the whole process of buying from them intimidating. But, silly me, I had made the mistake of telling them what I wanted and buying accordingly. I have since found that when you bother to solicit their advice, you are rewarded with an animated smile and a fount of knowledge is put at your disposal. I no longer trot along with any fixed ideas, but rather ask what I should buy and often, when faced with the more bizarre varieties, how to cook it. I have specified snapper in this recipe as it's so readily available, but you can use any oily sea-fish.

Polenta was forced upon me by my customers. I had always regarded it as a rather drab carbohydrate, like edible Blu Tack. As I refuse to sell anything which I do not understand myself, I have made it a little project over the last few years to collect increasingly delicious ways of preparing the stuff. I have to say, it is a great foil for this spiced fish. Again, this is enough for 4 people.

for the fish:
4 medium red snappers, scaled, gutted, and the nasty sharp bits cut off
2 dessertspoons tamarind paste
2 dessertspoons peanut oil (or olive, but peanut's nicer here)
2 green chillies (or ¼ habanero), chopped
2–3 cloves garlic, chopped
handful chopped fresh coriander
little knob ginger, chopped finely
salt and pepper

for the polenta:
750ml vegetable stock
½ teaspoon ground saffron
170g cornmeal/instant polenta
handful fresh parsley, chopped
olive oil, salt and pepper

Wash the snappers and pat them dry. Make two or three diagonal slashes in each side of each fish and lay them in a shallow dish. Mix the tamarind and peanut oil together and add the chillies, garlic, coriander, ginger, and a sprinkle of salt and pepper. Spoon this marinade over the fish, rubbing it in with your hands until all parts of it are coated. Cover the dish and refrigerate for a minimum of 2 hours.

In the meantime, make the polenta. This, too, needs some 'chilling' time. Bring the stock to the boil, add the saffron, then pour in the cornmeal in a slow, steady trickle, stirring all the while. Cook until the mixture thickens and starts to pull away from the sides of the pan. Stir in the parsley and season to taste. Spread it out on a greased baking tray (20cm x 18cm works well) to a depth of about 1cm and leave it to set somewhere cool for an hour.

The fish is just perfect cooked over fire, but a really hot domestic grill will do the trick. Oil the grill first and only turn the fish when the first side is properly cooked and the skin beginning to crisp. This way, the fish shouldn't stick. Cook the snappers for about 6 minutes each side, then pop them in the oven (on low) to keep warm. Brush the top of the polenta with olive oil, and cut it into 12 squares with a sharp knife before putting the tray under a hot grill. Cook until lightly browned, and then turn the squares over and repeat the exercise the other side.

Serve the polenta slices and snappers with a fresh green salad and lime wedges.

به سبک جدید

Persian Spiced Risotto (Italian *Biryani*)

This dish was evolved to habilitate one of my favourite dishes, risotto, into the Iranian diet. It took one look at the in-laws' faces to know my standard preparation with Parmesan and white wine was not going to be acceptable. To touches of Iranian cookery, it adds elements of our greengrocer's *biryani* recipe. *Biryani* is extremely popular with our Kashmiri and Afghan neighbours, as it enables rice, meat and sauce to be cooked in one pot, and feeds hordes of staff easily and cheaply.

The Persian equivalent of arborio rice is grown in Iran – in the rice-growing north they prepare a breakfast dish with 'sticky' rice, saffron, milk and dates, but it really is not part of the national cuisine. This should be enough for 8–10 people.

for the lamb bit:
1 small, lean shoulder of lamb
1 large onion, chopped
5–6 dried limes, washed and pricked
1½ teaspoons ground turmeric
salt and pepper
for the rice bit:
2 large onions, chopped
4–5 cloves garlic
butter
250g raisins, soaked in water for 15 minutes
2 tablespoons nibbed almonds
2 tablespoons nibbed pistachios
150g pine nuts
2 teaspoons ground cardamom
1 teaspoon ground cinnamon

غذاهای مخصوص ایرانی

2 teaspoons crushed dried rose petals
1200g arborio rice (or 150g per person), washed and drained
1 teaspoon ground saffron steeped in boiling water
salt and pepper
chopped parsley to garnish

Get your butcher to bone the lamb for you and then to cut the bone into 3–4cm pieces (the bone-marrow is a great delicacy). Cut the meat into small chunks (2cm) and place it in a large pan together with the bone. Cover with water to about 8cm above the surface, then add the onion, dried limes and turmeric before bringing to the boil. Reduce the heat to a simmer. Leave it alone for around an hour and a half before seasoning to taste.

Once this time is up, start the risotto. Fry the onion and garlic in a little butter until soft, and then add the raisins, nibbed nuts and pine nuts. Cook for 2–3 minutes and then add the cardamom, cinnamon and rose petals, followed by the rice, stirring constantly. Using a ladle, add stock from the lamb pan – you will need about 2½ litres of fluid altogether, so if you exhaust the lamb stock, add plain water. You need to add the stock slowly until liquid is no longer absorbed and the rice is soft to taste. At the point where the rice is nearly cooked, stir in the saffron, mixing thoroughly, and check the seasoning.

To serve, spoon the lamb and bones into the bottom of a large dish, and then pile all the rice on top. Garnish with a big handful of chopped fresh parsley, and serve with yoghurt, pickled chillies and lemon wedges.

به سبک جدید

Persian Pizzas

There are now so many Iranian pizzerias in London that this is a must. Of course, most of them just offer the 'deep pan or crispy, Four Seasons or Hawaiian, coleslaw on the side' type of menus, but one or two are starting to incorporate some decidedly Iranian touches, with delightful results.

For the base

Use either *barberi* bread (for a deep(ish) pan effect), or *taftoon* (for a really light, thin and crisp number) – the recipes for both can be found in Chapter One, or you can buy ready-made, thickish *naan*.

Topping 1 (to make 2 pizzas)

1 small onion, chopped
200g minced lamb
1 dessertspoon tomato purée
1 teaspoon garam massala
½ teaspoon ground cinnamon
¼ teaspoon ground cumin
salt and pepper
2 dessertspoons capers, roughly chopped
4–6 Iranian pickled cucumbers, roughly chopped
50g black olives, stoned and roughly chopped
few fresh chillies, chopped (optional)
2 dessertspoons kashk *(or plain yoghurt)*
sprinkling cheese (optional)
1 teaspoon dried mint
fresh herbs

غذا های مخصوص ایرانی

Fry the onion in a dash of oil and then add the mince, stirring well to break it up. When it is sealed, stir in the purée and spices, and season to taste. Spread in a thin layer over the *naan*. Scatter with the chopped capers, gherkins, olives, and optional chillies, and drizzle the *kashk* or yoghurt over the top. Dot some cheese on top, and sprinkle the dried mint on top of that. Bake in a moderate oven (gas mark 4/180°C) for 5 minutes. Serve strewn with shredded fresh herbs.

Topping 2

Simply spread the *naan* with *mirza ghassemi* (see p. 228) – but do not mix the eggs in. Crack them directly on to the aubergine mix on the pizza. Top with goats' cheese and mozzarella, and sprinkle with a little dried oregano. Bake at gas mark 5/190°C until the eggs are just set; around 6 minutes should do it.

Topping 3

You will need for 2 pizzas:

> *juice of 2 lemons*
> *¼ teaspoon saffron, steeped in boiling water*
> *salt and pepper*
> *4 cloves garlic, peeled and chopped*
> *handful fresh dill, washed and chopped*
> *about 20 fat, raw prawns*
> *4 scallops, halved*
> *bunch of fresh spinach, washed*
> *butter*
> *tomato sauce comprising 1 tablespoon each of Patent Persepolis*
>   *Tomato Sauce, tomato purée and chopped tinned tomatoes*
> *approximately 20 black olives*
> *handful grated mozzarella*
> *1 teaspoon caviar or other roe (optional, but really fun on a pizza of*
>   *all things)*

به سبک جدید

Mix the lemon juice with the saffron, seasoning, garlic and dill (retaining a little of this latter for garnish), then pour it over the scallops and prawns as a marinade. Refrigerate for 3–6 hours.

Blanch the spinach in boiling water for 2–3 minutes; drain well. Take the scallops and prawns out of the marinade, and sauté gently for about 5 minutes in a dessertspoon of butter (peel the prawns if necessary).

Spread the *naan* bases with tomato 'sauce', followed by a thin layer of spinach. Distribute the fish evenly over the spinach, and dot with olives. Sprinkle with mozzarella, and garnish with the reserved dill and the caviar. Bake at gas mark 4/180°C for 5–6 minutes.

Persepolis Muesli

In Iran they eat *aghil* – sweet or salted mixed nuts and seeds – by the bucket-load. Naturally, we sell it in the shop. As the Brits aren't too good with seeds that aren't already cracked open, my British clientele have taken more to the sweet 'silk trail mix', which features only kernels of things, and easily manageable chunks of fruit. It is not actually sweetened, it is just sweet by nature, comprising raw nuts as opposed to roasted and seasoned. It was an obvious next step to anglicize the mix by adding a few handfuls of grain and flakes. Thus Persepolis muesli was born. You can add any flakes you like to make this like a breakast cereal: rye, barley, oats, or wheat. My remit is simply to tell you about all the lovely dried bits and pieces that you could put in it if you 'go Persian'. Supermarket muesli will never taste the same.

Mulberries – dried white mulberries (*toot*) are extremely popular as an
    any-time snack in Iran. Unlike the black variety, the white ones taste

much nicer dried. They look like small, fat caterpillars. Don't let this put you off.

Baby figs – unlike the squidgy, Turkish or Greek-style ones, these honey-flavoured numbers are plump, rounded and tiny, and usually much drier. They have a cult following.

Hemp seeds – stop sniggering. Hemp seeds are good for you and contain none of that funny stuff. They've been eating them in Iran for millennia to help with blood pressure, and as they are choc-a-bloc with omega-3 and omega-6 oil, they're also good for the brain.

Nibbed pistachios – bright green slithers of everyone's favourite nut. They will enliven any dish.

Green sultanas – exceedingly posh, and very long. Great in muesli.

Raw cashews and brazil nuts – most muesli has plenty of almond and hazelnut bits, but cashew and brazils are good too.

Walnuts – there's walnuts and walnuts. Iranian ones are dear, but oh-so-creamy. In Iran they soak them before flaking off the inner skin, though this is perhaps excessive for muesli. A few walnuts a day do help to control high blood pressure.

Chick peas – soaked, and then dry roasted (but not salted). Look out for the pretty pastel-coloured sugar-coated ones in Turkish shops.

Fresh or dried dates – well, yes, we know a lot of muesli has bits of chopped dates – but if you haven't tasted Iranian dates, then you really haven't tasted dates at all. Even the dried ones are tastier, with a slight honied flavour, but it is the fresh dates from Bam for which the country is famous. These soft, velvety fruits taste too good to qualify as fruit; they surely release at least as many endorphins as chocolate. We do not actually put them in our trail mix – they are sticky and need to be kept chilled – but they are awfully good chopped into the bowl at the last moment. These are one of our biggest single imports. Dates are one of the staple foods of the Middle East, and have particular significance during Ramadan when they are used to break fast. Fortunately, both for date fans and the citizens of Bam (for whom they are an important source of livelihood), the date crops were not

به سبک جدید

destroyed by the devastating earthquake of 2004.

Pine nuts, sunflower, melon and pumpkin seed kernels, dried apricots, peaches and prunes – we're sure you already put these in your cereal anyway.

غذاهای مخصوص ایرانی

CHAPTER FOURTEEN

ای پزشکی

THE MEDICINAL PANTRY

God did not send down any disease without also sending the remedy for it.

Hadith, the body of tradition concerning the sayings of Mohammed

There are no incurable diseases; only lack of human will.
There are no worthless herbs; only lack of knowledge.

Avicenna

Iranians love tablets, and they love doctors. All parents secretly want their children to be doctors. All Iranians also secretly believe that they themselves know better than the doctor. Their relationship with the profession is very much love-hate. At the root of this is the fact that herbalism and ancient dietetics are very deeply entwined in Persian culture and this sometimes clashes with the medical profession.

While the British have lost a lot of their traditional remedies and culinary lore, Iranians have retained theirs. Most Persian households have a store-cupboard of non-pharmaceutical remedies at their disposal. Things like valerian root, marigold, borage, nettle, starch, even sugar – these (fairly easily obtainable) items, and a whole lot more, comprise the Persian medicine chest.

Most importantly, the Persians have a unique way of classifying food and balancing their diet. Put very simply, they believe that all foods have either 'hot' or 'cold', and 'wet' or 'dry' properties. If you consume too many foods from one category, your body will develop an imbalance, and a lifetime of eating the wrong stuff can actually lead to some fairly serious illnesses. If bells are already ringing, that is because the system closely resembles the Eastern ideas of the duality of *yin* and *yang*, and also the three *doshas* of ayurveda. The Persian concept is known informally as *sardi/garmi* (literally 'cold/hot'); it is as good as 3,500 years-old but, unlike Chinese and ayurvedic healing, there are currently no books available on it in English. In fact, there are but few in Persian. Amazing as it may seem, this is lore still passed on by oral tradition.

The origins of balance were laid down in the times of Zoroaster (see Chapter Four), who preached that just as it was the powers of good and evil who created the universe and thus an eternal duality, there is a similar duality in all things, and an awareness of balance is required. I quote here from the *Zend Avesta* (chiefly because it is a powerful piece of work, but also because it is not the sort of thing people quote from every day). The text is ancient, largely fragmentary, so the prose may not flow as well as that of other holy books.

> [the souls of animals] are the most effective amongst the creatures of the two spirits, they the good, strong, beneficent *Fravashis* [souls] of the faithful, who stood holding fast when the two Spirits created the world, the Good Spirit and the Evil One.
>
> *Zend Avesta*, Part II, from the *Farvardin Yast;*
> translated by James Darmesteter 1882

Zoroastrians also believe in the rhythm of nature, and that nature has an answer to everything. Again, the *Avesta* states:

> One may heal with Holiness, one may heal with the Law, one may heal with the knife, one may heal with herbs, one may heal with the Holy Word.
>
> from the *Ardibehist Yast*

The concept of good and bad, and good and bad foods, was thus born. I mention this at some length, because the origins of *sardi/garmi* are sometimes a bit muddled. The system was undoubtedly refined as the

غذا های مخصوص ایرانی

centuries trotted by, but the underlying belief in balance in all things stems from these very ancient times, and I believe that it is because it has such a deep foundation that it remains proudly unwritten, but unbowed by time or subsequent learning, at the heart of Persian society today.

It was not for another thousand years that any further significant developments were made, courtesy of Hippocrates of Cos. He is generally (and quite rightly) acknowledged as the father of medicine – although he came out with some preposterous theories, thus:

> We should purge upward in summer and downward in winter.

And even better:

> In women, blood collected in the breasts indicates madness.
> (these both from the 'Aphorisms' of the Corpus Hippocratus)

But he was the first medical chap to look at the body as a whole, and to understand that symptoms may be indicators of underlying sickness rather than finite occurrences. He took some of the magic out of medical practice, and turned the art of healing into the beginnings of a science. Crucially, for our purposes, he was the first to take the idea of opposites and develop a theory of the four humours. He suggested:

> The body of man has in itself blood, phlegm, yellow bile and black bile; these make up the nature of his body and through these he feels pain or enjoys health. Now he enjoys the most perfect health when these elements are perfectly proportional to one another in respect to compounding, power and bulk, and when they are perfectly mingled. Pain is felt when one of these elements is in defect or excess, or is isolated in the body without being compounded with all the others.

If there are four fluids or humours controlling the body, this is reflected

in the seasons, the elements, the ages of man, and the character of man as expressed in the chart below.

Humour	BLOOD	YELLOW BILE	BLACK BILE	PHLEGM
Element	AIR	FIRE	EARTH	WATER
Season	SPRING	SUMMER	AUTUMN	WINTER
Age	CHILDHOOD	YOUTH	MATURITY	OLD AGE
Character	SANGUINE	CHOLERIC	MELANCHOLIC	PHLEGMATIC

PROPERTIES

	BLOOD	YELLOW BILE	BLACK BILE	PHLEGM
HOT	◆	◆		
WET	◆			◆
DRY		◆	◆	
COLD			◆	◆

Hippocrates suggested that everyone is a mixture of these four humours, but there were any number of influences which could cause them to become unbalanced. To be considered were climate and geography, disposition, emotional state, pressures of work and the time of year. It was the job of the physician to find a way of redressing the balance before the body could develop disease.

Owing to frequent cultural-exchange programmes (invasions) between the Greeks and the Persians, it was only a matter of time before Hippocrates' refined ideas travelled to Iran and mingled with the primitive Zoroastrian concepts. It is believed that the Persians also managed a brief interface with the Chinese in the second and third

غذاهای مخصوص ایرانی

centuries AD, and thus the much older belief in yin and yang (which developed quite independently of other doctrines) would in some way have made its mark.

There were no further significant developments until about 1500 years later, when up popped Avicenna (Ibn Sina, in Persian). He was born in Bokhara in Afghanistan in AD980, and grew to be one of the finest medical minds the world has ever seen. His great achievement was to write down every bit of medical knowledge he could lay his hands on (much to the Persians' chagrin, he did this in Arabic, although he lived and worked in Iran and is properly regarded as Iranian). His collected works are known as *Al Qanun fi'-al at Tibb* (The Canon) and they are massive. It was Avicenna who developed dietetics, and it was he who formalized this belief in hot and cold and wet and dry foods. He wrote: 'Most illnesses arise solely from long-continued errors of diet and regimen.' His work in this sphere has not been surpassed – his teachings in fact reigned supreme in the medical world until the nineteenth century with the development of modern medicine and those tablets we all know and love. His work is carried on today by the Unani (literally, Greek) Foundation (based in America) as well as the Central Council for Research in Unani Medicine in India, and by assorted *hakims* (wise men) in rural Afghanistan and Iran – and every Iranian housewife.

What is the science behind it? How does it work? You notice that I refrain from asking simply, 'Does it work?' You may regard it as archaic, or even farcical, but there does seem to be something in it. It is basically about the speed at which the body breaks foods down. Avicenna observed that the body 'cooks' food. That which we eat is subjected to a whole range of enzyme action in its journey from the mouth to the stomach and liver. Various types of enzyme action contribute the various bodily fluids of the four humours. Hot foods are digested quickly and dealt with much more effectively than cold foods. They increase the metabolism. Cold foods hang around in the system more, and are slow to digest; they lower the metabolism. Too

many hot foods make the system race too much, which can put a strain on the heart and blood pressure. Too much cold food leaves the body with too much residue to handle, which can lead to things such as migraine, bowel disorders and arthritis. If the body cannot digest foods properly, the excess waste can lead to a build up of toxins. At the very least, these will bring on a nasty outbreak of spots. A further problem is that the wrong balance of foods distracts the enzymes from a lot of their normal healing and maintenance duties, leaving the body more open to disease than usual.

In addition to these simple facts, i.e. the need for a balanced diet, one should consider the constitution (*mazarj*) of a person. Those with a naturally cold constitution will be ill if they binge on cold foods, and the same applies to those who are 'hot'. My mother-in-law reckons that I have a cold constitution. This based on empiric observation of my eating habits and the fact that I am pale skinned and come from a cold country. I fought this diagnosis at first (many of my favourite foods are cold), but I must admit that I think she is probably right. I feel much better since I reduced my coffee consumption; alcohol (except wine, 'Hodar al shokhr') disagrees with me; and if I dine exclusively on my favourite foods – lentils, fish, salad, blackberries – I feel really washed out the next day. My husband Jamshid has a hot constitution, and over-indulgence in hot foods (the worst culprit being garlic) seriously disagrees with him. Incidentally, most alcohol is very cold; a hangover is a manifestation of cold imbalance, and the difference in the constitutions of various people explains why some can drink and others cannot. Hot and cold foods are sometimes wrongly associated with high and low blood pressure; there is no direct relation, but those of a hot or cold constitution can be adversely affected by eating too much food of the same category.

The remedy for such imbalances is to treat them with foods from the opposite camp. Fever (an obvious symptom of too much heat) is treated either by fasting or consumption of cold foods (melon, cucumber): hence our expression 'feed a cold, starve a fever'. Light-headedness, on

غذاهای مخصوص ایرانی

my part (as I am 'cold'), I treat with the 'hot' *nabat*, Persian rock sugar. This is the most wonderful substance, as it seems to lift everything from the dodgy tummy to the raging hangover. It comes either plain or with saffron, and is dissolved in boiling water or tea and sipped very slowly. One can also eat preventatively, compensating for the rigours of each season by altering one's diet (see the separate section below).

This system of dietetics and healing is known as allopathic, i.e. it treats ailments with opposite remedies, and is thus the opposite of homeopathic healing, which treats like with like.

Unfortunately, in the West we have lost contact with our inner body mechanisms which scream 'enough', and all too seldom realize that the remedy for our general malaise is within our grasp. There is more of a general realization that 'we are what we eat', but most treatises on the subject look at one angle or another (cholesterol, or blood pressure, or losing weight) and lose sight of the bigger picture. Another problem is that we eat so much food out of season that our natural biorhythms are utterly confused.

The *sardi/garmi* system is undoubtedly full of holes and based on some extremely quaint principles. There must be a thousand different scientific reasons why the whole thing should be consigned to quackville....and yet...and yet....

The human body is infinitely more complex than the entire universe.

Avicenna

Hot and Cold
The List

HOT FOOD

Apple; Asparagus; Avocado
Bananas; Basil; Beef; Black tea; Butter
Cheese; Cherries; Chick Peas; Chives; Cinnamon; Coconut; Cumin
Dates; Dill; Duck
Eggs; Fats; Fenugreek; Figs
Garlic; Ginger
Hen; Honey
Kashk
Lamb
Mango; Mint; Mulberries; Mung beans; Mushrooms
Nigella seeds; Nuts in general
Oils; Okra; Olives; Onions; Oregano
Peppers
Quince
Raisins; Rose Water
Saffron; Salt; Sesame seeds; Spices; Sugar; Sweetcorn
Tarragon; Turnip
Vanilla
Walnuts; Wheat
Yellow split peas

NEUTRAL FOOD

White cheese

غذاهای مخصوص ایرانی

COLD FOOD

Alchohol; Apricot; Aubergine
Barberry; Barley; Beef; Beetroot; Blackberry; Blueberry; Broad beans;
Broccoli
Cabbage; Cardoons; Carrot; Cauliflower; Celery; Cockerel; Coffee;
Coriander; Cornflour; Courgettes; Cucumber; Cumin
Fish
Green Tea
Kidney Beans
Lentils
Marjoram; Milk
Parsley; Peas; Pinto beans; Pistachios
Radish; Rhubarb; Rice
Sour cherries; Soya; Spinach; Sumak; Sweet potato
Tamarind; Tomato; Turkey; Turmeric
Veal
Water-melon
Yoghurt

Cigarettes
Gallyun (hubbly-bubbly)
Opium

COOL FOOD

Lemon; Sweet lemon (lime)
Nectarine
Orange
Peach; Pear; Pomegranate

به سبک جدید

Other useful stuff

There are a myriad useful plants and substances which the Persians use as medicine. Suffice it to say that nearly every plant has a beneficial, alternative use, and Iranians are more aware of this, at a very basic level, than most other nations. I have here but outlined the most common, the ones that every Iranian knows about, the ones in every Persian pantry.

Infusions to drink as tea
(or decoction, as we say in the trade)

❀   *Gul Mohammadi* – rose petals (*Rosa damascena*). As well as the obvious culinary uses of rose petals, the Iranians have used them medicinally for centuries. They are reputedly a good tonic for the heart and the nerves, and help the body's natural healing processes. Undoubtedly their fabulous fragrance works as an anti-depressant. Use clean, dried Damascene rose petals. Steep in boiling water for 5 minutes, whether on their own or mixed with *tea* tea. Enjoy with honey.

❀   *Gul* (which is the Persian word for flower) *Gavzaban* – borage (*Borago*). This plant is apparently making a comeback as a cash crop in Britain – something to do with the convolutions of the Common Agricultural Policy. Borage is well known in Iran as a 'blood strengthener', fortifying the weak. Its high concentrations of potassium mean that it is good for all the major organs. Most usefully it is taken at the first sign of the onset of a cold (along with sweet lemons/limes), a sort of Persian Lemsip. Once again, steep the dried leaves in boiling water, and drink as a tea, sweetening with honey to taste.

❀   *Gul-e-Khatmi* – (the flowers of the) marshmallow (*Althaea officinalis*). Like a lot of herbal remedies, this is cold and dry, i.e.

غذاهای مخصوص ایرانی

slightly laxative. It is very good at softening unwanted hard matter in the body, and so eases the whole of the digestive tract. It is also beneficial to those with excess phlegm or mucous (especially on the chest), as it helps to expel these from the body. It is best to steep the flowers in boiling water, sweeten to taste, and then allow to cool before drinking.

❀ *Taranjabin* – (seeds of the) camel thorn (*Alhagi persarum*). This seems to act as a general bodily expectorant. It works for dry coughs and constipation, as well as inducing sweating for those with an incipient fever. It is decocted and consumed cold.

❀ *Torkhmeh Beh* – quince seeds (*Cydonia*). One of Allah's cleverest fruits: not only does it smell alluring and taste divine, but it's also one of the good guys. The seeds are good for bronchial complaints. Steep them in boiling water, leave for 24 hours or so, and then drink the water. Quince products are also an aid to blood clotting.

❀ *'Onab* – jujube berries (*Ziziphus jujube*). Jujube berries have a pleasant smell and flavour, which probably contributes to their reputation as an anti-depressant and an anti-insomniac. They also work as a laxative, and are good for bronchial and catarrhal complaints. Boil the berries in water, and drink the resulting decoction as a tea. It is also prepared with barley and eaten as a sort of porridge.

❀ *Sonbol 'atib* – valerian root (*Valeriana*). The effects of this are legendary. It is more powerful than chamomile as a sleep inducer. The singularly unprepossessing roots are steeped in boiling water and drunk as a tea. It is also utterly irresistible to cats and rats – it was reputedly the secret weapon of the Pied Piper of Hamlyn, the scent of it luring on the wretched rodents. My cat goes berserk for the stuff – catnip is so last-year.

❀ *Chahar torkhmeh* – four-seed remedy. This is a real homely remedy, as it seems that no-one can truly agree which seeds are used. In the old *materia medica* they are variously listed as pumpkin, gourd,

به سبک جدید

melon, and cucumber, or pumpkin, water-melon, mustard and quince. The mixture which we import seems to contain the seeds of fennel, quince, (a cousin of) mustard and apple. The idea, I believe, is simply to hit any encroaching 'meecrobes' (as all bugs in Iran are called) with everything you can throw at them. The remedy is used primarily for colds, but is recommended for all sorts of infections. The seeds are boiled in water, and then ground into an emulsion, which is then supped slowly (inevitable, I should imagine, as they invariably taste less than wonderful).

More other useful stuff

Neshasteh, starch, is an odd but extraordinarily effective measure for really dry coughs and the ensuing soreness. Mix a little starch powder with warm (i.e. boiled and then cooled) water or milk, and sip slowly. My mother-in-law forced this on me once (I must have been poorly as I didn't object) and it did seem to help.

Khakshir, flixweed (*Sisymbrium sophia,* a sort of hedge mustard), as the name suggests, is classified as a controlled weed in many countries. One man's weed is another man's herbal remedy. This plant is great, and in truth a pleasant drink. It is consumed in Iran when the weather is stinking hot – when you feel your brain is cooking from within. *Khakshir* cools you right down. It is a remedy for fever, and is good for asthma too. It should be mixed with cold water and served over ice.

Golpar is Persian hogwort (*Heracleum persicum*). *Heracleum* in general is on the FBI's most wanted weeds list. Hogwort is apparently destroying whole swathes of Western Virginia. Furthermore, it is guilty of phyto-phototoxicity in the first degree (i.e. gives you a very nasty rash). Its Persian cousin is not only innocuous, it is one of Iran's favourite ingredients. Its seeds are used in pickling, and also ground into a spice for use on broad beans, jacket potatoes and so forth (see Chapter Eight). The reason it is in this section is because it is an enemy of *sardeghi*,

coldness, and thus of flatulence. So the next time you are having a beanfeast, reach for your (Persian) hogwort.

Herbal distillates

Distilled anything is known as *arak* in Persian, including sweat, which can lead to some funny translations. We once imported a container of willow water bearing the legendary words 'bottled sweat'; sales were a little slow.

Herbal distillates are big in Iran. Quite apart from the famous rose and orange blossom waters, there is a core range of herbs which are distilled (four times for purity and concentration) and kept in the medicine cabinets of most Persian homes. These include:

Mint water: classically for flatulence and gripe;
Cumin water: also for digestion;
Fennel water: aids digestion, and reputedly good for lactating women or those with erratic periods;
Chicory water: reduces fever and aids circulation; also a good toner for oily skin;
Dill water: used to reduce high blood pressure;
Salix Egyptia (willow): a mild sedative, good for palpitations and frayed nerves;
Cameleum water: used as a diuretic;
Fumitory water: to cleanse the blood, and as a remedy for eczema.

These distillates are usually taken diluted with water before breakfast. As they are so pure and plant-based, a lot of Iranians use them as remedies for children. I sell loads of the stuff, and I am assured that they are efficacious in every way.

به سبک جدید

Preventative foods and seasonal remedies

Chicken soup

It may be hardly original – umpteen cultures in the world rate it as a panacea and whole books cover the subject – but Iranians do it too.

At the first sign of a sniffle, my mother-in-law whips out her soup pan. Everything but the kitchen sink goes in there – a leg of chicken, all the (fresh, frozen or tinned) veg. she can lay her hands on, vermicelli-style soup noodles – all boiled together with a dash of lemon.

It is of course likely that any benefits derived from this wondrous pottage are psychological – the ritual of preparation at the hands of someone who cares, the cosseting, the notion of comfort food generally – it's enough to cheer the most morose. If you happen to believe in the magic, even the direst placebo can work.

It is also true that the heat and steam of the soup (actually any broth) are very effective at dislodging the mucous of a cold, opening the passages of the chest, clearing the head, and soothing the throat.

But there may be more in it than that. Chicken soup was first used as a cold-cure by the ancient Egyptians, but was truly launched by a gifted Jewish scholar called Maimonides in the twelfth century AD. This may explain why it is so much a part of Jewish culture today. He wrote that it 'has virtue in rectifying corrupted humours'. In recent years, the theory has been examined more rigorously. Stephen Rennard MD of the University of Nebraska carried out a whole range of tests on both on his mother-in-law's soup and a range of tinned and packaged varieties. He concluded that chicken soup does have anti-inflammatory properties as it helps something called neurophils (after that, the science weighed heavy, too heavy for our purposes).

Sweet lemons (limes) – *Citrus limettioides* Tanaka

These are fascinating if somewhat insipid little numbers, with the flavour of a sort of natural lemon squash. They are very pithy and pippy,

but full of juice. They are much beloved by the Iranians as they are regarded as God's own Lemsip – at the first sign of a slight fever or sniff, the average Iranian will consume 4–5 of the things with a view to zapping the *meecrobes* before they can get a hold. The skin contains a very soothing oil which is beneficial in the treatment of eczema.

Melon, water-melon and cucumber

These are all eaten in large quantities when they are in season, as they provide a sort of natural cooling system to the body. The first time I saw my significant other's family tucking into a water-melon, I was flabbergasted. They ate nearly all of it at a sitting: I am full after two pieces. Cucumbers (baby, when available) are peeled and salted and devoured in infinite number. The consumption of both water-melon and cucumber I understand, for they are cold, wet foods in the *sardi/garmi* system and counteract the summer's heat. Sweet melon, however, is also eaten for its cooling effect, even though it is classified as neutral or warm and wet in the *sardi/garmi* spectrum. There are three main varieties. The spring brings *guermec* melons, the summer *talebi*, and the late summer *kharbozeh*. They seem to be eaten as a tonic as much as anything. Sir John Chardin relates the tale of two Arab doctors passing through Isfahan looking for work:

> they came there exactly in the season of those guermec, and seeing the street full of this kind of fruit, they said to one another, 'Let us go further on, don't let us stay here, there is nothing for us to do in this place; these people have a remedy for all distempers.'

Walnuts

The walnut we know and love seems to have originated in Iran. It certainly gets everywhere in Persian cuisine.

Walnuts are widely eaten in Iran by mature teenagers (the over-50s)

to control high blood pressure. The inimitable Dr Khoshbin does not mention this, but says that walnuts are good sources of potassium, magnesium, carotene, copper and vitamins A, C and E. They are also beneficial in the treatment of lung disease, gall and kidney stones, worms, memory loss and spasm. He stresses that those of a hot disposition should not have too many as they are hot and dry. Nor do studies in the West mention anything about high blood pressure, but rather sing the walnut's praises in terms of its ability to lower cholesterol. Suffice to say that they are rather nice and, as long as you don't eat too many, they're jolly good for you.

Courgettes and dill

These are both believed to lower cholesterol and blood pressure, and again are consumed aplenty by those of an age to worry about that sort of thing. Mother-in-law actually went through a phase of juicing them, but this was utterly foul so we're back now to eating them normally.

Turnips

Dr Khoshbin gets very excited about turnips in his book *Miraculous Herbs*, and rates them as one of the very best foods to come out of Allah's kitchen. They are naturally antibiotic, antibacterial and full of antioxidants. He recommends them, if you're sitting comfortably, for spots (drink turnip water), the plague, sore throats, reducing high blood pressure, strengthening bones, thyroid problems (they are a good source of iodine), curing impotence, shrinking kidney stones and short-term memory loss, to name but a few on his list. Most importantly, Iranians consume vast quantities of them in the winter as a cough and cold preventative. They act to 'soften phlegm' and make sure that mucous doesn't lodge itself anywhere.

Beetroot

The benefits of beetroot consumption are understood even in Britain – at least in trendy juice-bars. It is one of Mother Nature's greatest detox tools, cleansing not only the kidneys but also the blood and the gall bladder. The problem is that Westerners eat things like this with such a holier-than-thou attitude that they feel like punishment. If they were simply part of our national (regional and seasonal) diet, I'm sure that we'd all be a lot healthier. In Iran, beetroots are consumed with passion and pleasure whenever available.

I end with a disclaimer.

This chapter is merely a report of the author's perception of Persian herbal remedies and diet. This is in no way intended as an authoritative source of alternative medical knowledge, and should not be regarded as a substitute for visiting a real doctor for a real diagnosis and remedy. Furthermore, dramatic changes to the diet should never be made without prior consultation with a physician.

به سبک جدید

Glossary

A few useful Persian words: even if they haven't all been used in the book, they will be useful when you go shopping for ingredients.

ab-gusht – meat (or poultry) stock
abureh – sour grape juice
advieh – spice
albaloo – sour cherries
aloo bohkara – plum
anar – pomegranate
ash – thick soup with herbs
assal – honey
badam - almond
bademjun – aubergine
bastani – ice cream
beh – quince
berenj – uncooked rice
bogoli – broad beans
chai – tea
chelow – cooked plain white rice
chir - milk
chirin – sweet
chirinee – sweeties, specifically Persian cookies
chiveed – dill
darchin – cinnamon
dolmeh – stuffed stuff
doogh – fizzy, salted yoghurt drink
esfanaj – spinach
esphand – wild rue, for burning
faloodeh – sorbet

gallyun – water-pipe or hubble-bubble

garmi – 'hotness'

gaz – nougat

geshneez – coriander

golpar – Persian hogwort

gerdu - walnuts

hel – cardamom

jaffaree – parsley

jigar – liver

jo – barley

kashk – whey, usually liquid

katteh – (over)cooked sticky rice

khalal-e-badam/pesteh – nibbed almonds/pistachios

khiarshoor – pickled cucumber

khorak – thickened sauce

khoresht – casserole

khormah – date

kookoo – omelette

kufteh – meat balls

limoo armani – dried lime

lubia – beans

mahi – fish

miveh – fruit

morabah – jam

morgh – chicken

must – yoghurt

naan – bread

nabat – crystallized sugar

na'nah – mint

narghil – coconut

Nowrooz – (literally 'new day') Iranian New Year

paneer – cheese

pulao – cooked rice, usually with herbs or vegetables stirred through it

reshteh – noodles
reyhan – basil
rob – concentrate, purée, paste
sabzi – herbs
sardi – coldness
sekanjabin – a mint cordial
sharbat – cordial/syrup
sir – garlic
sofreh – table cloth/spread
sumac – a slightly sour spice used on rice, kebabs or bread
tahdik – golden crusted rice
takhte-Jamshid – Persepolis, the ancient capital of Iran
tarkhoun – tarragon
taruf – politeness
toot – berry, usually mulberry
torkhmeh – seeds, usually roasted and salted
torsh – sour
torshi – pickle
zaffaran – saffron
zard chubeh – turmeric
zereshk – barberries
zireh – cumin

Useful addresses

Iranian shops

North London
    Caspian, 30 Vivian Avenue, Hendon, NW4 3XP.
    Super Tehran (Lily's Food), 565 Finchley Road, NW3 7BN.
    Anzali, 1063 Finchley Road, Temple Fortune, NW11 0PU.
South-east London
    Persepolis, 28–30 Peckham High Street, SE15 5DT.
West London
    Super Mazandaran, 201 Uxbridge Road, Ealing, W13 9AA.
Central London
    Super Zaman/Bahar, 347–9 Kensington High Street, W8 6NW.
    Super Massoud, 9a Hammersmith Road, W14 8XJ.
    Sara Food, 7 Hereford Road London W2 4AB.
Birmingham
    Super Pars, 201a Hagley Road, Edgbaston, B16 9RE.
Cheltenham
    Anna's Food, 18 Winchcombe Street, GL52 2LX.
Leeds
    Super Shandiz, 229 Roundhay Road, LS8 4HS.
Sheffield
    Super Pars, 54–6 Infirmary Road, S6 3OD.
Glasgow
    Little Persia, 11–13 Commerce Road, G5 8AB.

Iranian restaurants

North London
    Hafez 2, 559 Finchley Road, NW3 7BJ (020 7431 4546).
South-east London
    Iran-e-Mah, 30 Borough Road, SE1 0AJ (020 7620 0100).

West London

Pars, 370 Harrow Road, Maida Vale, W9 2HU (020 7289 2023).

Ealing Kebab, 179 Uxbridge Road W13 9AA (020 8840 2811).

Central London

Hafez 1, 5a Hereford Road, W2 4AB (020 7229 9398).

Mohsen, 152 Warwick Road, W14 8PS (020 7602 9888).

Patogh, 8 Crawford Place, W1H 5NE (020 7262 4015).

Alounak, 10 Russell Gardens, W14 8EZ (020 7603 1130).

Scheherezade, 346 Kensington High Street, W14 8NS
(020 7371 1919).

Birmingham

Festival Restaurant, 14 Villagers' Walk, B3 3HJ (0121 200 1504).

Manchester

Persia Restaurant, 255 Barlow Moor Road, Chorlton M21 7GJ
(0161 860 6864).

Hull

Saffron Restaurant, 157 Kingston Road, Willerby, HU10 6AL
(01482 650280).

Middle-eastern shops

South West London

Suroor Market (Iraqi), 113 Robin Hood Way,
Roehampton, SW15 3PW.

West London

Damas Gate (Syrian), 81 Uxbridge Road, W12 8NR.

Lebanese Food Centre, 65 Stirling Road, W3 8DJ
(their kebabs are pretty cool too).

Dokal and Sons (Indian), 133–5 The Broadway, Southall, UB1 1LW
(tell them we sent you).

East London

Quality Foods (Indian) – 118–26 Ilford Lane, Ilford, IG1 2LE
(a sort of spice hypermarket).

North London
> MFA Cash and Carry (Turkish), 89–91 Turnpike Lane, N8 0DY (worth a visit for connoisseurs of good salesmanship).

Central London
> Manar (Iraqi), 351 North End Road, Fulham, SW6 1NN.
> Greenfields (Egyptian), 25 Crawford Street, W1H 1PL.

Nice things in and around Peckham

Ganapati (the coolest Indian restaurant ever), 38 Holly Grove SE15 5DF (020 7277 2928).

Il Giardino (a cosy Sardinian restaurant run by Spaniards; we love it), 7 Blenheim Grove SE15 4QS (020 7358 9962).

Bar Story (Peckham's cutting-edge watering hole; a bit experimental at times, but always good fun; includes an art gallery extension), Railway Arches Blenheim Grove, SE15 4QL (020 7635 6643).

Petitou (Peckham's take on Totnes, a licensed café with wholesome food and friendly staff), 63 Choumert Road, SE15 4AR.

Area 10, Project Space, Eagle Wharf, Peckham Hill Street, SE15 5JT: the quirkiest art collective, inhabiting an old timber yard; they put on fabulous exhibitions and performances several times a year; check out <www.area10.info>.

Review (a fine community bookshop), 131 Bellenden Road, SE15 4QY.

And in London as a whole

Southall Broadway: a joyous riot of colour and aroma, this stretch of the Uxbridge Road is a celebration of all things Indian, Pakistani and Afghani. There are restaurants galore, but it is the shopping that always lures me – beautiful fabrics, mouth-drooling sweeties, heady spices and the best of Bollywood at silly prices.

Green Lanes, Haringey: Greeks and Turks jostle for space in this busy shopping thoroughfare. This is the place to get Greek or Turkish supplies – food, drink, pastries, handicrafts.

The Lantern Taverna, 5 Grosvenor Parade, Ealing Common W5 3NN (020 8992 4207): pure nepotism this, as it is run by a Greek Cypriot friend of ours. If you want a really fun night out with live music and meze, this West London venue may well be for you.

Golborne Road: just off the more famous Portobello Road. Jamshid and I had a stall there selling Persian foods for about a year; we were fair-weather traders, just doing Fridays and Saturdays. Jolly hard work, market trading. Golborne Road is a real treasure, full of Portuguese and Moroccan delights.

Bumblebee, 30, 32 & 33 Brecknock Road, Kentish Town, N7 0DD (020 7607 1936): a fabulous organic and wholefood empire spread out over several shops; they used to buy lots of goods from us, and we don't know why they don't any more – so if you see them don't forget to ask.

به سبک جدید

Suggestions for further reading

Food and cookery

Ghillie Bhasan, *The Middle Eastern Kitchen* (London, Kyle Cathie, 2001).

Rosa Montazami, *Honar-e Ashpazi* (The Art of Cooking). This classic book is not available in English. First published in Tehran in 1961, it is now in its 44th edition. The publisher today is Ketabe Iran, Tehran. It is in two volumes, 1725 pages, and the ISBN is 964 9168001.

Nesta Ramazani, *Persian Cooking. A Table of Exotic Delights* (first published in 1974, now issued by Ibex Publishers, Washington DC, 1997).

Claudia Roden, *The Book of Middle Eastern Food* (London, Penguin Books, 1968).

Jill Tilsley Benham, 'Is that Hippocrates in the Kitchen?' a paper in *Oxford Symposium on Food and Cookery 1984 & 1985, Cookery: Science, Lore and Books* (London, Prospect Books, 1986).

Margaret Shaida, *The Legendary Cuisine of Persia* (London, Grub Street, 1992).

Travel

Andrew Burke, Mark Elliott and Kamin Mohammadi, *Iran* (London, Lonely Planet, 2004)

Jason Elliot, *Mirrors of the Unseen* (London, Picador, 2006).

R. W. Ferrier, *A Journey to Persia. Jean Chardin's Portrait of a Seventeenth-century Empire* (London, I.B. Tauris, 1995).

Joseph Knanishu, *About Persia and Its People. A Description of their Manners, Customs and Home Life* (Piscataway, New Jersey, Gorgias Press, 2001). This book, by a Persian expatriate, was first published in 1899 by the Lutheran Augustana Book Concern in Rock Island, Illinois.

Alison Wearing, *Honeymoon in Purdah. An Iranian Journey* (London, Pan Books, 2000).

Religion

The Holy Qur'an, translated by Abdullah Yusuf Ali (London, Wordsworth Editions, 2000).

Zend Avesta, translated by James Darmesteter and L.H. Mills in 1882, now published in Delhi by Motilal Banarsidass Publishers.

Paul Kriwaczek, *In Search of Zarathustra: The First Prophet and the Ideas That Changed the World* (London, Orion, 2002).

The World Zoroastrian Organisation has a very informative website: <www.w-z-o.org>.

History and politics

Vesta Sarkhosh Curtis, *Persian Myths* (London, British Museum Press, 2003).

Gene R. Garthwaite, *The Persians* (Oxford, Blackwell, 2004).

Stephen Kinzer, *All the Shah's Men: An American Coup and the Roots of Middle East Terror* (Hoboken, New Jersey, John Wiley & Sons, Inc., 2003).

John Simpson and Tira Shubart, *Lifting the Veil, Life in Revolutionary Iran* (London, Coronet Books, 1995), one of the best introductions to Iran ever written.

Literature

Peter Washington, ed., *Persian Poems* (London, Everyman, 2000).

Abbas Aryanpur Kashani, *Odes of Hafiz, Poetical Horoscope* (Costa Mesa, California, Mazda Publishers, 1984).

Ferdowsi, *The Epic of the Kings: Shah-Nama the National Epic of Persia*, translated by Reuben Levy (London, Routledge & Kegan Paul, 1967). There are several editions of this translation (and a later revision by Amin Banani) published by Routledge and Arkana/Penguin in London, and Mazda Publishers or the University of Chicago Press in the USA.

Jalaluddin Rumi, *Words of Paradise: Selected Poems by Rumi – New Interpretations by Raficq Abdulla* (London, Frances Lincoln, 2000).

Farid al-Din Attar, *Conference of the Birds: Extracts from Attar's Sufi Classic* (London, Frances Lincoln, 2002).

Omar Khayyam, *The Rubaiyat*, translated by Edward Fitzgerald (New York, Dover Publications Inc., 1991, first published in 1859).

Language

Yavar Dehghani, *Farsi (Persian) Phrasebook* (London, Lonely Planet, 2001).

John Mace, *Teach Yourself Modern Persian* (London, Teach Yourself Books, 1988). There is a more recent edition in this series, written by Narguess Farzad, 2004.

Medicine

Being too much of a hypochondriac myself to buy any books on the subject, my recommendations consist entirely of websites.

<www.unani.com> covers very alternative medicine.

<www.etext.library.adelaide> contains a good translation of Hippocrates' aphorisms by Francis Adams.

<www.afghan.network> has lots of good stuff, particularly a biography of Avicenna)

Botany and herbalism

Dr Sohrab Khoshbin, *Giahan Mojezegar* (Miraculous Herbs) (Tehran, Nashreh Salez, 2005). This is currently unavailable in English although a translation, as *100 Miraculous Herbs*, is mooted (see the website <www.drkhoshbin.com>).

Kazem Moghadam, *Miveh Darmani* (Healing Fruit) (Qom, Bargozideh, 2006). Not available in English.

V. Mozaffarian, *Dictionary of Iranian Plant Names: Latin, English, Persian* (Tehran, Farhang Mo'aser, 1996).

<www.pfaf.org> is a superb plant database with particular reference to their medical uses.

غذاهای مخصوص ایرانی

Index

Abbas I, Shah, 12
ab-gusht, 152; with chicken, 154; with lamb, 153
ab-naranj, 216
Achaemenid dynasty, 11
Afghan lamb and turnip casserole Persian-style, 148
Afghan-style spiced meatballs with tortilla wraps and avocado and kiwi salsa, 364
Agha Mohammed Khan, 13
albaloo pulao, 218
almonds
 carrot jam with pistachio and almond, 350
 rose, raspberry and almond roulade, 250
apricots, 277
Arabian lamb hotpot, Persepolis-style, 141
ash reshteh, 93
ash-e-mash, 109
ash-e-miveh, 98
Attar, 319
aubergines
 chicken and aubergine boats, 138
 fried, 228
 kookoo, 69
 marinated, 230
 preserve, 342
 sandwiches, 84
 with whey, 42
 stuffed, 82
Avicenna, 387
avocado and kiwi salsa, 364

baby *chelo* kebabs wrapped in *lavash* bread with relish, 40
baklava, Persian, 305
bamya, 302
bandari marinated olives, 347
bandari sausages, 85
barberi naan, 37, 113
barberry jelly, 334
barberry rice with chicken, 206
barley
 chicken porridge, 91
 soup, 102
 stuffed peppers, 78
bastani, 256
Batmanghelidjh, Camilla, 301
batter, *doogh*, 187
batter cakes, 302
bazaari bogoli, 227
beans
 baked beans with cheesy meatballs, 155
 herb, noodle and bean soup, 93
 see also broad beans; French beans; kidney beans; mung beans; pinto beans
beef steak with fenugreek and chive butter, 121
beetroot, 225, 399
beh-limoo, 320
berenj, 199
big *barberi* burgers, 115
biryani, Persian spiced risotto, 374
biscuits, elephant's ears, 309
bogoli, 226
bogoli pulao, 154, 204

borage infusion, 392
borani-ye esfanaj, 49
brains, fried, 161
braised sweet gem lettuce with
     sekanjabin, 233
bread, 33ff.
breakfast rice, 73
broad beans, 226
     broad bean balls, 132
     broad bean rice with dill, served
     with chicken or lamb, 204
     Tom's, 53
bulghur wheat, 134
burgers, big *barberi*, 115
butter, fenugreek and chive, 121

cakes, batter, 302
caleh-pah-cheh, 160
calf's tongue à la mother-in-law, 162
camel thorn infusion, 393
cameleum water, 395
cardamom
     Persian winter fruit pudding with
     saffron and cardamom suet, 262
     quince jam with cardamom, 349
cardoon stew, 151
carpets, Persian, 243f.
carrots
     carrot jam with pistachio and
     almond, 350
     carrot salad with nibbed pistachios,
     234
     extremely exotic carrots, 235
casseroles, 137ff.
caviar, 178
celery
     chicken soup with quince, celery
     and saffron, 107
     stew, 151
chador, 15

chahar torkmeh, 393
chai, 283, 322ff.
chai khaneh, 324
Chardin, Sir John, 210, 397
cheese
     persimmons filled with spiced
     cheese, 276
     spinach, walnut and Tabriz cheese
     salad, 242
chelo kebabs, baby, 40
chelow, 200–201
     suya chelow with jerk chicken, 358
     tuna *chelow*, 62
cherry, see sour cherry
cheshm, 22
chick peas
     chick pea shortbread, 254
     salt cod with Iranian herbs and
     beans, 370
chicken
     ab-gusht with, 154
     barberry rice with chicken, 206
     broad bean rice with dill, served
     with chicken or lamb, 204
     chicken and aubergine boats, 138
     chicken and rice cake, 57
     chicken on a bed of prunes and
     spinach, 164
     chicken porridge, 91
     chicken soup, 396
     chicken soup with quince, celery
     and saffron, 107
     Greek lemon chicken with dill,
     362
     jerk chicken with *suya chelow*, 358
     Persepolitan roast and stuffed,
     128
     plum hotpot with chicken, 146
     rice and French beans with
     Andiwornee chicken, 208

Somali-style *molohiya*, 366
spring chicken marinated with lemon and saffron, 120
chicory water, 395
chilled cucumber and herb soup, 104
chips, spiced, 191
chirin pulao, 214
chirinee, 283
   chirinee keshmeshee, 288
chive butter, fenugreek and, 121
chunky fish with split peas and sour grapes, 178
chutney, Jo-Jo's, 336
cinema in Iran, 236f.
cinnamon ice-cream with *gaz*, 260
citrus-infused vegetable hotpot, 245
citrus limettioides Tanaka, 396
clotted cream ice-cream, 256
cobbler, tamarind lamb and mushroom, 166
coconut and walnut *couloucheh*, 307
cod, see salt cod
coffee, Turkish, 325
cookies
   coconut, 307
   saffron, 288
   walnut, 307
cordial
   lemon or lime, 320
   orange, 320
   quince and lemon, 320
   rose, 321
cottelettes, 88
couloucheh, 307
courgettes, 398
   marinated, 231
cream
   clotted cream ice-cream, 256
   lime and pistachio cream, with

noon khameii, 252
croquettes, 88
cucumber, 397
   cucumber and herb soup, chilled, 104
   cucumber, mint and cucumber syrup, 318
   yoghurt with cucumber, 50
   pickled cucumbers, 346
cumin water, 395
Cyrus the Great, 11

dates
   date pickle, 344
   lentil rice with date fudge, 217
dill, 398
   dill water, 395
   broad bean rice with dill, served with chicken or lamb, 204
   Greek lemon chicken with dill, 362
dizee', 152
dolmeh, 77ff.
doogh, 315
   haddock cooked in *doogh* batter, 187
dried fruit
   Persian winter fruit pudding with saffron and cardamom suet, 262
drugs in Iran, 328
duck with walnut and pomegranate sauce, 143

Earl Grey ice-cream with chick pea shortbread, 254
egg and onion soup, Persian, 105
eggs
   Takht-e-Jamshid eggs, 71
elephant's ears, 309
eshkeneh, 105

espand, 23
everyday lentils, 240
extremely exotic carrots, 235

faloodeh, 258, 274
Farsi, 100f.
feet, lamb's head and, 160
fennel water, 395
fenugreek
    steak with fenugreek and chive butter, 121
Ferdowsi, 318, 324
fish
    chunky fish with split peas and sour grapes, 178
    fish 'Pahlavan' with a walnut and tarragon *tarator*, 180
    fried fish with herbed rice, 172
    herb and tamarind fish stew, 177
    southern-style spiced fish, 196
    Khanum Sohaila's stuffed fish, 192
flixweed, 394
four-seed infusion, 393
frankfurter sausages, 122
French beans
    rice and French beans with Andiwornee chicken, 208
fried brains, 161
fried fish with herbed rice, 172
fruit, dried, Persian winter fruit pudding with saffron and cardamom suet, 262
fruit soup, 98
fudge, saffron, 304
fumitory water, 395

gallyun, 326
garlic, spring, yoghurt with, 51
garlic pickle, 345

gaz, 260
ghormeh sabzi, 144
golpar, 23, 226–227, 394
goosh-e-fil, 309
grapes, see sour grapes, verjuice
Greek lemon chicken with dill, 362
guests, unexpected, 271ff.
gul-e-khatmi, 392
gul gavzaban, 392
gul Mohammedi, 251, 392

haddock cooked in *doogh* batter, 187
Hafez, 318
hafte-bijar pickle, 339
halal-e-naranj, 216
halal meat, 114
halim, 91
halwa, 308
head, lamb's, and feet, 160
heart, lamb's liver, kidney and, on sticks, 125
hejab, 15
hemp and sesame crumble, pan fried fillet of mackerel coated in, 188
herb and bean casserole with lamb, 144
herb and tamarind fish stew, 177
herb, noodle and bean soup, 93
herbal waters, 395
herbed rice with fried fish, 172
herbs, 39
    chilled cucumber and herb soup, 104
Hippocrates, 385–386
hospitality, Iranian, 271ff.
'hot' and 'cold' foods, 384ff.
hotpot
    Arabian lamb hotpot, Persepolis-style, 141
    citrus-infused vegetable, 245

plum hotpot with chicken, 146
hubbly-bubbly smoking, 326f.

ice-cream
  cinnamon, 260
  clotted cream, 256
  Earl Grey, 254
Ilkhanid dynasty, 12
infusions, 392–394
Iran
  cinema, 236f.
  drugs, 328
  fish, 171
  history, 11ff.
  hospitality, 271ff.
  importing from, 65ff.
  Islam, 116f.
  match-making in, 283–286
  meat, 114
  modern facts about, 14ff.
  mourning in, 309f.
  music, 86f.
  picnics in, 76f.
  smoking in, 326f.
  street food, 223ff.
  table manners, 24ff.
  traditional medicine, 383ff.
  weddings in, 210ff.
Iranians, modern character of, 18ff.
Islam, 116f.

jam
  carrot jam with pistachio and almond, 350
  quince jam with cardamom, 349
jelly, barberry, 334
Jo-Jo's chutney, 336
jujeh kebab, 120
jujube berry infusion, 393

Karim Khan Zand, 13
kash-e-bademjun, 42
kashkul, 25
kebabs
  baby *chelo* kebabs, 40
  lamb fillet kebab with pomegranate salsa, 118
  spring chicken marinated with lemon and saffron, 120
kebab-e-barg, 118
khakshir, 394
Khanum Sohaila's stuffed fish, 192
kharbozeh, 277
khastegari, 283–287
Khayam, Omar, 318
khaysi, 277
khiar shoor, 346
khorak-e-morgh, 208
khoresht, 137ff.
  khoresht aloo Bokhara, 146
  khoresht-e-bademjun, 138
  khoresht-e-fessenjun, 143
  khoresht-e-gharch, 166
  khoresht-e-rivas, 150
  khoresht ghaliheh mahi, 177
Khoshbin, Dr Sohrab, 224, 398
kidney beans
  herb and bean casserole with lamb, 144
kidney
  lamb's liver, heart and kidney on sticks, 125
Kids Company, 301
kiwi fruit salsa, avocado and, 364
Knanishu, Joseph, 34, 210, 284
kookoo, 182
  kookoo burger, 68
  kookoo sabzi, 69
  kookoo-ye-bademjan, 69
  sweet *kookoo*, 70

korma shalgam, 148
kufteh Number One, 130
kufteh Number Two, 132
kufteh Tabrizi, 130

laboo, 225
lamb
    ab-gusht with lamb, 153
    Afghan lamb and turnip casserole
    Persian-style, 148
    Arabian lamb hotpot, Persepolis-
    style, 141
    broad bean rice with dill, served
    with chicken or lamb, 204
    fried brains, 162
    head and feet, 160
    herb and bean casserole with lamb,
    144
    lamb fillet kebab with pomegranate
    salsa, 118
    lamb sausages, 122
    liver, heart and kidney on sticks,
    125
    tamarind lamb and mushroom
    cobbler, 166
    tongue à la mother-in-law, 162
lavash, 35, 40
lemon
    Greek lemon chicken with dill,
    362
    lemon or lime cordial, 320
    quince and lemon cordial, 320
    spring chicken marinated with
    lemon and saffron, 120
lentils
    everyday lentils, 240
    lentil rice with date fudge, 217
    sausages and lentils, 122
    spiced red lentil purée, 239

lettuce
    braised sweet gem lettuce with
    sekanjabin, 233
    lettuce with mint syrup, 232
    sweet minted lettuce, with orange
    sorbet, 279
lime and pistachio cream, *noon khameii*
    with, 252
limoo armani, 152
liver, heart and kidney on sticks, 125
Lorry Food One, 62
Lorry Food Two, 64
lubia chitti, 155, 238
lubia pulao with *khorak-e-morgh*, 208

macaroons, coconut, 307
macaroons, walnut, 307
mackerel, pan fried fillet, coated in
    hemp and sesame crumble, 188
Maimonides, 396
marinated aubergines, 230
marinated courgettes, 231
marinated olives, *bandari*, 347
marshmallow infusion, 392
mash, saffron, 193
match-making in Iran, 283–285
meat, *halal*, 113f.
meatballs
    Afghan-style spiced, 364
    cheesy meatballs with baked
    beans, 155
    spiced mung bean and meatball
    soup, 109
    very big meatballs, 130
melokhia, Somali-style, 366
melon, 277, 397
    see also water-melon
meze, 33
mint
    mint and cucumber syrup, 318

mint syrup, 232–233
mint water, 395
orange sorbet with sweet minted
    lettuce, 279
mirza ghassemi, 228
molohiya, Somali-style, 366
Montazami, Rosa, 157, 238, 307, 344
mourning in Iran, 309f.
moussir, 51
muesli, Persian, 378
Mullah Nasruddin, 113, 171, 278
mung beans
    spiced mung bean and meatball
    soup, 109
mushrooms
    tamarind lamb and mushroom
    cobbler, 166
must-e-moussir, 51
must-o-khiar, 50, 149, 196

naan, 33ff.
naan-e-barberi, 37
naan-e-lavash, 35
naan-e-sangak, 38
Nader, Shah, 13
nazr, 265
neshasteh, 394
New Year, Persian, 174–176
noodles
    herb, noodle and bean soup, 93
noon khameii with lime and pistachio
    cream, 252
noon pangareii, 261, 286
Norrington-Davies, Tom, 9, 53
nougat, 260
Nowrooz, 174–176

offal, 157ff.
oh-my-God-how-many-relatives-etc?
    pudding, 269

oliveiyeh salad, 74
olives, marinated *bandari*, 347
omelette, see *kookoo*
onab, 393
onions
    Persian egg and onion soup, 105
opium, 328
oranges, 216
    orange cordial, 320
    orange sorbet with sweet minted
    lettuce, 279

Pahlavi dynasty, 13
pan fried fillet of mackerel coated in
    hemp and sesame crumble, 188
peaches, squashed, 277
pears, baby, 277
peas, see split peas
peppers, stuffed, 78
Persepolis, Iran, 55f.
Persepolis, the shop, 9, 10, 26ff., 193ff.,
    355ff.
Persepolis muesli, 378
Persepolis patent piquant tomato
    sauce, 331
Persepolis special *torshi*, 337
Persepolitan roast stuffed chicken,
    128
Persian *baklava*, 305
Persian carpets, 243f.
Persian egg and onion soup, 105
Persian hogwort, 394
Persian pizzas, 376
Persian poetry, 318ff.
Persian spiced risotto, 374
Persian wedges, 190
Persian winter fruit pudding with
    saffron and cardamom suet, 262
persimmons filled with spiced cheese,
    276

به سبک جدید

pesto, Persian, with smoked salmon, 52

pickles, 205
    date pickle, 344
    garlic pickle, 345
    hafte-bijar pickle, 339
    Persepolis special *torshi*, 337
    pickled cucumbers, 346

picnics in Iran, 76f.

pinto bean salad, 238

pistachios
    carrot jam with pistachio and almond, 350
    carrot salad with nibbed pistachios, 234
    noon khameii with lime and pistachio cream, 252

pizza, Persian, 376

plantain and sweet potato slosh, 360

plum hotpot with chicken, 146

poetry, Persian, 318ff.

polenta, saffron, with spiced red snapper, 372

pomegranates, 185f.
    duck with walnut and pomegranate sauce, 143
    lamb fillet kebab with pomegranate salsa, 118
    pomegranate paste, 184
    pomegranate sorbet with vodka, 258
    pomegranate soup, 97
    vegetables in pomegranate sauce, 241

porridge, chicken, 91

potatoes
    jacket, 225
    Persian wedges, 190
    potato rice, 205
    potato salad, 74

saffron mash, 193
spiced chips, 191

potted shrimps with saffron and sabzi, 44

Pourandokht, Queen, 49

preserve, aubergine, 342

profiteroles, *noon khameii* with lime and pistachio cream, 252

prunes, chicken on a bed of prunes and spinach, 164

puddings
    oh-my-God-how-many-relatives-did-we-invite-for-dinner? pudding, 269
    Persian winter fruit pudding, 262
    rice pudding, 264

pulao, 154, 196, 200
    albaloo, 218
    bogoli, 204
    chirin, 214
    lubia, with *khorak-e-morgh*, 208
    sabzi, ba mahi, 172
    sib, 205
    zereshk, 206

purée, spiced red lentil, 239

Qajar dynasty, 13

quail, stuffed, with *chirin pulao* (sweet rice), 214

quince
    chicken soup with quince, celery and saffron, 107
    quince and lemon cordial, 320
    quince jam with cardamom, 349
    quince seed infusion, 393
    stewed quince with *bastani*, 256

Ramadan, 95f.

Ramazani, Nesta, 235

raspberry, rose and almond roulade, 250

غذاهای مخصوص ایرانی

red snapper, spiced, with saffron polenta, 372
refugees, 193ff.
Reza Khan, 13
rhubarb stew, 150
rice
  barberry rice with chicken, 206
  basmati, 199
  breakfast, 73
  broad bean rice with dill, served with chicken or lamb, 204
  chelow, 200–201
  chicken and rice cake, 57
  herbed rice with fried fish, 172
  lentil rice with date fudge, 217
  potato rice, 205
  rice and French beans with Andiwornee chicken, 208
  rice pudding unlike-mother-in-law-used-to-make, 264
  sadri, 199
  saffron rice with sour cherry sauce, 265
  salmon and saffron patties, with spinach and rice, 182
  smoked *sadri*, 199
  sour cherry rice, 218
  southern-style spiced fish with rice, 196
  stuffed quail with *chirin pulao* (sweet rice), 214
  suya chelow with jerk chicken, 358
  tahdik, 200, 202
  see also *pulao*
risotto, Persian spiced, 374
rob anaar, 186
rose, raspberry and almond roulade, 250
rose apples, 277
rose cordial, 321

rose petal infusion, 392
rose sorbet with tongue wafers, 274
roses, 251f.
roulade, rose, raspberry and almond, 250
roupush, 15
Russia, culinary influence of, 102
Russian salad, 74

Saberi, Helen, 33
sabzi, 39
sabzi pulao ba mahi, 172
saffron, 45
  chicken soup with quince, celery and saffron, 107
  Persian winter fruit pudding with saffron and cardamom suet, 262
  saffron cookies, 288
  saffron fudge, 304
  saffron mash, 193
  saffron polenta, with spiced red snapper, 372
  saffron rice with sour cherry sauce, 265
  salmon and saffron patties, with spinach and rice, 182
  spring chicken marinated with lemon and saffron, 120
salad
  carrot salad with nibbed pistachios, 234
  pinto bean salad, 238
  Shirazi salad, 115, 184
  spinach, walnut and Tabriz cheese salad, 242
salad *oliveiyeh*, 74
salmon and saffron patties, with spinach and rice, 182
salmon, smoked, with Persian pesto, 52

به سبک جدید

salsa
  avocado and kiwi, 364
  pomegranate, with lamb fillet
    kebab, 118
salt, 142
salt cod with Iranian herbs and beans,
  370
sandwiches, 75
  aubergine, 84
sardi/garmi, 384ff.
Sassanid dynasty, 12
sauce
  duck with walnut and pomegranate
    sauce, 143
  Persepolis patent piquant tomato
    sauce, 331
  sour cherry sauce, saffron rice and,
    265
  vegetables in pomegranate sauce,
    241
sausages, *bandari*, 85
sausages and lentils, 122
Savafid dynasty, 12
seer abi, 158
sekanjabin, 232–233, 279, 318
Seleucid dynasty, 11
sesame seeds
  pan fried fillet of mackerel coated
    in hemp and sesame crumble, 188
Shab-e-Yalda, 185
Shaida, Margaret, 102
shalgam, 224
sharbat, 316f.
  sharbat ab-limoo, 320
  sharbat portooghal, 320
sherbets, 316f.
shir berenj, 264
Shirazi salad, 115, 184
sholeh zard, 265
shortbread, chick pea, 254

shrimps, potted, with saffron and
  sabzi, 44
sib pulao, 154, 205
Simorgh, 290ff.
smoked salmon with Persian pesto,
  52
smoking in Iran, 326f.
sofreh, 25
sohan assali, 304
Somali-style *molohiya*, 366
sonbol 'atib, 393
sorbet
  orange sorbet with sweet minted
    lettuce, 279
  pomegranate sorbet with vodka,
    258
  rose sorbet, 274
soup
  barley soup, 102
  chicken soup, 396
  chicken soup with quince, celery
    and saffron, 107
  fruit soup, 98
  herb, noodle and bean soup, 93
  pomegranate soup, 97
  sour cherry soup with meringue
    'croûtons', 267
  spiced mung bean and meatball
    soup, 109
soup-e-jo, 102
sour cherries, 268
  cordial, 322
  jam with vodka, 348
  rice, 218
  sauce, saffron rice and, 265
  soup with meringue 'croûtons',
    267
sour grapes
  chunky fish with split peas and
    sour grapes, 178

غذاهای مخصوص ایرانی

sour grape juice, 140

southern-style spiced fish with rice, 196

spiced mung bean and meatball soup, 109

spiced red lentil purée, 239

spiced red snapper with saffron polenta, 372

spiced vinegar, 333

spinach

    chicken on a bed of prunes and spinach, 164

    salmon and saffron patties, with spinach and rice, 182

    salt cod with Iranian herbs and beans, 370

    spinach, walnut and Tabriz cheese salad, 242

    yoghurt with spinach, 49

split peas

    chunky fish with split peas and sour grapes, 178

starch, 394

steak with fenugreek and chive butter, 121

stew, 137ff.

    cardoon stew, 151

    celery stew, 151

    herb and tamarind fish stew, 177

    rhubarb stew, 150

stewed quince with *bastani*, 256

stock, 152

street food in Iran, 223ff.

stuffed aubergines, mother-in-law's recipe, 82

stuffed peppers, 78

stuffed quail with *chirin pulao* (sweet rice), 214

stuffed vineleaves, 80

suet, saffron and cardamom, 262

sumac, 189

suya chelow with jerk chicken, 358

sweet *kookoo*, 70

sweet lemons (limes), 396

sweet potato slosh, plantain and, 360

sweetcorn, 225

syrup

    mint, 233

    mint and cucumber, 318

taftoon, 35

tahcheen, 57

tahdik, 200, 202

tahini dip, 227

Takht-e-Jamshid eggs, 71

tamarind, 168

    herb and tamarind fish stew, 177

    tamarind lamb and mushroom cobbler, 166

taranjabin, 393

tarator, fish 'Pahlavan' with a walnut and tarragon *tarator*, 180

tarragon, fish 'Pahlavan' with a walnut and tarragon *tarator*, 180

taruf, 20

tea, 322ff.

tea house, 324

tomato sauce, Persepolis patent piquant, 331

Tom's broad beans, 53

tongue à la mother-in-law, 162

tongue wafers, 274

torkmeh beh, 393

torshi, 205

    Persepolis special *torshi*, 337

    torshi seer, 345

    torshi-ye-khormah, 344

tripe, 158

tuna
 tuna *chelow*, 62
 Persepolis barbecued tuna, 184
Turkish coffee, 325
turnips, 224, 398
 Afghan lamb and turnip casserole
 Persian-style, 148

unexpected guests, 271ff.
valerian root infusion, 393
vegetables
 vegetables in pomegranate sauce,
 241
 citrus-infused vegetable hotpot,
 245
verjuice, 140
vinegar, spiced, 333
vineleaves, stuffed, 80
vodka
 pomegranate sorbet with vodka,
 258
 sour cherry jam with vodka, 348

wafers
 tongue wafers, 274
 window wafers, 261, 286
walnuts, 397
 coconut and walnut *coucoucheh*,
 307

duck with walnut and pomegranate
 sauce, 143
fish 'Pahlavan' with a walnut and
 tarragon *tarator*, 180
spinach, walnut and Tabriz cheese
 salad, 242
water-melon, 278f., 397
 water-melon salsa, 278
 water-melon smoothie, 278
water-pipes, 326f.
weddings in Iran, 210ff.
whey, aubergines with, 42
wholemeal bread, 38
willow water, 395
window wafers, 261, 286
Winter Solstice, 185

yoghurt, 47, 315
 yoghurt with cucumber, 50
 yoghurt with spinach, 49
 yoghurt with spring garlic, 51

za'atar, 191
zabun, 274
zereshk pulao, 206
zoolbia, 302
zoolbia-e-bamya, 289ff.
Zoroastrianism, 126–128

The shopkeeper chills after a hard day behind the counter.